THE UNIVERSITY OF CHICAGO
SOCIOLOGICAL SERIES

Editorial Committee

ELLSWORTH FARIS   ROBERT E. PARK
ERNEST W. BURGESS

THE UNIVERSITY OF CHICAGO SOCIOLOGICAL SERIES, established by the Trustees of the University, is devoted primarily to the publication of the results of the newer developments in sociological study in America. It is expected that a complete series of texts for undergraduate instruction will ultimately be included, but the emphasis will be placed on research, the publications covering both the results of investigation and the perfecting of new methods of discovery. The editors are convinced that the textbooks used in teaching should be based on the results of the efforts of specialists whose studies of concrete problems are building up a new body of funded knowledge. While the series is called sociological, the conception of sociology is broad enough to include many borderline interests, and studies will appear which place the emphasis on political, economic, or educational problems dealt with from the point of view of a general conception of human nature.

THE TAXI-DANCE HALL

THE UNIVERSITY OF CHICAGO PRESS
CHICAGO, ILLINOIS

THE BAKER & TAYLOR COMPANY
NEW YORK

THE CAMBRIDGE UNIVERSITY PRESS
LONDON

THE MARUZEN-KABUSHIKI-KAISHA
TOKYO, OSAKA, KYOTO, FUKUOKA, SENDAI

THE COMMERCIAL PRESS, LIMITED
SHANGHAI

THE
TAXI-DANCE
HALL

*A Sociological Study in Commercialized
Recreation and City Life*

By PAUL G. CRESSEY

*Formerly Special Investigator, Juvenile
Protective Association*

THE UNIVERSITY OF CHICAGO PRESS
CHICAGO · ILLINOIS

COPYRIGHT 1932 BY THE UNIVERSITY OF CHICAGO
ALL RIGHTS RESERVED. PUBLISHED MAY 1932
PAPERBACK EDITION 2008
17 16 15 14 13 12 11 10 09 08   1 2 3 4 5

ISBN-13: 978-0-226-12051-5 (PAPER)
ISBN-10: 0-226-12051-1 (PAPER)

COMPOSED AND PRINTED BY THE UNIVERSITY OF CHICAGO PRESS
CHICAGO, ILLINOIS, U.S.A.

♾ THE PAPER USED IN THIS PUBLICATION MEETS THE MINIMUM REQUIREMENTS OF THE AMERICAN NATIONAL STANDARD FOR INFORMATION SCIENCES—PERMANENCE OF PAPER FOR PRINTED LIBRARY MATERIALS, ANSI Z39.48-1992.

TO MY PARENTS
ROGER FRED AND EMMA GOALBY CRESSEY

TABLE OF CONTENTS

FOREWORD *By Jessie F. Binford* xi

INTRODUCTION *By Ernest W. Burgess* xiii

AUTHOR'S PREFACE xix

PART I. THE TAXI-DANCE HALL: WHAT IT IS
I. A NIGHT IN THE TAXI-DANCE HALL 3
II. THE TAXI-DANCE HALL AS A TYPE 17

PART II. THE TAXI-DANCER AND HER WORLD
III. THE TAXI-DANCE HALL AS A SOCIAL WORLD 31
IV. THE FAMILY AND SOCIAL BACKGROUNDS OF THE TAXI-DANCER 54
V. THE LIFE-CYCLE OF THE TAXI-DANCER 84

PART III. THE PATRON AND HIS PROBLEMS
VI. THE PATRON: WHO HE IS; WHY HE COMES 109
VII. THE FILIPINO AND THE TAXI-DANCE HALL 145

CONTENTS

PART IV. THE NATURAL HISTORY AND ECOLOGY
OF THE TAXI-DANCE HALL

VIII. The Origins of the Taxi-Dance Hall 177
IX. The Taxi-Dance Hall Meets the Public 196
X. Competition, Conflict, and Specialization among
    Taxi-Dance Halls 210
XI. The Location of the Taxi-Dance Hall 224

PART V. THE TAXI-DANCE HALL PROBLEM

XII. Personal Demoralization 237
XIII. The Taxi-Dance Hall and Social Reform . . 262

Index 297

FOREWORD

It is gratifying indeed to an organization like the Juvenile Protective Association of Chicago when community conditions about which it is especially concerned become the subject for extensive study and research. Paul G. Cressey while serving as a case-worker and special investigator for the Juvenile Protective Association was requested during the summer of 1925 to report upon the new and then quite unfamiliar "closed dance halls." This book is in a sense the outgrowth of those assignments. While our interpretation of the taxi-dance hall problem may not coincide entirely with Mr. Cressey's, this possibility does not make us less appreciative of the great contribution he has made.

Mr. Cressey's initial investigations revealed, as do other studies, the complexities which social agencies face in the urban situation, when in the interests of young people they are called upon to control and regulate doubtful social centers. His reports indicated clearly that certain amusement places came into existence because of our lack of social resources and that only through increased experimentation and study can we learn to meet more wholesomely the needs which call the taxi-dance hall into existence.

Social agencies have failed signally to take community conditions into account, and even when such a point of view has been accepted, there has been little effort to analyze and interpret these conditions. "Case work" has not yet been applied to the community. Few social agencies realize the importance or have the resources for "eternal vigilance" and for this very necessary research and experimentation.

If the experience and case material of other agencies could be utilized and interpreted as Mr. Cressey has here done, these studies should make possible not merely intelligent regulation and control but—what is of far greater importance—the substitution of wholesome acceptable social centers, commercial, as well as private and municipal, to meet the recreational needs of young people.

JESSIE F. BINFORD, *Executive Director*
Juvenile Protective Association

INTRODUCTION

The taxi-dance hall is almost unknown to the general public. What little is reported in the press, by social workers, and by exploring visitors is colorful, but damning and shocking. Little wonder that crusades have been directed against the taxi-dance hall in several American cities, and that it has been outlawed in the city of its origin, San Francisco.

The campaign against the taxi-dance hall has run true to the traditional American pattern of reform, namely, reaction to the external aspects of a situation without any real understanding of the social forces underlying its origin and growth.

The present study, undertaken under the assumption that knowledge should precede action, had a threefold purpose. The first object of the inquiry was to give an unbiased and intimate picture of the social world of the typical taxi-dance hall with its owner and manager, with its bevy of pretty, vivacious, and often mercenary "instructresses," with its motley array of patrons: Orientals, older men, isolated and socially handicapped youth, eager for association with feminine beauty at "a dime a dance."

The second purpose of the study was to trace the natural history of the taxi-dance hall as an urban institution, to discover those conditions in city life favorable to its rise and development, and to analyze its function in terms of the basic wishes and needs of its male patrons.

The third objective of the study was to present as impartially as possible the present kinds of control operating to maintain order, to create codes of conduct, and to enforce standards, whether on the part of managers, instructresses, patrons, police, social workers, or the press.

The candid reader of this volume will, I believe, agree that Mr. Cressey and his assistants have had a fair measure of success in achieving all three of these objectives. The reader is given an entrée into the social world of the taxi-dance hall such as the casual visitor never gains. Vicariously, he may imagine himself in the place of the taxi-dancer or her patron, participating, as it were, in their experiences, and getting some appreciation of their outlook and philosophy of life.

The reader secures a lively appreciation of the interesting way in which the taxi-dance hall arose to meet the demands for feminine society of homeless and lonesome men crowded into the rooming-house districts of our larger cities. He realizes that the owners of these enterprises are exploiting this interest of the patrons for financial gain. In the competition between various establishments for attendance, standards are lowered and the interest in sexual stimulation tends to find expression in unwholesome forms without control.

Normally an institution develops its own system of control from the inside which is enforced not only by its functionaries but also by its members. In the case of the taxi-dance hall the only control is external. The managers as a rule are foreigners, unacquainted with American standards, intent upon "giving the public what it wants" in terms measured by financial receipts. The code of the taxi-dancer tends also to be commercialized, for her earnings are 50 per cent of her total receipts at ten cents a dance. The patrons are a true proletariat of foot-loose, generally propertyless persons, who attend as an aggregation of individuals with little or no sense of the influence of group control. In fact, the only

INTRODUCTION

effective control is exerted by the presence of a policeman or "bouncer."

This study has a significance that goes far beyond the taxi-dance hall situation. It raises all the main questions of the problem of recreation under conditions of modern city life, namely, the insistent human *demand for stimulation*, the growth of *commercialized recreation*, the growing *tendency to promiscuity* in the relations of the sexes, and the failure of our ordinary devices of social control to function in a culturally heterogeneous and anonymous society.

In the city, the expression of the fundamental human craving for stimulation appears often to be dissociated from the normal routine of family and neighborhood life. In the village of past generations, all activities, both of work and of play, were integral parts of a unified communal existence. The desire for stimulation and adventure normally found wholesome expression in the varied program of events of village life, or in pioneering in the settlement of the West. But with the passing of the frontier, the bright-light areas or "the jungles" of the city become the *locus* of excitement and new experience. Family and neighborhood recreation have declined in direct proportion to the growth of city-wide enterprises intent upon commercializing the human interest in stimulation. The result has been the growing tendency to make the pursuit of thrills and excitement a segmented interest detached from the other interests of the person.

To grasp the tremendous social change that has taken place in our leisure-time habits in the last fifty years, it suffices to enumerate in brief review certain outstanding enterprises and facilities for recreation, most of which were nonexistent at the beginning of the period: the growth of professional baseball, the building of stadiums seating tens of thousands for university football contests, the emergence of championship prize fights as national events, the mounting number of automobiles which now average almost one to a family, the rapid increase in the number of radios, the replacement of the neighborhood saloon by the "blind pig" and the speakeasy, the expansion of the motion picture with its twenty thousand theaters, "Miss America" beauty contests, endurance contests including dance marathons, the construction of magnificent dance palaces in our large cities, the night club, and the roadhouse.

In all of these the center of interest has gravitated from the home and the neighborhood to the outside world, in nearly all of them the effect of participation goes little beyond the stimulation of individual emotion and has little or no function for social integration, and practically all of them are operated on a basis of commercialization.

The predominant place of commercialization in present-day recreation has much the same consequences as indicated in the study of the taxi-dance hall. Commercialization of recreational activities tends almost inevitably, in the competition for patronage, to increase the emphasis upon stimulation. Stimulation for stimulation's sake tends to become a goal in itself as a profit proposition. Stimulation, under these conditions, ceases to be a natural and wholesome accompaniment of an activity of the entire personality. Not only in the taxi-dance hall but in all public dance halls and to a greater or less extent in all recreational life in the city, the factor of the commercialization of stimulation is complicated by the fact of promiscuity.

By "promiscuity" is meant intimate behavior upon the basis of casual association. The promiscuity of city life has its extreme example in prostitution. Promiscuity, of course, does not necessarily end in vice, but it opens the door either to vice or to exploitation, or to both.

Promiscuity naturally arises under conditions making for casual acquaintanceship in city life. Conventional avenues for forming friendships are notoriously deficient in the city. The drive toward casual association, with the added piquancy of adventure and irresponsibility, is correspondingly strong. In the social relations of the sexes certain patterns of behavior come to be expected. These forms of behavior range in informality from the "pick-up" and the *gigolo* to the establishment of business bureaus to supply girl companions to visiting business men. Lonesome clubs in our large cities and matrimonial advertising journals are eloquent in their testimony either of the difficulty of making satisfactory acquaintances according to conventional modes or of the desire for romance outside of the usual and familiar.

The taxi-dance hall and all public dance halls are organized to exploit for profit a situation of promiscuity. This basic fact explains the essential problem of control in the public dance. Any solution of the problem that does not deal with this factor of promiscuity is, in the nature of things, external and superficial. A fundamental approach would grapple directly with the lack of provision for the social life of young people, and particularly of socially handicapped and lonesome persons in the large city.

The statement of the problem, as in this book, is the first step in its solution. It cannot fail to make evident the futility and stupidity of many of the current proposals of reform. As a matter of fact, crusades against the taxi-dance hall and other similar urban institutions are a part of the whole situation, since they are as chronic as the condition which they periodically seek to reform. But, as Mr. Cressey insists, the problem should be worked out experimentally and constructively in the light of the facts and in the interest of all the human values so clearly revealed in his study.

ERNEST W. BURGESS

AUTHOR'S PREFACE

Among the recreational institutions of the American city none perhaps reveals with as much clarity as many of the perplexing problems which make difficult the wholesome expression of human nature in the urban setting as does the public dance hall. In it can be found in bold relief the impersonality of the city, the absence of restraints, the loneliness and the individual maladjustment and distraction characteristic of the life of many in the urban environment.

It was with the belief that the public dance hall played a significant rôle in the life of the community which deserved more thorough study that the writer began this project in 1925. The taxi-dance hall was selected for special study because it was at the time a very new and questionable type of establishment with which even social workers were not familiar, and because it seemed to represent in their extreme many of the forces which shape behavior in all public dance halls. Since the study was begun taxi-dance halls have increased in number and in importance until they are now the dominant type of dance hall in the business centers of our largest cities.

Most of the data upon which this study is based was secured from the case records of social agencies, notably the Juvenile Protective Association, and from the reports of observers and investigators. Published material upon such a new phenomenon as the taxi-dance hall was found to be scanty and of little value; and formal interviews were abandoned as unsatisfactory. When the interests of the interrogator were revealed the proprietors and their associates were all found to be unwilling to co-operate and often to be unable to understand adequately the purpose of this research. It was apparent that this study, if it were to be completed, had to be conducted without any co-operation from the proprietors and despite the deliberate opposition of some of them.

Observers were sent into the taxi-dance halls. They were instructed to mingle with the others and to become as much a part of this social world as ethically possible. They were asked to observe and to keep as accurate a record as possible of the behavior and conversations of those met in the establishments. Each observer was selected because of his past experience, his training, and his special abilities. These investigators made it possible to gather significant case material from a much more varied group of patrons and taxi-dancers than could have been secured through any one person. The investigators functioned as anonymous strangers and casual acquaintances. They were thus able to obtain this material without encountering the inhibitions and resistance usually met in formal interviews. Further, the independent reports from different observers upon their contacts with the same individual made possible a check upon the consistency of the documents obtained. Moreover, this information concerning patrons and taxi-dancers made it feasible to secure much ancillary social data from the records of social agencies.

The desirability of securing statistical data was early recognized. But the inability of obtaining the co-operation of proprietors and the great cost in time and money which extensive individual investigations entail made this impossible. Nevertheless the considerable amount of case material which has been amassed through the experiences and observations

AUTHOR'S PREFACE

of investigators over a five-year period afford a reasonable basis for the validity of the generalizations made. It should be noted that the documents included within this book are but a portion of the case material and observations assembled in this study.

The writer wishes to take this opportunity to express his great appreciation for the assistance of the many friends, agencies, and institutions which has made this book possible. To Professor E. W. Burgess he owes a special debt of gratitude. If it had not been for his willingness to give generously of his time and advice and to give encouragement at many times during the past years, this book would never have been completed. To Professors Robert E. Park and Ellsworth Faris the writer is indebted for numerous suggestions and ideas which have been incorporated into this book. To Miss Jessie F. Binford, director of the Juvenile Protective Association of Chicago, and to Mrs. Catherine Wright Page, formerly case-work supervisor for that organization, he is grateful for the original opportunity to study these dance halls and for their support of his work throughout the years. To the Juvenile Protective Association of Chicago he is indebted for financial assistance at different times and for the privilege of quoting extensively from their records. The writer also wishes to express his gratitude to the Local Community Research Committee and the Department of Sociology of the University of Chicago for making it possible for him to pursue this study further through an appointment as a research assistant.

To Professor Frederic M. Thrasher and to Dean E. George Payne of the School of Education of New York University, the writer wishes to acknowledge an indebtedness for advice and counsel in the preparation of the manuscript. For tech-

AUTHOR'S PREFACE

nical assistance in the preparation of the manuscript he is also indebted to Dr. Ruth Shonle Cavan and Dr. Elinor Nims. Dr. Paul Frederick Cressey of McGill University also assisted in evaluating the material used in this study. For help in gathering and interpreting the material the writer is especially obligated to Mr. Philip M. Hauser, Mr. Phillips B. Boyer, Dr. Francisco T. Roque and Miss Ruzena Safarikova. Acknowledgment is due Miss Eveline Blumenthal for preparing the manuscript for the printer and also Mr. James F. McDonald for his assistance in completing the maps. And for valuable assistance in revision and the correcting of the proofs, the writer wishes to express his appreciation to Mr. Lewis L. McKibben and Mr. Jay Beck. If space permitted he should mention others who as investigators and in other ways have contributed materially to this study.

PAUL G. CRESSEY

NEW YORK UNIVERSITY
April 28, 1932

PART I
THE TAXI-DANCE HALL: WHAT IT IS

CHAPTER I

A NIGHT IN A TAXI-DANCE HALL

Taxi-dance halls are relatively unknown to the general public. Yet for thousands of men throughout the United States who frequent them they are familiar establishments. Located inconspicuously in buildings near the business centers of many cities, these taxi-dance halls are readily accessible. They are a recent development and yet already are to be found in most of the larger cities of the country and are increasing steadily in number. Today, under one guise or another, they can be discovered in cities as different as New Orleans and Chicago, and as far apart as New York, Kansas City, Seattle, and Los Angeles.

In these halls young women and girls are paid to dance with all-comers, usually on a fifty-fifty commission basis. Half of the money spent by the patrons goes to the proprietors who pay for the hall, the orchestra, and the other operating expenses while the other half is paid to the young women themselves. The girl employed in these halls is expected to dance with any man who may choose her and to remain with him on the dance floor for as long a time as he is willing to pay the charges. Hence the significance of the apt name "taxi-dancer" which has recently been given her. Like the taxi-driver with his cab, she is for public hire and is paid in proportion to the time spent and the services rendered.

In Chicago, with which this study is chiefly concerned, the taxi-dance halls almost invariably seem to have incorporated the name "dancing school" or "dancing academy" into their title as though to suggest that systematic instruction in dancing were given. The Eureka Dancing Academy may be considered typical of Chicago taxi-dance halls.[1]

THE EUREKA DANCING ACADEMY

The Eureka Dancing Academy is lodged unimpressively on the second floor of a roughly built store building on an arterial street, but a half-block from an important street-car intersection. Only a dully lighted electric sign flickering forth the words "Dancing Academy," a congregation of youths and taxicabs at the stairway entrance, and an occasional blare from the jazz orchestra within indicate to the passer-by that he is near one of Chicago's playgrounds. But a closer inspection reveals a portable signboard on which is daubed the announcement, "Dancing Tonight! Fifty Beautiful Lady Instructors."

Before long the patrons and taxi-dancers begin to arrive. Some patrons come in automobiles, though many more alight from street cars. Still others seem to come from the immediate neighborhood. For the most part they are alone, though occasionally groups of two and three appear. The patrons are a motley crowd. Some are uncouth, noisy youths, busied chiefly with their cigarettes. Others are sleekly groomed and suave young men, who come alone and remain aloof. Others are middle-aged men whose stooped shoulders and shambling gait speak eloquently of a life of manual toil.

[1] The following is not a description of any specific taxi-dance hall in Chicago but is rather a delineation of what could be seen in 1927 and 1928 in almost any Chicago taxi-dance hall. In order to present a more complete picture for the reader many of the personal impressions and reactions of the observer have been retained. A more objective treatment will be found in the succeeding chapters.

A NIGHT IN A TAXI-DANCE HALL

Sometimes they speak English fluently. More often their broken English reveals them as European immigrants, on the way toward being Americanized. Still others are dapperly dressed little Filipinos who come together, sometimes even in squads of six or eight, and slip quietly into the entrance. Altogether, the patrons make up a polyglot aggregation from many corners of the world.

The girls, however, seem much alike. They wear the same style of dress, daub their faces in the same way, chew their chicle in the same manner, and—except for a few older spirits—all step about with a youthful air of confidence and enthusiasm. But one soon perceives wide differences under the surface. Some approach the entrance in a decorous manner, others with loud laughter, slang, and profanity. The girls most frequently alight from street cars, sometimes alone, often in groups of two and three. Some seem to live within walking distance, and a few arrive in taxicabs, with an occasional girl perched in the forward seat beside the driver. Frequently an overflowing taxicab conveys three or four girls, accompanied by an equal number of men. The girls, trim in their fur coats and jauntily worn hats, hurry across the sidewalk, through the entrance and up the stairs, followed by their escorts. When the escorts are Filipinos, they too hasten toward the doorway, themselves the object of a none-too-friendly gaze from the men about the entrance.

Admission to the dance hall is easy to secure. In a narrow glass cage at the head of the stairs sits the ticket-seller, with immobile countenance. He indicates by a flicker of the eyelids and a glance toward the sign stating the admission fee that entrance will be granted upon the payment of the prescribed charge of $1.10. Stuffing into convenient pockets the long strip of dance tickets, the patron is then ushered through the checkroom and into the main hall.

It is a long narrow room with a low ceiling festooned with streamers of red-and-green crêpe paper. Wall panels of crudely painted pastoral scenes serve only to accentuate the rude equipment. On a platform at one end of the hall the five musicians of the orchestra wriggle, twist, and screech. But their best efforts to add pep and variety to the monotonous "Baby Face, You've Got the Cutest Little Baby Face" win no applause. The dancers are musically unappreciative, entirely oblivious to the orgiastic behavior on the orchestra stand.

Most of the two hundred men in the hall do not seem to be dancing. They stand about the edge of the dance space or slouch down into the single row of chairs ranged along the wall and gaze fixedly upon the performers. No one speaks. No one laughs. It is a strangely silent crowd. The orchestra stops with a final squawk from the saxophone. The couples dissolve, and for the next half-minute the crowded dance floor becomes a mass of seething, gesticulating figures; sideline spectators dart hither and thither after girls of their choice, while other men slump down into the vacated seats. Above the commotion the ticket-collector shouts loudly for tickets. As soon as the girl receives a ticket from the patron, she tears it in half, gives one part to the ubiquitous ticket-collector; and the other half she blandly stores with other receipts under the hem of her silk stocking—where before the evening is over the accumulation appears as a large and oddly placed tumor. She volunteers no conversation; as the music begins, she nonchalantly turns toward her new patron ready for the dance with him.

This time the orchestra offers the snappy little jig, "I Like

A NIGHT IN A TAXI-DANCE HALL 7

Your Size, I Like Your Eyes, Who Wouldn't?" The newly elected couples move out upon the floor, and the side-line spectators again line up to ogle. Ogling, in fact, seems here to be the chief occupation of the male. Twice as many men ogle as dance. They jostle each other for room along the side line and gradually, involuntarily, they encroach upon the dance space. "Back to the line, boys, back to the line!" An Irish policeman in uniform walks along the side lines pushing back the overzealous with vigorous, persistent shoves. The men retreat, only to press forward a moment later.

The dance-hall girl, on closer inspection, seems to represent a type in more than appearance. She may be either blond or brunette, but apparently she is required to be slender, lithe, youthful, and vivacious. She perhaps need not be thought virtuous, in the conventional sense; she must at least be considered "peppy." Occasionally a girl more brazen than the rest, with cynically curled lips and too generously applied rouge, dances by, exhibiting in her actions a revolt against the conventional. But for the most part the dancers appear to be giddy young girls in the first flush of enthusiasm over the thrills, satisfactions, and money which this transient world of the dance hall provides. Their stock in trade seems to be an ability to dance with some skill a great variety of dance steps, and, more important, sufficient attractiveness to draw many patrons to the hall. They apparently seek to enhance their attractiveness by every feminine device—rouge, lipstick, and fetching coiffures. Even the silken dress seems sometimes to serve its mistress professionally. When business is dull the unchartered girls frolic together over the floor, their skirts swish about, the side-line spectators gape and reach for more tickets.

The taxi-dancer's job is an arduous one. The girl must

have almost unlimited physical stamina to stand up indefinitely to the many forms of physical exercise which the patron may choose to consider dancing. As a matter of fact, dancing is anything but uniform in the taxi-dance hall. Some couples gallop together over the floor, weaving their way in and around the slower dancers; others seek to attain aesthetic heights by a curious angular strut and a double shuffle or a stamp and a glide. Still others dance the "Charleston," and are granted unchallenged pre-emption of the center of the floor. Some couples are content with a slow, simple one-step as they move about the hall. At times certain dancers seem to cease all semblance of motion over the floor, and while locked tightly together give themselves up to movements sensual in nature and obviously more practiced than spontaneous. These couples tend to segregate at one end of the hall where they mill about in a compressed pack of wriggling, perspiring bodies. It is toward such feminine partners that many of the men rush at the end of each dance; these are the taxi-dancers who, irrespective of personal charm, never seem to lack for patrons. "It's all in the day's work, and we are the girls who get the dances," would seem to be their attitude.

A majority of the patrons, however, do not appear to be seeking this type of activity. Many obviously enjoy dancing for its own sake. Others frankly crave youthful feminine society of a sort which can be enjoyed without the formality of introduction, and are willing to pay liberally for it. A few appear to be those who have taken the "dancing academy" advertisement seriously, and have come to be instructed. The girls make no attempt to teach these men, but simply walk them about the hall in an uncertain manner. But for most men attending this "dancing school" it is certainly a place of amusement, not of instruction.

A NIGHT IN A TAXI-DANCE HALL

The patrons of the taxi-dance hall constitute a variegated assortment. The brown-skinned Filipino rubs elbows with the stolid European Slav. The Chinese chop-suey waiter comes into his own alongside the Greek from the Mediterranean. The newly industrialized Mexican peon finds his place in the same crowd with the "bad boys" of some of Chicago's first families. The rural visitor seeking a thrill achieves his purpose in company with the globe-trotter from Australia. The American Negro remains the only racial type excluded from the taxi-dance hall.

Age likewise involves little or no restriction for the patron of this dance hall. Gray-haired, mustached men of sixty dance a slow, uncertain one-step in response to the vivacious jigging of their youthful companions, or, perhaps, sit alone in some corner puffing at a cigar. Then there are pudgy men of forty or fifty who dance awkwardly but obviously with great pleasure to themselves; and a few spectacled, well-groomed, middle-aged gentlemen who move quietly, politely, and discreetly among the others. Then also there is the florid-faced, muscular giant of middle years, uncouth in manner and dress, who occupies a prominent place on the side lines, his huge hairy paws extended over the shoulders of his diminutive partner. And standing a little removed from the others is the anemic little man, short of stature, meekly getting out of everyone's way.

Young men are there too, boisterous youths who enter in groups of three and four and hang together at the outskirts of the side-line spectators. They dance little, but instead seem preoccupied in noisy disputes with one another. At first impression they do not seem to be interested in the taxi-dancers. But when they address a girl it is with a certain directness of manner which frequently seems to win favor.

They draw her to one side where with appropriate display of braggadocio they press their suit, collectively or singly. Failing in their quest, they seek out other favorites. But should success attend their efforts, they conduct themselves more quietly, very probably awaiting closing time when they will be able to escort from the hall the girl of their choice. The taxi-dancer in question meanwhile goes on about her business—collecting dance tickets.

In addition to the old or middle-aged and the young men there are "rough and ready" fellows of marriageable age who seem to be unable to assimilate completely some of the modes of city life. In a more rustic setting they may have been the Brummels of the party; in the impersonal contacts of city life they play a more obscure rôle. Many appear to be recent industrial recruits from the country, eager to experience some of the thrills of city life. Others may be foot-loose globe-trotters, hobo journeymen "traveling on their trade," for whom the normal steps in feminine acquaintanceship must be sped up. Still others, however, constitute a different type and suggest the sleekly groomed, suave young "business men" of questionable antecedents. A man of this last type will stand politely at the side lines smoking his cigarettes, and, when wishing to dance, will select invariably the prettiest and youngest of the girls. Finally, there are a few men, handicapped by physical disabilities, for whom the taxi-dancer's obligation to accept all-comers makes the establishment a haven of refuge. The dwarfed, maimed, and pock-marked all find social acceptance here; and together with the other variegated types they make of the institution a picturesque and rather pathetic revelation of human nature and city life.

The orchestra passes from the snappy little jig "I Like

A NIGHT IN A TAXI-DANCE HALL 11

Your Size, I Like Your Eyes, Who Wouldn't?" to "Honey Bunch, You Know How Much I Love You; Honey Bunch, I'm Always Thinking of You"; and then to "I Wish I Had My Old Girl Back Again; I Miss Her More than Ever Now." This last offering is a slow, dreamy waltz, and seems popular with the patrons. There is a scurry for partners; laughter and conversation cease, and except for the shuffling of feet and the labored measures from the orchestra, nothing disturbs the rhythmic movements of the dance. Overhead lights go out, and from one corner a spotlight throws a series of colors over the revolving figures. They appear weird shapes, gliding in and out of the kaleidoscopic colorings, one moment in a blaze of color and the next instant retreating to ashen-gray hulks in the dusk that enshrouds the room. Here are mystery, fantasy, and romance. A strange quiescence pervades all. But only momentarily. The incandescent clusters again light up the room, the saxophone croons forth its final notes, and the dance is done. The spell over, all are back again in a practical, money-making world. Girls disengage themselves from their erstwhile captors, and hurry unescorted to the side lines or to a prearranged rendezvous with other partners. Patrons, grown suddenly active, finger hurriedly for tickets, and pace up and down the row of unappropriated girls along the side lines seeking out favorites. The traffic in romance and in feminine society is again under way.

It is a mercenary and silent world—this world of the taxi-dance hall. Feminine society is for sale, and at a neat price. Dances are very short; seldom do they last more than ninety seconds. At ten cents for each ninety seconds of dancing, a full evening would total the man a tidy sum. Since the average patron does not seem to belong to the social class of easy affluence, he spends much of his evening on the side lines balancing his exchequer against new stimulations in the dance—apparently with the result that his exchequer loses. The more popular taxi-dancer accumulates an enormous number of tickets in the course of an evening. These young girls by a few hours of dancing each evening may secure a weekly income of at least thirty-five or forty dollars. By the sale of nothing more than their personal society for a few hours each evening they may earn twice or three times as much as they could by a long disagreeable day in a factory or store.

There is little conversation. The patron may sit for hours beside others of his sex without conversing with them. Instead, the attention of all patrons focuses upon the jigging couples in the center of the floor. The girls, likewise, when not dancing stand for long periods beside each other without talking. Conversation, at best, does not seem to be a highly developed art in this taxi-dance hall. Even when dancing couples do not converse, although it is almost the only situation in the dance hall in which men and girls may become acquainted.

The evening in the dance hall is coming to a close. It is past one o'clock in the morning and the "dancing academy" adjourns at two. The jazz musicians, now thoroughly tired, grind out their music mechanically. It is now a matter of physical endurance. So it is also for the taxi-dancer. Her vivacity and enthusiasm—so evident earlier in the evening—are now gone. She stands indifferently on the side lines, shoulders drooping, or shuffles toward a chair where she slouches dejectedly, awaiting closing time, when she will be permitted to leave. Many patrons also show signs of fatigue. Some who have imbibed too freely sleep noisily in their

A NIGHT IN A TAXI-DANCE HALL

chairs. A few vigorous ones, however, remain dancing upon the floor.

Some of these men are obviously dancing for sheer enjoyment. But they are in the minority. More often they seem to be seeking a certain girl for a "date" after closing hour. They dance on, dance after dance, apparently supplied with an endless number of tickets. The periods of "dancing" are shortened from ninety to sixty seconds, but the interested patrons continue undaunted by the change, in some cases apparently not even realizing that a shortening of the dance has occurred.

Financial considerations for the time are thrown to the winds as patron after patron responds to the dancing of the girls. They overlook completely the momentary pause between dance numbers, and frequently cease all semblance of movement upon the floor. "Get off that dime," good-naturedly shouts a taxi-dancer to a girl chum and her overzealous patron. The man pays no attention, and the girl grins but replies nothing. A minute later the patron shuffles away. But there are other clients waiting their turn. Among these the ticket-collectors continue to circulate, oblivious to everything save the all-important bits of pasteboard. Overhead in conspicuous places along the walls large black-lettered signs bear the injunction, "No Improper Dancing Permitted," while up and down the line of spectators stroll three uniformed officers of the law, "supervising" activities.

Suddenly there is a rush of spectators and taxi-dancers toward one corner of the room. The dancing and music continue, but there is a craning of necks, and exclamations and conjectures are heard above the music. A moment later the pack of excited revelers divides and two angry youths of swarthy complexion emerge, flanked on either side by officers of the law, who project them down the stairway. "Guess they got in a fight over one of these 'broads'!" is the explanation offered by a bystander. The excitement over, the spectators again return to their previous center of interest—the spectacle provided by the dancers in the center of the floor. The orchestra comes finally to the "home waltz," and without more ado the taxi-dancers hurry to the box-office, where they deposit their accumulations of tickets, and scurry to the wardrobe. The men, now disgruntled or expectant—depending upon their luck with the girls—make their way toward the checkroom and the exit. Flourishing their clubs, the uniformed officers pace up and down the hall, urging the stragglers toward the door. "All out now! All out for tonight!"

On the sidewalk at the foot of the stairway stands a little semicircle of youths, either those having a prearranged "date" with a taxi-dancer or those still hoping to secure one. A dozen taxicabs purr at the curb, waiting for fares. The girls descend, sometimes in two's and three's, sometimes alone. As each girl appears, her favored man steps forward, takes her by the arm, and steers her toward a waiting cab or private car. A few girls do not seem to have escorts. They ignore the solicitations from the sidewalk suitors and walk briskly toward the street car.

And so it goes, the sidewalk board of review dwindling, until finally a blue-coated policeman locks the door and ungrammatically advises those remaining to "Go on home! All the girls has went!"

PROBLEMS THE TAXI-DANCE HALL PRESENTS

A visit to this resort raises more questions than it answers.

A NIGHT IN A TAXI-DANCE HALL

What are the characteristics of taxi-dance halls? What distinguishes them from other dance halls? What function have they in urban life?

Who are the young girls who at such an early age have been drafted into this dubious occupation? By what channels were they enabled to find their way to these questionable places? What does this life mean for these young girls and what will be the consequences in later life? Where will their dancing career end: in other more legitimate occupations, in marriage, or in prostitution? And the family backgrounds of these young women—from what types of families do they come? What has been the kind of rearing provided them in their homes? What types of relationships of the girl to her family, her relatives, and the community make it possible for her to enter, and remain, in this dance-hall life?

And then the men of the establishment, the patrons and the proprietors—who are these men who freely spend considerable money for just a few minutes of entertainment? Why are they so attracted? By what stress of circumstances are they willing to pay so dearly for even this transitory feminine society? What does this dance hall mean in the lives of the young boys, the older men, the European immigrants, and the youthful Filipinos? What is the effect of this experience upon their later conduct and their conceptions of life? Who are these proprietors who operate the establishment? What has been their influence in the development of this unique form of dance hall?

Where did this type of dance hall first develop? How was it diffused throughout the country and how was it brought to Chicago? What is its relationship, if any, with prostitution, with police corruption, and with mismanagement of city government? Are there conditions of city life which explain—and perhaps even justify—the taxi-dance hall, properly supervised? Or should it be denied a place in the structure of city life?

These and other questions immediately present themselves and bid for answer.

CHAPTER II

THE TAXI-DANCE HALL AS A TYPE

Until very recently the taxi-dance hall was not recognized as a distinct type of public dance establishment. It was a new and rather specialized type of dance hall and so did not touch directly the lives of most of the people of the city. To the passer-by or the casually interested citizen it no doubt appeared as merely "another dance hall." For others more inquiring the almost universal and erroneous use of the term "dancing academy" in the names given these resorts served further to allay suspicion. There was at first no generic name to describe them, nor was there a clear understanding among patrons or taxi-dancers as to the factors differentiating this type of dance hall from others.

The first efforts of its clientèle to provide a satisfactory name for the taxi-dance hall resulted in such descriptive phrases as "dime-a-dance halls," "stag dance," and "monkey hops." At the same time the taxi-dancer in Chicago, because her revenue from each separate dance had been fixed at five cents, was awarded the apt title "nickel-hopper"—a nickname that has remained with her until the present time. But it was left for the social workers of the country to provide the first comprehensive name for the new type of resort. This term, "closed dance hall," seems to have arisen quite naturally among social workers. For them it served to indicate what they apparently considered the most significant characteristic of the institution—that it was *closed to women patrons*. A former social worker of San Francisco writes as follows of her first knowledge of the term (about 1920): "I never had any uncertainty as to what it meant. It has always meant to me a dance hall where women are employed to dance with male patrons and where other women—for all practical purposes—are excluded."[1] However satisfactory the term may have been to social workers, it was not probable that such an ambiguous phrase would ever gain acceptance with the general public. Certainly the more recently invented term, "taxi-dance hall," because of its aptness and clarity, gives promise of being the name by which this type of establishment will be known in the future.

The taxi-dance hall is but one of a dozen or more types of public dance establishments that may be found in the modern metropolitan city. If the taxi-dance hall is to be distinguished from these other places it must be done through a review of the basic factors which differentiate one type of dance hall from another. Even a brief study of the problem suggests that there are at least seven such factors that must be considered. These include: first, the type of ownership or management, whether publicly or privately owned and operated; second, the dominant motive actuating the management, whether the chief interest is in business profits, professional standards and service, or in social welfare; third, the methods of payment and the relative cost of attendance; fourth, the type of patronage, how homogeneous, whether younger or older people, whether exclusively masculine or both masculine and feminine; fifth, the association of the dancing with other services and activities in the establishment, whether dancing is incidental to other activities or is the center of attention; sixth, the type of physical equip-

[1] Maria Ward Lambin, formerly director of the Dance Hall Survey of San Francisco in a personal letter to the writer.

THE TAXI-DANCE HALL AS A TYPE 19

ment provided, whether expensive or inexpensive, whether making possible dancing throughout the year or only during certain seasons; and, finally, the location of the dance establishment in the urban structure, whether typically in the central business district, in the "bright-light areas" outside, or perhaps beyond the city limits.

A consideration of any dance establishment reveals that it may be classified in terms of these basic factors. Thus the "dine and dance" restaurant is to be differentiated from the commercially operated ballroom primarily because dancing in it is only incidental to the dispensing of food. The cheaper commercialized pavilion dance hall can be distinguished from the "million-dollar wonder ballroom" on the basis of the relative inexpensiveness of equipment and because of its seasonal character. This same commercially operated pavilion dance hall may likewise be differentiated from the Chicago Municipal Pier dance pavilion, for instance, because the latter is municipally owned. In the same manner the roadhouse can be distinguished from the cabaret or the "dine and dance" establishment because of its typical location beyond the boundaries of the city but within automobile-driving distance for its clientèle.

A review of the information available reveals that, according to the foregoing classification, there are at least fourteen types of public[1] dance establishments to be found in a

[1] It should be noted that reference is here made only to those dance establishments which are "public," i.e., open to the patronage of the general public. There are many "private" dances and dance establishments which obviously are not considered. Likewise, there are marginal establishments about which it is not so easy to decide. The term "night club," for instance, has come to be used to denote both the "*public* cabaret" and the "*private* club," to which admission is granted only to "members." But where the "private club" is a club in name only, is operated by one or more enterprisers

metropolitan city such as Chicago, of which the taxi-dance hall is but one. The following classification, prepared by the writer, while only tentative, is at least based upon what appear to be the fundamental structural differences among these public dance halls.

1. *Municipal ballroom or pavilion.*—Owned and operated by the city with an objective of social welfare. Equipment usually inexpensive, small admission fees, located on public property and within easy access of those living in the more congested parts of the city.

2. *Dancing academy.*—Operated privately by teachers with a recognized professional status who have definite methods and programs for instruction in dancing and whose interest therefore is professional. Dancing is the center of interest, fees are relatively high, adults of all ages attend, and the establishments are usually located in or near the central business district or in the major "bright-light" areas outside the central business district.

3. *Social-service dance.*—Sponsored by social agencies or other humanitarian groups to meet specific social needs with the ideal of social service. Admission fees are low, the patronage is restricted to the special groups which the activity is designed to serve, and the dances are given at a location which at once identifies the dances as being sponsored by the social agency or group and as being a recognized part of their program.

4. *Fraternal or "benevolent" dance.*—Public or semipublic dances conducted by certain fraternal orders as a means for promoting social gatherings and for financing worthy causes. Thus, the "charity ball," the "lodge dance," or the dance sponsored by an athletic club may be of this type; admission fees are relatively high, patronage is of one cultural group and of approximately the same age-span.

---

for private profit, and where "membership cards" are sold promiscuously, it is clear that the "night club" is in reality a *public* dance establishment. Inasmuch as virtually all so-called night clubs are reported to provide a vaudeville program, food, and refreshments as well as an opportunity to dance, such *public* night clubs may also be classified as cabarets. But where the "night club" is a bona fide private club it is obviously not a public dance establishment and is therefore beyond the scope of the accompanying classification.

THE TAXI-DANCE HALL AS A TYPE

5. *Pseudo-club dance.*—Operated under the guise of a bona fide club but in reality a public dance operated for private profit by one or more people who have a dance following. Such names as "The Koo Koo Klub," "The Jolly Steppers," and "Campus Club" may be used, and create the impression that the patrons constitute a stable "primary group" or that the dance is exclusive. These dances are usually given periodically in a rented hall with fair equipment, located in the more congested parts of the city or near a center of mobility and retail trade, to which a certain clientèle is attracted. Patrons tend to be a rather homogeneous group and admission charges are fairly high.

6. *Hotel dance.*—Public or semipublic dances given by residential hotels for their guests but to which others appearing to be socially desirable or the acquaintances of guests are also admitted. No admission charges are usually made and the equipment is whatever the hotel building affords. People of all ages may attend though otherwise the dancers are at least as homogeneous as are the hotel guests.

7. *Dine-and-dance restaurant.*—A commercially operated restaurant with provision for dancing usually including an orchestra. The dancing is thus regarded as merely incidental to dining and is enjoyed chiefly during the meal. Such restaurants are relatively expensive though sometimes without a special cover charge. They are usually located in the central business district or in other "bright-light" areas, and usually have attractive, expensive quarters. The patrons are heterogeneous; they attend independently as small groups and have little interest in others seen at the restaurant.

8. *Cabaret or "night club."*—The cabaret is to be distinguished from the dine-and-dance establishment by the presence of vaudeville entertainment. Interest of patrons is not only in dancing but also in dining and in witnessing vaudeville acts. It is operated as a commercial enterprise, attendance is costly and usually involves a cover charge. Equipment is showy though sometimes not expensive. Such establishments are located in areas of high mobility which will tolerate them, near the central business district, in the "area of deterioration" surrounding the central business district, or in outlying "bright-light" areas. Patrons are exceedingly heterogeneous, they differ greatly in age, financial resources, cultural attainments, and in dominant interests and purposes. In the case of the so-called "black and tan" cabarets, for instance, this heterogeneity extends to admitting Negroes as well

as other non-Caucasian groups. When the term "night club" denotes a *public* dance establishment, providing refreshments, food, and a vaudeville program, it can be considered synonymous with the cabaret.

9. *Dance palace.*—A large, spacious ballroom, representing large outlays of money, attractively equipped and operated as a private commercial venture. Located chiefly in outlying "bright-light" areas, near focal transportation points and in the vicinity of good residential property. Admission is expensive and the patrons are rather heterogeneous. Interest is focused in the dancing and in the social contacts, though refreshments may be an incidental service in the establishment.

10. *Dance pavilion.*—In contrast with the dance palace the commercially operated dance pavilion represents a small expenditure of money, is a rudely equipped open-air dance platform or pavilion, located in an outlying part of the city where low rents can be secured. It is seasonal, provides an opportunity for summer dancing only, and has low admission charges. Frequently associated with amusement parks and picnic grounds, it provides an opportunity for young people of the poorer classes to attend. The patrons are a more homogeneous group than in the cabaret or the dance palace.

11. *Roadhouse.*—A commercially operated resort located outside the city limits but within auto-driving range of the city. In equipment it may range from a slightly remodeled saloon to a large and attractive farm dwelling. Dancing is only an incidental service, the major functions being the dispensing of refreshments, food, and the provision of vaudeville entertainments similar to that offered by cabarets. The patrons are a rather heterogeneous group though a pecuniary selectivity is afforded through the high charges in many places and through the necessity for automobile transportation.

12. *Rent party.*—As a means of paying the rent, according to common report, some impecunious city people have developed the practice of opening their homes occasionally for a public dance. Admission charges are low, equipment inadequate, located presumably in the poorer, more congested sections of the city. This type of public dance is as yet reported only among city Negroes, but there is no reason to believe that it will not become a practice among certain classes of white people as well.

13. *Pleasure-boat dances.*—Dancing as an incidental service is provided on commercially operated excursion boats. The dancing is seasonal, is relatively inexpensive, attended by a rather heterogeneous

THE TAXI-DANCE HALL AS A TYPE 23

crowd, though mostly by young people. The physical equipment is usually inadequate.

14. *Taxi-dance hall.*[1]

The taxi-dance hall is to be differentiated not only from the other chief types of public dance establishments found in the larger cities but also from the exceptional dance hall which, on first impression, may be confused with it.

Consider, first of all, the dance establishment at which girls are employed to dance with patrons on the ticket-a-dance plan and which seems to be characteristically a taxi-dance hall except that it claims to be a "*private* club"—not a public resort at all—because it sells admissions only to "members" and to those "indorsed" by them.

The Sunglade wasn't on the Bowery, nor on Second Avenue, New York. It was on Riverside Drive and overlooked the Hudson River. Up two flights. Press a button at the side of the locked door and an eye-hole opens. My companion was a Columbia boy of dark complexion, with a card from a well-known patron of the "club." We were admitted. A stuffy nine-room apartment split into three rooms; a four-piece orchestra, shaggy lights, and a few tattered tables were the equipment. Seventy men were in the "club," and about half that number of girls. The dues were $1.00 plus war tax—if the government ever gets it. Tickets, three for a quarter. But there wasn't much dancing. The swarthy-faced men sat at the tables and grinned at the girls.[2]

The policy of admitting only "members" and their friends is used chiefly as a ruse to avoid public notice and routine police surveillance. But even here the profit motive will no doubt be sufficient to induce the proprietors to admit as many patrons as they dare, and to distribute "membership cards" as promiscuously as seems expedient. And, as the es-

[1] This is the type to be considered in this study, a definition of which is to be found at the end of this chapter.

[2] J. B. Kennedy, "Devil's Dance Dens," *Collier's*, LXX (September 19, 1925), 12.

tablishment comes, actually, to admit almost any man who may present himself, it becomes in reality a taxi-dance hall. Then, and only then, may the individual establishment be considered unquestionably a taxi-dance hall.

A second variant from the taxi-dance hall type is the establishment where both women patrons and taxi-dancers are to be found. In some cities the dance palaces have made provision for the man who cannot easily secure dance partners on the ballroom floor by having "hostesses" on hand for him to employ.[1] These "hostesses" or taxi-dancers are not, however, the only women in the establishment, and from this fact arises a very important difference. While the dance palace with professional "hostesses" may serve the same function as the taxi-dance hall for many men, the fact that the professional dancers may not be the dominant woman's group makes it impossible to consider a dance palace with "hostesses" a characteristic taxi-dance hall.

A third divergence from the taxi-dance hall is to be found in the establishment which secures its revenue from other sources than a pro rata charge upon the patron's dances and which reimburses its "hostesses" by other methods than a commission upon their dancing. The most striking instance of this is to be found in "the '49 dance hall" or "the '49 camp," a heritage from the days of the Gold Rush and of San Francisco's "Barbary Coast." In "the '49 dance halls" the dancing was free and the partners or "hostesses" secured their income not from the dancing, but upon the amount of liquor which they could persuade the patrons to buy at the

[1] Institutions of this type are to be found in many cities of the country, notably in Seattle and New York. This hybrid between the taxi-dance hall and the dance palace is not found in Chicago, where the desire of the proprietors of the dance palaces has been to keep their establishments free from the type of man who must pay to secure a dance partner.

THE TAXI-DANCE HALL AS A TYPE 25

adjoining bar. At one time this kind of dance hall was distributed throughout the Pacific Coast region.

The older police officers state that very early in Seattle's history, especially during the Alaska Gold Rush, many dance halls were in existence in connection with bars. The girls in attendance were there working on commission, and received their money from the drinks sold, not as taxi-dancers. . . . . . Later, as a term of condemnation in the newspapers these were called " '49 Dance Halls."[1]

In its later history the " '49 Camp," as it came to be called, was not found exclusively in the Far West. In Chicago this type of establishment was known as the "concert hall saloon," and many resorts of this character were to be found in it even later than 1900.[2] In the South, with the advent of local-option legislation, this type of dance hall became a special attraction of the traveling carnival.

Until very recently in the South the smaller towns were visited almost yearly by a traveling carnival, one of the chief attractions of which was a " '49 Camp." Almost every carnival had a " '49 Camp." It occupied a separate tent, to which admission was charged. On the inside was a little raised platform on which the local boys were invited to dance with the girls attached to the show. At the end of the platform stood a little bar which dispensed everything the law allowed— but at double prices. At the close of each dance the manager called, "Up to the bar, boys! Just as in the days of '49."[3]

Even now, several " '49 Camps" are reported[4] to be made up each year in Chicago to visit the mining towns of northern Michigan, Minnesota, and Idaho. However, these " '49 dance halls" are not to be confused with the taxi-dance hall.

[1] Mrs. E. W. Harris, superintendent, Women's Division, Seattle Police Department, in a personal letter dated April 22, 1927.

[2] From information supplied by Dr. Nels Anderson, Columbia University.

[3] Edgar Thompson, Department of Sociology, University of Chicago.

[4] From information furnished by an official of a well-known traveling carnival having offices in Chicago.

While serving very much the same function, the structural organization is entirely different. The girl receives her pay as a commission upon the drinks she can induce the men to buy and dancing is thus only incidental to the consumption of liquor.

Another variant from the taxi-dance hall is the institution which does not use the ticket-a-dance plan and which does not permit the patron to choose his dance partner. The best instance of this is seen in some of the methods used for mass instruction in dancing.

Monday was announced as "Beginner's Night" at the Cinderella Gardens. The admission charge was only a dollar for the entire evening. The dance floor was roped off into two sections. In one enclosure young men were lined up awaiting their turn for a circuit about the floor with some of the young women acting as instructresses. In the other section young men wearing instructors' badges were taking women—old and young, portly and slender—for a circuit around the floor. At the end of each trip the couples separated without even a nod in parting, the instructor's card was punched, and he was ready for another "pupil."

No choice in instructors was allowed. The two burly attendants at the meeting of the two lines of "pupils" and "instructors" saw to that. As each "pupil" and "instructor" appeared at the head of the lines they were shoved together and forced to dance out a circuit together; whether they were matched as to height and age was of no consequence. People did not appear to be in the least interested in each other and their dancing was automatic and without spirit. It was clearly not an immediate recreational interest which attracted them.[1]

When the patron's dance partner is arbitrarily selected for him, it is probable that his interest in the dancing will be instructional and artistic. But when he is permitted to choose his dance partners, it seems inevitable that the recreational interest will become dominant. If to this is added the ticket-a-dance plan, with very short dance periods and a

[1] Records of an investigator.

chance for frequent selection of dance partners by the patrons, interests other than recreation and romance seem virtually to disappear. A "dancing academy," for instance, which embarks upon a ticket-a-dance plan with the opportunity for frequent reselection of "instructresses" has been found to swing irresistibly over to a situation where all instruction is made ineffective and where the interest becomes social and recreational. Maria Ward Lambin, director of the San Francisco and the New York dance-hall surveys, writes of her experience as follows: "I have found that the use of the dime-a-dance ticket system in a dancing school tends to make it really a closed dance hall [taxi-dance hall]. Where partners are changed every two minutes little dancing instruction can be expected to be given—and as a rule little is given."[1] The taxi-dance hall as a place of recreation, and not of instruction, appears thus to be inevitably associated with the use of the ticket-a-dance plan and with the opportunity for a frequent reselection of dance partners.

From a comparison of these marginal institutions the basic characteristics of the taxi-dance hall type can now be seen more clearly. It is apparent that a taxi-dance hall is an establishment to which only the masculine "public" is admitted, and in which the income of the establishment and the taxi-dancers is derived from dancing. Further, the ticket-a-dance plan and the opportunity for a frequent reselection of dance partners are inextricably bound up with the taxi-dance hall. A formal definition may now be offered.

A taxi-dance hall is a commercial public dance institution attracting only male patrons, which seeks to provide them an opportunity for social dancing by employing women dance partners, who are paid on a commission basis through the ticket-a-dance plan, and who are expected to dance with any patron who may select them for as few or as many dances as he is willing to purchase.

[1] Personal letter to the writer, April 12, 1927.

PART II

THE TAXI-DANCER AND HER WORLD

CHAPTER III

THE TAXI-DANCE HALL AS A SOCIAL WORLD

For those who attend the taxi-dance hall, even irregularly, it is a distinct social world, with its own ways of acting, talking, and thinking. It has its own vocabulary, its own activities and interests, its own conception of what is significant in life, and—to a certain extent—its own scheme of life. This cultural world pervades many avenues of the habitué's life, and some of its aspects are readily apparent to even a casual visitor at the halls.

I had expected almost anything at this dance hall but even then I was surprised. It was the most speckled crew I'd ever seen: Filipinos, Chinese, Mexicans, Polish immigrants, brawny laborers, and high-school boys. More disturbing was the cynical look which the men directed at the girls and the matter-of-fact way they appropriated the girls at the beginning of each dance. The girls, themselves, were young, highly painted creatures, who talked little—and when they did speak used strange expressions to accentuate their talk. They spoke of "Black and Tans," "Joe's Place," "Pinoys," "nigger lovers," and used other terms with which I was not familiar. My attempts to get acquainted with several of the girls met with indifference on their part, while at the same time they each seemed very much alive to a few men and several girls in the place. To everyone else they seemed polite, coquettish, but really quite indifferent. I left the place feeling that I had been permitted to witness but not to participate in the real life revolving around the hall.[1]

So well is the vital world of the dance hall veiled by conventionalized conduct that a person may attend regularly

[1] Impressions of an investigator on his first visit to a taxi-dance hall.

without perceiving it. Unless he is initiated into the meaning of certain activities, of certain words and phrases, of certain interests and standards of conduct, he may as well not try to understand the human significance of the taxi-dance hall. For many factors aid in making the world of the taxi-dance hall a moral milieu rather completely removed from the other more conventional forms of city life.

1. FUNDAMENTAL WISHES OF PERSON FULFILLED

Perhaps the most important aspect of this dance-hall world making possible its moral isolation is the completeness of the interests and satisfactions afforded in it. Especially for young girls removed from home influences and living with other taxi-dancers the dance-hall life proves sufficient to meet satisfactorily most of their dominant interests and wishes.

After I had gotten started at the dance hall I enjoyed the life too much to want to give it up. It was easy work, gave me more money than I could earn in any other way, and I had a chance to meet all kinds of people. I had no dull moments. I met bootleggers, rum-runners, hijackers, stick-up men, globe-trotters, and hobos. They were all different kind of men, different from the kind I'd be meeting if I'd stayed at home with my folks in Rogers Park. .... After a girl starts into the dance hall and makes good it's easy to live for months without ever getting outside the influence of the dance hall. Take myself for instance: I lived with other dance-hall girls, met my fellows at the dance hall, got my living from the dance hall. In fact, there was nothing I wanted that I couldn't get through it. It was an easy life, and I just drifted along with the rest. I suppose if something hadn't come along to jerk me out, I'd still be a drifter out on the West Side.[1]

Not only economic gain, but opportunities for excitement, masculine conquests, intimacies, and masculine affection are

[1] Case No. 11.

TAXI-DANCE HALL AS A SOCIAL WORLD

all provided in the taxi-dance hall. The dancers may even identify themselves with the dance-hall life so completely that when they return after an absence they experience a feeling of joy and satisfaction in "getting back home again."

You can't imagine how happy I felt to get back to the "school" again after two weeks at home in Wisconsin. Of course I was glad to see my mother, but then you know we don't have so much to talk about any more. And as for that old German stepfather of mine—the less I see of him the better. I don't feel like I belong back in Wisconsin any more. But up at the "school" I just feel at home. . . . . I know how things go, I have my friends who are always glad to see me come back, and who are really interested enough to spend their money on me. There are a lot of fellows up there who don't amount to much, but—just the same—I have more real friends there than in all the rest of the world put together.[1]

The fundamental desire for recognition, for status, along with the desire for intimacy or response, and for new experience and excitement, all find some satisfactions in the taxi-dance hall. In fact, the desire for security is the only one of Thomas' "Four Wishes"[2] which does not have a place in the life of the efficient taxi-dancer.

2. UNIQUE ACTIVITIES AND VOCABULARY

A second fundamental aspect of the world of the taxi-dance hall helping to maintain its moral isolation is its distinctive patterns of behavior and vocabulary. Even minor characteristics of a person's behavior and manner may become, to the dance-hall world, the means for identifying him as either an "insider" or an "outsider." Thus a taxi-dancer suggests some of the clues which she used to identify an outsider:

[1] Case No. 10.

[2] See W. I. Thomas' statement of the "Four Wishes" in *The Unadjusted Girl*, chap. i.

34   THE TAXI-DANCE HALL

The first time I saw you I knew right away you didn't belong on West Madison Street. You didn't act like the other white fellows who came up to the hall. The other strange men would come in and be very quiet or act like they weren't sure of themselves. They wouldn't talk very much. But you did. You'd even go up and talk straight out to the boss, but none of the others would have done that until after they'd known him.

Then when you'd come over to me you'd first ask me to dance—not just hand me a ticket like the others did. Then you danced differently. . . . .

I also discovered right away you talked differently, used different words, and while you didn't brag about yourself like most of the others do, I got the feeling that you thought you were somebody, and yet you weren't ashamed to be caught in the hall. That's the way I got the idea you were a "professional" of some sort.[1]

The special vocabulary of the dance-hall world is itself a means of identification, as well as communication. It reflects the special interests, judgments, and activities which center about the establishment. To a considerable extent the vocabulary is constructed from common slang and from the "West Side dialect." But in addition there are other picturesque words and phrases which have their chief usage in the dance-hall world. Many of these words or phrases find almost universal usage among all patrons, but others are used exclusively by one group. The Filipinos, for instance, have their own words and phrases; while the white youth of the West Side also has his special vocabulary. Likewise, the taxi-dancer has her words and phrases by which she describes both the Filipino and the West Side youth. This whole special vocabulary, however, blends together and reveals a unique world of interests and activities, in which the focus of interest is sensual and commercial. While a complete glossary is not presented, the significance of this vocabulary in

[1] Comment of a veteran taxi-dancer to an investigator.

TAXI-DANCE HALL AS A SOCIAL WORLD

the dance-hall life can be seen from the following list of picturesque words and phrases.

Africa.—The Black Belt, especially the colored cabarets.
Playing Africa.—Clandestine prostitution in the Black Belt.
Staying in Africa.—Living in the Black Belt, presumably for purposes of prostitution.
Bata.—Tagalog word for "baby," used by Filipinos to describe a Filipino's white sweetheart.
Black and Tan.—A colored and white cabaret.
Buying the groceries.—Living in clandestine relationship.
Class.—Term used by Filipinos to denote the taxi-dance halls.
 I have a class.—I'm going to the dance hall.
 Let's go to class.—Let us go to the dance hall.
Colegiala.—Spanish word for "coed" used by Filipino to denote taxi-dancer.
Escuela.—Spanish word for "school" used by Filipinos to denote taxi-dance halls.
Fish.—A man whom the girls can easily exploit for personal gain.
 To fish.—To exploit a man successfully for personal gain.
Flip.—Filipino's name for himself. Of American origin.
Fruit.—An easy mark.
Hot stuff.—Stolen goods.
Line-up, the.—Immorality engaged in by several men and a girl.
Make, "to make."—To secure a date with.
Monkey-chaser.—A man interested in a taxi-dancer or chorus girl.
Monkey shows.—Burlesque shows having chorus girls.
Monkeys.—Dancing girls, either chorus girls or taxi-dancers.
Nickel-hopper.—A taxi-dancer.
Nigger.—West Side term for Filipino.
Nigger lover.—A girl who "dates" Filipinos.
On the ebony.—A taxi-dance hall or taxi-dancer countenancing social contacts with men of races other than white.
Opera, "the opera."—A burlesque show.
Paying the rent.—Living in clandestine relationship.
Picking up.—Securing an after-dance engagement with a taxi-dancer.
Pinoy.—Filipino's name for himself. Of native origin.
Playing.—Successfully exploiting one of the opposite sex.

Professional.—An investigator. One visiting the dance hall for ulterior purposes.
Punk.—A novitiate; an uninitiated youth or young girl, usually referring to an unsophisticated taxi-dancer.
Puti.—Filipino's word for white man.
Racket.—A special enterprise to earn money, honestly or otherwise.
Shakedown.—Enforced exaction of graft.
Staying white.—Accepting dates from only white men.

3. UNIQUE MEANINGS OF CONVENTIONAL ACTIVITY

Not only have a new vocabulary and a distinct type of personal behavior in the world of the taxi-dance hall developed, but old, well-established phrases and customs have acquired new meanings and purposes. An outward conformity to well-established customs often cloaks conduct in conflict with the moral standards of society. Such thoroughly acceptable conventions as courting and "dating" take on new meanings. The date, a conventionally accepted means for young people to become acquainted, comes to have, in the environment of the taxi-dance hall, a suggestion of immorality. While the first date with a taxi-dancer may only give rise to speculation concerning its significance, several dates together are accepted by many as proof that an illicit relationship has been established.

They've been going together now for two weeks. . . . . You don't suppose he's spending his evenings up here, and taking her home every night, unless there's something doing? . . . . Say, listen Big Boy, there ain't no Santa Claus![1]

Not only the date itself, but many other forms of conventional behavior come to have new meanings in the taxi-dance hall.

"Well, of course they're sweet on each other," Mildred exclaimed in answer to my suggestion that Hazel and Arthur seemed well ac-

[1] Case No. 12.

TAXI-DANCE HALL AS A SOCIAL WORLD

quainted. "Haven't you noticed she gives him all her free dances, and that he's jealous whenever any fellow dances more than two dances with her? Art doesn't dance with anybody else now, you notice. He just comes up and sits around and gives her his tickets. . . . . I don't suppose you've noticed that new dress she's got, and her new fur coat. Well, a girl doesn't get a fur coat at a nickel a dance," she concluded sardonically.[1]

The taxi-dance hall has its own body of judgments and experiences by which the activities revolving about the establishment are interpreted.

4. THE TAXI-DANCER DOMINANT IN THE TAXI-DANCE HALL

The most distinguishing aspect of the taxi-dance hall is the position of prominence and prestige occupied by the successful taxi-dancer. Far from feeling herself exploited commercially, the taxi-dancer responds to the stimulation of the situation and the admiration of the patrons and for a time finds satisfaction in them.

Of course it's an easy life, no work, sleep late in the morning, more money than I could earn by day work—and all that. But that's not all that makes me like it. There's something about the hall that makes me feel good. I may be as blue as indigo when I go down there but before long I feel all peppy again. I don't think it's the music. I like to be with people and up at the hall the fellows—especially the Filipinos—treats me real nice.[2]

Especially where the patrons are seeking to win a girl's favor, with the hope of securing late night engagements, they are polite and courteous. Since the girl's society outside the dance hall—so much sought after by many of the patrons—can be secured only through the dubious process of courtship rather than through the more dependable method of

[1] Records of an investigator. [2] Case No. 12.

bargaining, the popular taxi-dancer has a favorable status in the taxi-dance hall which seems to arise in part from the very uncertainty of her favors. Even with those patrons who very evidently have no desire or expectation of securing a date, the taxi-dancer usually has satisfactory associations. Their contacts are of either an impersonal character or a friendly camaraderie.

More completely even than in other types of dance establishments the taxi-dancer dominates the social world, because of the peculiar organization of the taxi-dance hall. The patrons are, for the most part, transient and casual in their attendance. The girls, on the other hand, have a definite and rather permanent economic relationship to the establishment. In their contacts with one another and with the patrons they set the mode, provide a certain scheme of life, and set the immediate standards of conduct for both taxi-dancers and patrons. External standards of conduct may be maintained by the management, but the most direct control remains with the group of girls who dominate the life of the establishment and who have evolved certain codes and techniques of control. These are transmitted from experienced girls to newcomers through casual contacts in the dance hall. Naturally enough, the restroom during intermissions provides one place for the transmission of this code.

I'll never forget my first night at the hall. As you know, I wasn't much of a Sunday-school kid when I hit that place, but they sure made me think I was. During the intermission I went back to the restroom and found the girls powdering, painting, using lipstick, swearing, smoking, and drinking. One girl was pretty drunk, and she was cussing and saying the worst things I'd ever heard. The others were listening to her and laughing at everything she said. The whole thing made me sick and I left.

I didn't go back to the restroom for almost a week. When I did, one evening, a tough-looking Polish girl yelled out at me, "Big Blond Mamma thinks she's stuck up, don't she?" I was so mad I didn't know what to do, so I just turned and walked out. But it didn't take long to get used to things. I gradually got to using their talk and now when I get back there I talk just like the rest of them.[1]

5. THE EXPLOITATION MOTIF

Another basic characteristic of the social world of the taxi-dance hall—already implied in much of the previous discussion—is the existence in it of unique "schemes of life." The schemes of life typical of the taxi-dance hall are in part products of the establishment itself and of the type of life necessary because of its social structure and the interests of its personnel. They represent the ways by which the people most closely identified with the taxi-dance hall seek to achieve through it what they consider significant in life. Their methods are somewhat standardized, and when fully matured are associated with a certain "philosophy of life" or "rationale" by which these activities, and the methods used, are justified. The dominant scheme of life for both patrons and taxi-dancers grows out of the combined commercial and romantic interests and the necessary casual intimacies with many patrons. It is represented in the motive of exploitation toward the other sex, prominent in the minds of most seasoned taxi-dancers and of not a few patrons.

An important aspect of the scheme of life is the attitude which taxi-dancer and patron adopt toward each other. The impersonal attitudes of the market place very soon supersede the romantic impulses which normally might develop. Under the spur of commercialism the taxi-dancer, for instance, very soon comes to view the patrons, young or old,

[1] Case No. 13.

not so much as *ends*, but rather as *means* toward the achievement of her objectives—the recouping of her personal fortunes. Romantic behavior, along with other less desirable forms of stimulation, becomes merely another acceptable method for the commercial exploitation of the men.

The patron's point of view is the complement of the taxi-dancer's. He is interested in securing an attractive young woman with whom he may dance and converse without the formality of an introduction and without many of the responsibilities entailed at other social gatherings. Frequently he desires a young woman who gives promise of other contacts later in the night. Thus, from the special interests of the patrons and the commercial aims of the taxi-dancer a competitive struggle develops between man and woman for an advantage over each other. In many instances the struggle is a conscious one in which any means, fair or foul, are used in exploiting the other.

All these girls are after is the money they think they can get out of a fellow. They'll "gyp" a guy if they can. But they don't get far wid me. I'm on to them. . . . . But it's not that I care about. I can take care of myself. I'm not just trying to keep them from putting something over on me; I'm trying to put it over on them. I know what I'm after and I'm out to get it. That's me all over.[1]

With the seasoned taxi-dancer this philosophy of exploitation, the zealous practicing of her techniques, the revengeful impulses arising from blasted dreams and romances, and her honest though carefree view of her own unconventional conduct blend together to make of her a distinct personality type, interesting in itself. While individualized and somewhat egocentric, able quickly to find the character faults in others who would seek to take advantage of her, she is un-

[1] Conversation of a patron with an investigator.

TAXI-DANCE HALL AS A SOCIAL WORLD

able, apparently, to discover the major faults in herself. But neither taxi-dancer nor most patrons perceive that the most basic explanation for these unfortunate associations, these unpleasant experiences, is to be found not so much in the original character of the individuals themselves as in the very social structure of the present-day taxi-dance hall.

Unable to perceive these basic yet unseen social forces which shape her life, the taxi-dancer becomes something of a drifter, gaining what satisfactions she can from the transient thrills of the day and from the skilful practicing of her devices for exploitation. The following report by a clever newspaper woman who served for a time as a taxi-dancer of her contact with "Dorothy" depicts concisely the experiences, the attitude toward herself, the philosophy of life, and the proud use of her devices for exploitation typical of the seasoned taxi-dancer.

"What's your name?" she asked.
"Lillian," I answered.
"Are you going to work here all the time?"
"I don't know. This place looks kinda cheap to me."
"Well, you're right. I never saw such a lousy bunch of cheap skates. . . . .
"Why don't you move up with me? Every afternoon I come down Sheridan Road. There's always a couple of good suckers just waiting to be taken, and we could have some fun besides. I used to have a steady boy friend, but he tied the can to me, and now I'm foot-loose. They're all the same, anyway.

"I'd never tie up with another sap. They make you sick. Boss—boss—boss—all day and night. Then they take your dough, and you can go without even a decent rag to your back. After this what I get is mine. And what they have is mine, too, if I am smart enough to get it."

"Come on—let's go back out," I said. "I have had about 30 dances now, but so far I can't brag about the big-heartedness of the boys."

"Yeh? Well, leave it to little Dorothy. I'll show you how to take their socks away. Watch me and have a fur coat in a week." We walked out and little Dorothy put her hands on her hips and started looking over the prospects.

"I'll take that one. You watch me and then go over to that big papa in the corner and 20 to 1 you'll hit the bull's eye." Little Dorothy walked over to a little dark-skinned boy and looked him over, and said: "You look aces to me. Come on." She put her arms around him, took two tickets, and then laid her cheek up against his and started murmuring in his ear. The strategy of a street-walker and taxi-dancer combined. The dance was over before I could stop watching her attempt to practice her tricks.[1]

6. ORIENTALS AS "FISH"

The motive toward exploitation is seen most clearly in the attitude toward "dating" and dancing with Orientals. These young men, frequently because of the absence of satisfactory young women of their own races in the United States and because they are denied free social contacts with white Americans, find their problem of social contacts with young women a distracting one. Frequently this restriction reaches such a point that it becomes a matter of absorbing curiosity and even a mark of pride to secure contacts with white American women. Under such circumstances many Orientals are willing to pay exorbitantly for even casual contacts with taxi-dancers. The girls, however, often regard them as "fish," as persons to be exploited.

I was invited into the parlor of the Malowiski home where Sophie was entertaining a rather uncouth Chinese fellow who claimed to be a waiter in a chop-suey restaurant. They did not converse. He merely sat and looked. Nor did he dance..... Sophie and I began moving toward the doorway but in an instant she hesitated. "We mustn't get so far away. My 'fish' might get jealous!" "Your fish?" I asked. "What is that?" "Oh, that Chinaman over there." "Why

[1] Jane Logan, *Chicago Daily Times*, January 31, 1930.

do you call him your 'fish'?" I persisted. "Oh," she replied, "he gives me about twenty dollars every time I ask him, and he only spends two evenings a week up here."[1]

Orientals, and especially Filipino young men, prove to be such lucrative sources of income that many young women, under the spur of opportunism, lay aside whatever racial prejudices they may have and give themselves to a thorough and systematic exploitation of them. They may even develop techniques for exploitation.

Lila .... told me that the Filipino boys were good suckers and spent a lot of money on the girls, providing the girls act jealous and start a fight over them once in a while. "If I had to live on the money I made in this joint I'd starve to death. But you can always get money from these Filipinos.

"My sister works here too, but she is sick tonight. She tried to drink everything she could get her mits on . . . . and then fought with a couple of girls over her Chink. He goes to the university and works as a waiter. He gets a little money from home, but my sis keeps him busy so she can get a lot of bucks out of him.

"I keep my bozo busy, too. He is an interne at a hospital and works in a barber shop, too. He bought me this dress last week after I told him I would cut his throat if he danced with any other dame. These white guys that come up here are all the bunk. They wouldn't give a girl a dime if it killed them, so don't waste your time.

"I'll introduce you to a new one that just came over. He still has a little cash from home, and you can take it away from him if you're smart. One girl that used to work up here went with a Filipino who was a boxer. She took $1200 away from him and then blew to California. When she got there she wrote him and told him to go to hell, that he was a dum sucker and that she was going into the movies."[2]

Among her own white friends it is necessary for the taxi-dancer to explain her interests in Orientals. Here the justification is found again in terms of exploitation.

[1] Report of an investigator.
[2] Logan, *op. cit.*, January 30, 1930.

"Oh, these "Niggers" [Filipinos] and "Chinks" [Chinese] are just "fish" to the girls. They say to us fellows, "You don't mind if I play around a little with these fellows, do you? They're all right, and give us presents, too. We don't mean nothing with them."
The girls just keep them on the string for what they can get out of them. One girl told me she had three of them. She'd get Christmas presents from them, see? These guys are mostly Filipinos. They have a lot of jack [money]. Most of them go to college, I guess.[1]

However, there are many taxi-dancers who will not accept dates from Orientals, and occasionally one may even object to being in the same dance hall with them. For these girls "staying white," as it is called, is of supreme consideration.

The "Flips" [Filipinos] are all right for anybody that wants them. They're a lot more polite than most of the other fellows who come up here. But they're not white, that's all. Of course, I'll dance with them at the hall. But I won't go out with them. I'm white, and I intend to stay white.[2]

7. NIGHT CLUBS AND CABARETS

The motive toward exploitation is also associated with attendance at night clubs and cabarets. Men are useful, in part, because they may be induced to escort girls to these resorts and to pay the bills. To go cabareting is a mark of prestige, and it becomes almost mandatory upon the young girl who would be regarded as a person of consequence to visit certain resorts. However, there are only a few cabarets and restaurants that are considered to be worth patronizing. Among them the "black and tan" cabarets of the colored belt are favored. No doubt this was originally because the escorts, so frequently Filipinos and Chinese, find these resorts hospitable to racially mixed couples. Also certain resorts are

[1] Comment of a Polish youth to an investigator.   [2] Case No. 10.

TAXI-DANCE HALL AS A SOCIAL WORLD 45

avoided because manners of dress or conduct are more cultured or sophisticated than those to which the patron of the taxi-dance hall is accustomed.

The two couples of us were starting forth for an early morning cabaret party. "Where shall we go?" LaBelle asked. "Let's go to the Rendezvous," I suggested. "No!" yelled Big Bill Hanson, the ironmaker. "We don't wanta go to no 'soup 'n' fish' place. Let's go to Kelly's Stables." The girls seemed to favor Big Bill's suggestion, and so we told the taxicab driver to head for Bert Kelly's.[1]

As a result of this restricted selection the taxi-dancer, getting her introduction into the amusement life of the city via the taxi-dance hall, comes into contact almost exclusively with the most demoralizing establishments in the city. An illustration of this fact is the following:

> I've not been around so much in Chicago. I've been to the "black and tans." I was at the Rex Café once. . . . . But I never was to a show downtown; I've been to the little movie near where we live. . . . . I never went to the big dance places. I always wanted to but nobody of our crowd ever goes.[2]

A few of the more notorious "black and tan" cabarets, several establishments in Chicago's tenderloin, and one or two notorious places in the demoralizing sections of the Lower North Side have constituted the night resorts held in high esteem in the world of the taxi-dance hall.

8. SENSUAL DANCING AND EXPLOITATION

The motive of exploitation even extends to the type of dancing which many taxi-dancers find it profitable to practice and encourage. Many girls who are anxious to increase their earnings adopt a standardized form of sensual dancing commonly practiced in many halls. The individual's de-

---

[1] From report of an investigator.   [2] Case No. 19.

cision as to whether or not to engage in this practice is more completely an economic adjustment—and less a moral decision—than is commonly thought. A typical attitude is expressed in the following excerpt:

> Up here you might as well sit in the corner if you don't dance that way. I stood on the side with thirty cents for the first two nights because I wouldn't, but now I'm like the worst of them. Two girls up here won't speak to me now, but I don't care. It's the money I'm after.[1]

From a frank accommodation to the economic situation in which the girl finds herself to a justification of her conduct on the basis of exploitation is a transition very easy to make. In the taxi-dance hall, where exploitation is thought of as any means of gaining money and gifts short of overt immorality, the idea of exploitation very readily affords a satisfactory rationalization for sensual dancing. Such conduct appears as but another means for "fishing" or exploiting the men.

9. THE "SEX GAME"

The exploitation motive which is characteristic of so many aspects of the life of the taxi-dance hall also has its place in the personal sex philosophy and practices of the taxi-dancer. The "sex-game," a term applied to this scheme of life,[2] denotes the battle of wits in which there is a careful stalking of the other sex and in which the woman frankly utilizes her sex attractions as an aid in winning the game.

This game arises very naturally as a fortuitous adjustment of the unattached woman in a world of transient contacts. In these casual associations utilitarian interests tend to take precedence over all others. For the girl trying to

---
[1] Case No. 20.
[2] See Frances Donovan, *The Woman Who Waits*, pp. 211-20.

make her way in such a world a readjustment in her code may seem mandatory. The philosophy of the sex game is the natural result.

Though often thought of and described as "gold-digging," the sex game is the characteristic scheme of life not only of the seasoned taxi-dancer but of many other groups of women who seek to make their way in a world of transient associates. The waitress, according to Frances Donovan,[1] finds it expedient to avail herself of some such practice. Were the information available, it is probable that it would also be found that the chorus girl, the cabaret entertainer, and even many salesgirls find some form of the sex game immediately advantageous.

While there is perhaps no basic pattern of life on which there is more agreement among seasoned taxi-dancers than in their sex philosophy, the uniformity cannot be said to be wholly a result of their dance-hall activities. It is, rather, a product of their very similar experiences prior to entrance upon dance-hall life. Even though from widely different cultural backgrounds, most of them have gone through very much the same experiences before entering the taxi-dance hall and have arrived at similar schemes of life. For the most part they have been young girls set adrift in a careless money-mad city life with little effective moral instruction to guide them and with no money-making skill or training, who have come to accept uncritically the standards of achievement represented in the shop windows and on the boulevards.

In the quest after the material equipment of life which seems of such prime importance, the girl becomes not only an individualist but also—frankly—an opportunist. Unable

[1] *Ibid.*, p. 213.

to buy many of the stimulations and material things which she craves through the money earned in conventional occupations, she has, in her resourcefulness, discovered financial possibilities in her own personality and feminine charm. This adjustment is merely a matter-of-fact adaptation to the exigencies of the situation in which moral considerations, in a surprising number of cases, have only secondary importance. In the words of one taxi-dancer, the problem becomes simply one of "making the most of what you've got."

I don't go to the hall to make friends. I go there to make money. I've been up there only a month, but I already know how to make the cash. I've got to look peppy and fast, but a girl doesn't have to dance immodestly to make the money. I get all the dances I want without, but maybe it's because I've got a good figure and wear the right kind of dresses. . . . . It's just a question of making the most of what you've got. All I've got to work with is my "sex appeal."[1]

10. FORMS OF SEXUAL ALLIANCE

The sex game very naturally results in considerable sexual irregularity. From these experiences have arisen several forms or patterns of sexual alliances which, although imported from the outside, nevertheless have become an integral part of the world of the taxi-dance hall. In some cases these importations have been considerably altered to meet the economic necessities of the situation. This is strikingly true in the case of the "plural alliance," an anomalous adjustment which has been reported from but few circles outside the taxi-dance hall, though it might develop equally well in other detached worlds.

The mistress.—The highest in point of status of these various extra-marital alliances is that of the mistress. Like the

[1] Case No. 15.

other forms of illicit sex activities associated with the taxi-dance hall, there is a considerable amount of personal interest and sympathy in the attitudes of paramours toward each other. Likewise there are rather definite and well-understood standards of loyalty and faithfulness. Very often there is little bargaining. It is rather a co-operative association in which the man, in the terminology of the dance hall, either "pays the rent" or "buys the groceries," or both. These alliances may last for some months.

The plural alliance.—A less frequent arrangement is what might be called the "plural alliance." Instead of being "true" to one man, the girl enters an understanding by which she agrees to be faithful to a certain three or four men, who may even come to know one another. Through separate arrangements with each man the financial requirements are met.

Ann wasn't what you'd call promiscuous. She had an understanding with four fellows by which she'd restrict herself to us four. She picked us out and then invited us into the arrangement. We each contributed something. Two of us paid her rent, another paid her groceries, and the fourth fellow bought some of her clothes. There never was any jealousy among us. Often we'd meet at her apartment and sit around together. It got to be quite a joke who'd get to stay. When midnight came she'd turn to the unlucky fellows and say, "Well, it's about time for you guys to go on home." Then the next night she'd pick on the other fellow. Nobody got jealous, because—we all knew Ann. .... As far as any of us ever knew she was faithful to this arrangement as long as it lasted—for over four months.[1]

The overnight date.—There is, finally, the overnight date —a rather frequent practice. However, activities of this sort, it should be noted, quickly take on the character of clandestine prostitution.

[1] Case No. 27.

11. THE ROMANTIC IMPULSE

It has been pointed out in the last pages that the taxi-dancer's scheme of life involves an emphasis, fundamentally, upon exploitation. Whether in the girl's attitude toward the patrons, the Orientals, attendance at night resorts, or in the "sex game," the attitude of exploitation—of getting as much as possible for nothing—is clearly seen. This is not only the taxi-dancer's own point of view, but—in its more conservative form—it is no doubt the attitude the proprietors desire that the girls take. In practice, however, the motive toward exploitation is constantly being checkmated by another force—the romantic impulse. Whether desired or not, the romantic impulse flowers forth with increased vigor in this setting—to such an extent that the proprietors have accepted it as an inevitable handicap in doing business.

For the first years that we ran our school we tried to keep the girls from leaving with the patrons. We even made it a rule that any girl who met a man at the foot of the stairs would be fired. But it did no good. They'd just meet them on a corner a block away. And if we told them they couldn't meet them on a corner they'd meet in a restaurant. Se we gave it up. As long as boys are boys and girls are girls they're going to get together somehow.[1]

Toward the patrons the taxi-dancer's general attitude may be that of exploitation, but before long she comes to make certain "exceptions." She comes to "like" certain men, and the rigid commercial system of the dance hall breaks down. Instead of demanding a ticket from her more favored suitors she frequently gives them "free dances," voluntarily renouncing her income from those whom she favors. Even the extensive system of "ticket-collectors," who circulate among the dancers during each dance number demanding from ev-

[1] Statement of a proprietor.

ery taxi-dancer a part of each ticket, is not sufficient to check this tendency. By one ruse or another the taxi-dancer finds a way of circumventing the system and succeeds in giving up at least part of the income received from dances with her special friends.

The romantic impulse also functions in the attitude of the girls toward Orientals, and especially Filipinos. At first regarding the Filipino as an object of exploitation, many before long come to take an entirely different attitude.

> The Filipinos are nice fellows. I don't know whether you know I'm engaged to a Filipino. I love him, too. Right now, I'm trying to make up my mind whether I love him enough to give up everything else for him. And if I marry him, I won't quit. Even if I find I've made a mistake, I'll stick by him just as long as he'll stick by me. I'm either going to marry for good or not at all.
>
> If we do marry we'll go to the Islands to live. There won't be so much prejudice over there, will there? . . . . I wouldn't mind having a baby a little brown. I've seen some of them. They're not so very different and they look awfully cute to me.[1]

The acceptability of the Filipino, in preference to other Oriental groups, is explained by such factors as his Occidental culture, represented in the Spanish influence in the Philippine Islands; his suave manners, dapper dressing, and politeness; and the romantic Spanish-lover rôle which it is possible for him to play. For the young girl with a limited knowledge of the world the Filipino especially appears as an attractive and romantic figure.

> I didn't know much when I started at the hall. I didn't even know what a Filipino was. I thought they were movie actors or something. They were always well dressed, and treated me nicely; I fell for them hard. They took me out to nice places, and took me riding in taxicabs all the time. I thought they must be rich.[2]

[1] Case No. 21.   [2] Case No. 19.

Especially when the girl is dissatisfied with her past, with the type of opportunities which her other men friends afford, or with their treatment of her, the politeness and deference of the Filipino help to give her an enhanced conception of herself. Under such circumstances the taxi-dancer very frequently becomes romantically interested in him.

In some instances the romantic impulse in its reaction to the sordid emphasis in the taxi-dance hall takes on additional strength, and may even extend to a naïve acceptance of an individualistic philosophy suggestive of "freedom in love" doctrines.

I believe in love, even though I've really never had any..... I know I've had a lot to make me not believe in it, but if I really didn't believe it was possible for me to have a real true love I believe I'd want to die..... I wouldn't care what kind of a man he was, just so I loved him. I wouldn't care what he did for a living either. I don't like drinking, but if he was a bootlegger, or even a garbage collector, and I loved him, I'd marry him. It wouldn't be anybody's business what my husband did. He'd be my husband, nobody else's.....

Love is a lot more important than getting married. What does marriage amount to anyway? A preacher says something over your head but it doesn't mean anything unless you love your man.[1]

The romantic interests cut across and negate, quite extensively, the impersonal commercial system of the taxi-dance hall. Yet the personal romantic interest of one day may become the utilitarian interest of the following. If the object of a taxi-dancer's affection is believed to attempt exploitation, disillusionment, cynicism, and resentment quickly supplant her sincere romantic interest.

Out of these conflicting impulses and disorganizing activities the taxi-dancers and patrons shape their standards and

[1] Case No. 12.

TAXI-DANCE HALL AS A SOCIAL WORLD

practices, their own schemes of life. The wide range of satisfactions in the taxi-dance hall, the distinct vocabulary and ways of acting, the interpretations of activities, the code, the organization and structure, and the dominant schemes of life are the basic factors in the social world of the taxi-dance hall, by which the activities, the conception of life, and philosophy of life of taxi-dancer and patron are molded.

CHAPTER IV

THE FAMILY AND SOCIAL BACKGROUNDS OF THE TAXI-DANCER

Although the experiences in the taxi-dance hall tend to mold the taxi-dancer into a type—"chic," "peppy," impersonal and somewhat disillusioned, with her own code of morals—what the taxi-dancer is can in part be explained also by her experiences before entering the dance hall. We may well ask who these young girls are who, out of the many different occupational opportunities of the city, choose to earn their living by dancing with all comers at a nickel a dance.

It should be noted in the first place that a large majority of these girls are Chicago products.[1] Though they may live in cheap rooming-houses and in apartments shared with other taxi-dancers, they often have near relatives living somewhere in Chicago. When apprehended a girl of this sort may present a fascinating and entertaining story of being an "orphan," who has had to "shift for herself since the age of three," or even of a "world-search for her mother" in which she is engaged. But in more than a majority of the cases it is safe to say that the parental families are somewhere in Chicago.[2]

Agnes Gretin, seventeen years of age, shared a cheap apartment in the Lower North Community with three other taxi-dancers and

[1] All names used in denoting taxi-dancers, members of their families, patrons, or proprietors have been disguised to prevent identification.

[2] See Maps I and II, pp. 56 and 57. Except for some girls living in furnished-room areas it will be noticed that the taxi-dancers have home addresses in residential districts.

several young men. The apartment was raided and Agnes told the social workers a romantic story of her life which she maintained with such prepossession and consistency that it was accepted for several months.

She told of being born in Belgium, of Belgian parents, and of being brought to Philadelphia where she had lived until the death of her parents in 1924. She insisted that she had no brothers and sisters and was entirely "on her own."

Only after several months was it discovered that her parents, both alive and well, along with nine brothers and sisters, lived in a house not more than six city blocks from the dance hall where she originally had been employed. She had deceived them into thinking that she was working in a laundry, and had been successful in keeping them uninformed of her dance-hall activities and of her difficulties with the law.[1]

A smaller number of girls are runaway girls from other cities or from the smaller towns and rural districts of the Middle West.

Mary Boris, a fifteen-year-old Lithuanian girl, lived with her mother and stepfather in a small town not far from Minneapolis. Life was "too dull" and so she used her savings to come to Chicago. She shortly made her way to the taxi-dance halls where she represented herself as being eighteen years of age. She wrote only irregularly to her family who remained ignorant of the life she was leading. When finally apprehended she was found to be diseased and living immorally with other taxi-dancers in a rooming-house.[2]

Christina Stranski, a seventeen-year-old daughter from a large Polish family in Pittsburgh, was not satisfied with the income she could gain by unskilled work in that city. She heard from relatives in Chicago that wages were much better and so left for this city. After living with relatives a short time she took a cheap room in a West Side rooming-house.

At the same time she began attending the "dancing schools" and very shortly blossomed forth as "Miss DeLoris Glenn, dancing teach-

[1] Summarized from information supplied by social workers.

[2] Adapted from records of the Juvenile Protective Association.

er." She had personal cards printed on which were given her new name and profession, and soon moved into better rooming accommodations. She broke all contacts with her Chicago relatives and corresponded only irregularly with her family in Pittsburgh. Only after several months were "Miss DeLoris Glenn, dancing teacher" and Christina Stranski discovered to be one and the same individual.[1]

Occasionally the taxi-dancer is found to be in reality an immigrant girl from some European country. Sweden, Holland, Germany, Belgium, and France have each supplied girls for the taxi-dance halls of Chicago.

Minnie Kuyper was a Dutch girl who came to this country about 1923. "There was no work at home," she had said, "so I came to America. I was in New York four months until I learned to speak English a little bit. Then I came to Chicago because my aunt lives here. But we don't get along good and I don't live with her now. .... I've done all sorts of things since I came to this country. I waited on table at a restaurant downtown for a while, but this is more fun, and I get to meet nicer fellows at the dance hall. . . . . I'm saving my money. I want to go back home and see my mother. She's not very well."[2]

I. THE CHICAGO RESIDENCES OF
THE TAXI-DANCERS

The accompanying maps show the residences of over seven hundred taxi-dancers. Except where they are located in the rooming-house areas of the city it is safe to assume that in most of the cases the locations upon the map represent the family residences of the girls. Map I indicates the residences of one hundred and four taxi-dancers, taken casually as the addresses could be secured. While it cannot be claimed to be truly a random sample, because of the personal equation and the limited number of instances, it is nevertheless as general a representation of all the taxi-dancers found in any

[1] Adapted from reports supplied from a Chicago city court.
[2] Records of an investigator.

MAP I

SHOWING THE RESIDENCES OF CHICAGO TAXI-DANCERS WITH REFERENCE TO NATIONALITY AND RACIAL GROUPS AND LOCAL COMMUNITIES

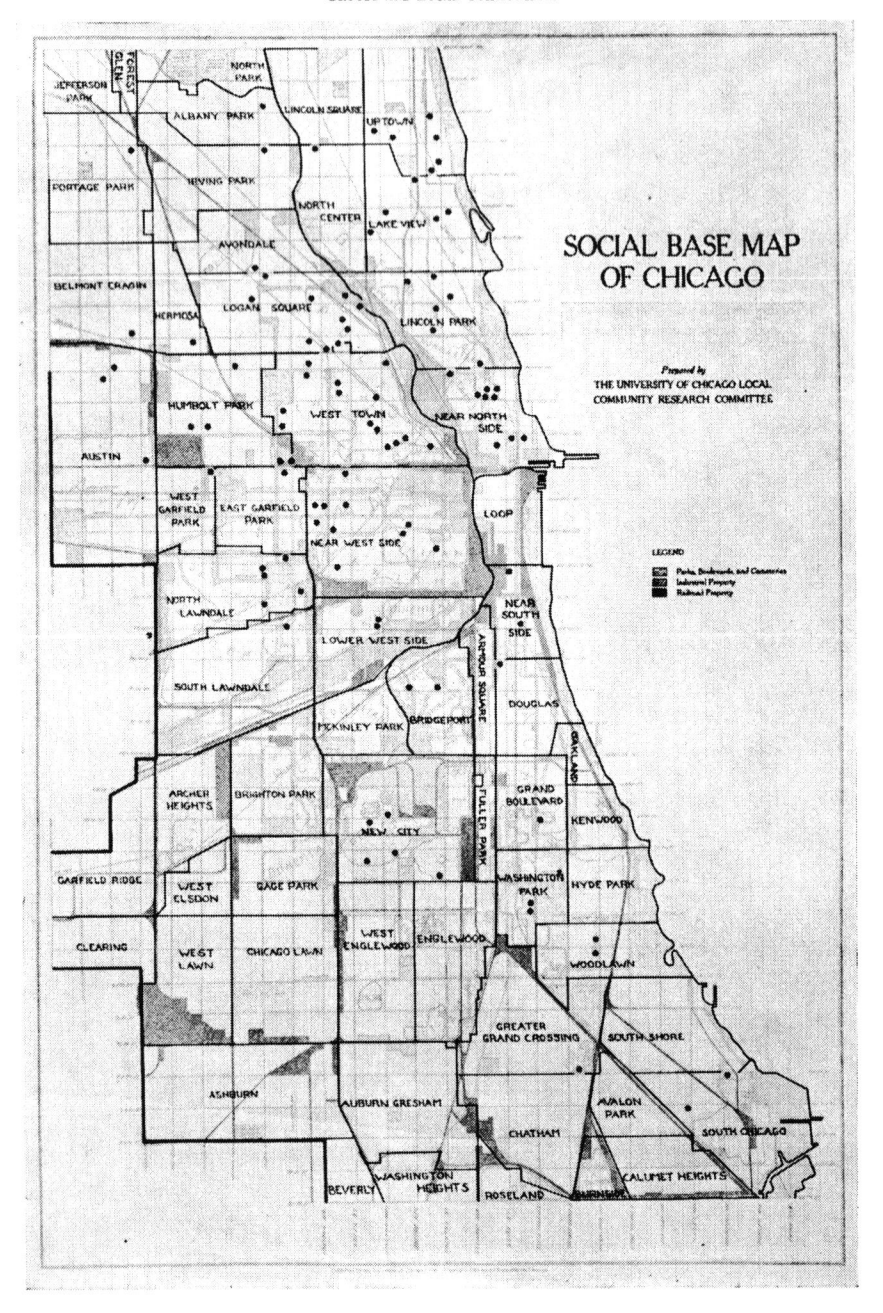

BACKGROUNDS OF THE TAXI-DANCER 57

of the halls of the city as could be secured. The second map shows the residences of over six hundred girls who were registered with the Lorraine Gardens Dancing School, which for a time operated on Clark Street near North Avenue. This is a much more adequate sample, but it is not certain that the distribution given here is representative of the taxi-dancers found in the other establishments of the city. A comparison of these two maps shows, however, that they are essentially in agreement.

Compare, in the first place, the distribution of residences throughout the city. Although the girls come from homes in nearly all parts of the city, a large majority reside on the North and Northwest sides. Much more important, however, is the observation that the taxi-dancers appear to be persons somewhat detached from the communities in which they have lived. This is revealed through Map I. Because of the sheer necessity of numbers on the North Side and the Northwest Side, Map I gives the impression that the girls may have local associates in their dance-hall adventure. This is not true, however. The addresses used in making these maps were obtained from the girls, clique by clique, group by group, rather than by an order arising purely from chance. Because of this fact any tendency for cliques of taxi-dancers to be composed of girls from the same neighborhood would have been revealed. Little evidence of neighborhood association was found, and as a result one is forced to the conclusion that the taxi-dancer's girl associates do not come from her own neighborhood within the city. When found in the dance hall the taxi-dancer is already considerably detached from her early neighborhood ties.

These maps also suggest something concerning the nationality and ancestry of these young girls. A surprisingly large number are from the Polish areas of the city. Hardly any girls come from the Italian areas or from the Jewish Ghetto. In the Jewish areas of second settlement, however, where the Jew moves first after leaving the Ghetto, one finds taxi-dancers. The striking contrast between the Polish group, on the one hand, and the Italian and the Ghetto groups, on the other, suggests the distinct cultural heritage of the Slavic group as compared with that of either of the latter two groups, and suggests the apparent ease with which the girl of Polish parents may be absorbed into the life of the taxi-dance hall.

2. THE TAXI-DANCER AND HER FAMILY TIES

When one observes the extreme youth of the majority of girls in taxi-dance halls, one may be led to the false assumption that they are as immature in their experiences as they are in years. A sample of thirty girls which was chosen as nearly as possible at random, despite its insufficiency for any scientific finality, serves to portray, roughly, the premature experiences which many have had. Investigation shows, for example, that two-fifths of them have been married, although only one-sixth remained with their husbands any length of time. Most of these young girls very shortly sought a divorce, and in many cases—in spite of their extreme youth—entered upon a second marriage.

The parental family life of the thirty girls generally has not been satisfactory. Less than a fourth of this group came from "normal families," in which both parents were still living and maintaining the family. Fully three-fifths came from broken homes, from nearly two-thirds of which the breadwinner (father) had been removed. The resulting economic instability of the family is perhaps an important factor in the

MAP II

SHOWING THE RESIDENCES OF THE TAXI-DANCERS OF THE LORRAINE GARDEN TAXI-DANCE HALL
IN RELATION TO NATIONALITY AND RACIAL GROUPS AND LOCAL COMMUNITIES

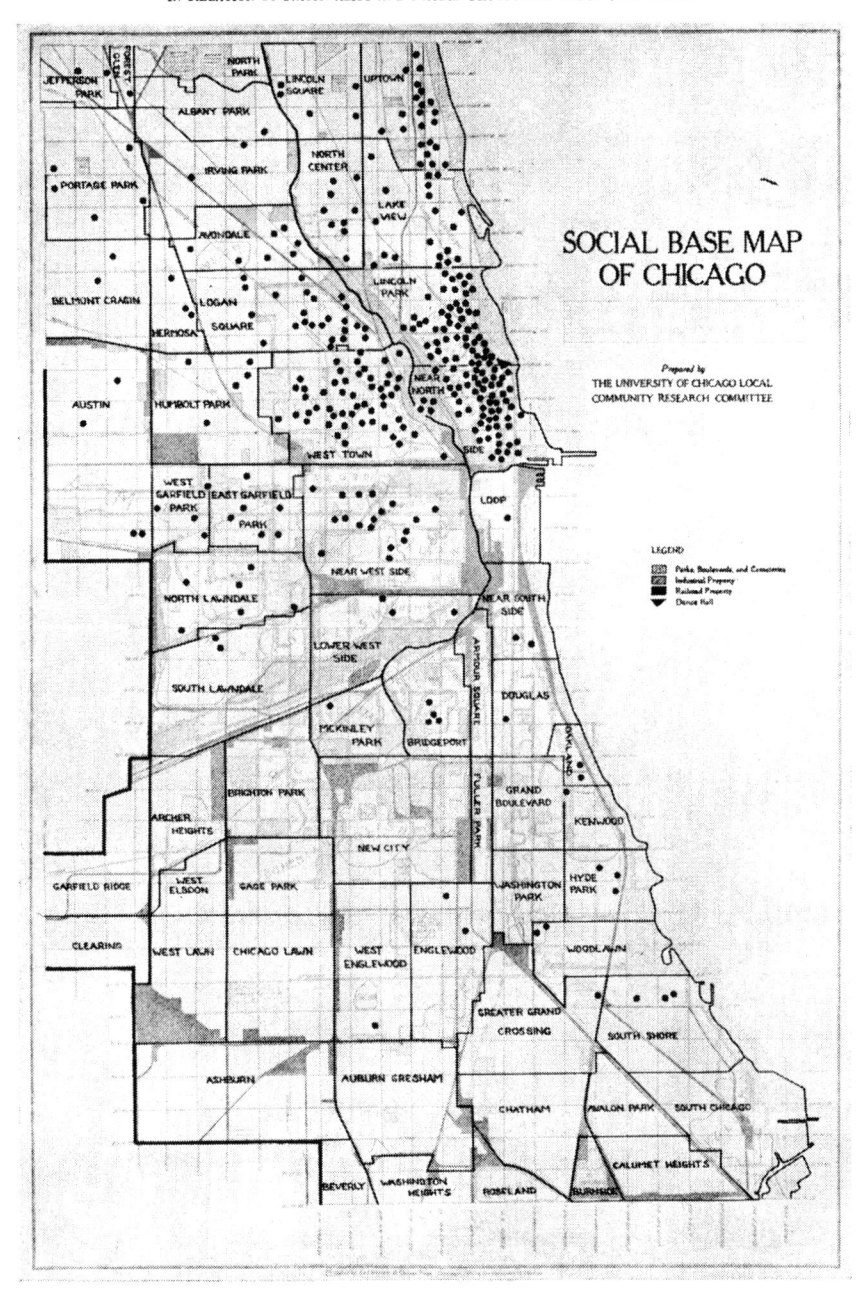

BACKGROUNDS OF THE TAXI-DANCER

girl's turning to the taxi-dance hall as a source of immediate and rather large remuneration.

The economic status of these girls, in relation to their family affiliations, is suggested in Table I.

TABLE I

THIRTY TAXI-DANCERS DISTRIBUTED ACCORDING TO THEIR ECONOMIC STATUS

Dependent member of parental family (if married, no permanent alliance established)	5
Self-supporting; living with parental family in Chicago (if ever married, relationship not maintained)	3
Self-supporting; parental family known to be in Chicago, but living away from parental family	6
Self-supporting; parental family believed to reside outside of Chicago; rooming; no marriage established	9
Self-supporting; married, but separated or divorced	5
Married and co-operating in support of conjugal family	2

3. TYPES OF TAXI-DANCERS' FAMILIES

Enough has already been said to suggest that most of the girls come from parental homes in which there have been severe conflicts. Conflict situations often arise in broken homes; for instance, where step-parents have entered. Again, conflicts arise when families are in stringent economic straits which prevent the girl from dressing as attractively as she wishes—in short, conflicts in standards of living. Various types of cultural conflicts arise—for example, between parents and children, in cases where the former were bred in a rural or European social world in contrast to the urban world in which their children have been reared. Many cases might be cited in which the perennial conflict between youth and age regarding moral standards, aesthetic standards, forms of recreation, has radically affected the family situations.

Perhaps one of the most difficult family situations in which a young girl can find herself is that in which parents are definitely psychopathic. A striking case in point—though in no sense typical—is that of Virginia Wilson, alias Peggy Stone, who was reared under conditions of unspeakable depravity.

Arthur Wilson, who later became the father of Virginia, first met the mother in 1900 when she was a waitress in a restaurant in Chicago. His boyhood sweetheart had recently spurned him and later he married this waitress. Mr. Wilson was then employed as a salesman. While his family ancestry was good, in Mrs. Wilson's heritage insanity was markedly present in previous generations, and two sisters were already inmates of state hospitals for the insane. It was soon discovered by case-workers that Mrs. Wilson was quite incompetent as a wife and mother—"she couldn't cook, sew, or keep house."

Nervous and mental instability became increasingly apparent in Mrs. Wilson, until, in 1908, the husband decided he could no longer live with her. "She was never satisfied—always wanted to be moving into another apartment." She was fretful, moody, and "insanely jealous" of her husband. Then began a period of fifteen years during which Mrs. Wilson constantly accused many different women of "stealing" her husband. In 1913, a psychiatrist adjudged her insane.

Arthur, the first-born, was observed to be mentally deficient when seven years of age, and vicious toward his baby sister, Virginia, born in 1907. Virginia, in turn, though only five years of age, was reported to be "mean and unmanageable."

In the years between 1910 and 1916 the two children were the "football" in the conflict between the two parents, in which social agencies, police officers, institutions, and courts were at times arrayed on either side. Mrs. Wilson was continually hounding her husband through the courts, seeking more support. He, on the other hand, was seeking to get the children away from her and placed in institutions. She dodged from rooming-house to rooming-house, fearing lest her children be

BACKGROUNDS OF THE TAXI-DANCER

taken from her. Mr. Wilson was constantly apprehensive lest his wife cause him loss of employment and friends.

Both children early developed bad sex habits, about which the mother knew and which she failed to correct. In fact, she laughed about them.

Virginia, thought by her father to be mentally normal, attended school only irregularly and did not get beyond the fifth grade. Despite the efforts of social agencies, courts, and institutions, Virginia spent her adolescent years with her demented mother. Arthur was finally committed to a state school for feeble-minded when Virginia was ten years of age. After Arthur's commitment, mother and daughter moved so frequently that social agencies had difficulty keeping on their track. For a time in 1921 they lived in a cheap flophouse in the Lower North Community, where the girl, apparently with the approval of her mother, spent much of her time visiting in the rooms of broken-down men who made the hotel their headquarters. Virginia, then fourteen, was already sexually irregular.

Legal obstructions for a long period prevented the separation of the two. Not until 1926—thirteen years after she was first adjudged insane—was Mrs. Wilson sent to an institution. Virginia, then nearly twenty years of age, was set adrift in Chicago, with little other than the training she had received at the hands of her incompetent mother. She was, for a time, in the taxi-dance halls of Chicago, where she soon became notoriously immoral and was later discharged.[1]

However, there are other types of psychopathic situations which may at times play a part in making it possible for the girl to embark upon a career in a taxi-dance hall. Religious fanaticism of the parent, for instance, may occasionally be a salient factor in a family situation which makes impossible any effective control of the girl by her family. Such was the case of Gertrude Pressley.

Gertrude Pressley when fifteen years old was reported to be out of school and staying away from home. Later it was discovered that she was spending nights with Filipinos. The mother, a religious fanatic, called upon the Lord frequently during the social worker's interview.

[1] Adapted from Juvenile Protective Association records.

She told an incoherent story of her difficulties and when asked why she did not do something to overcome them repeated that she was in the hands of the Lord and that she was willing to do anything he directed —in fact, that she would be glad if he saw fit to remove her from this earth. Finally she admitted that Gertrude had been away from home for a week, and that a certain girl friend was responsible for this. Gertrude left home, it was claimed, because her father drank and abused her. An older son was in prison serving a sentence for a murder. The family had spent all its resources in defending him. The house was reported as filthy and both Gertrude and her mother were said to be dirty. Later reports showed that there had been no improvement in the situation.[1]

A general condition of family demoralization in which the girl fails to receive even the simplest ideals of personal decency or even physical and household cleanliness is, in some cases, the basis for much of the girl's difficulties. The conflicting standards of home and community likewise have a place in such a deplorable household situation as that which has confronted Florence Klepka throughout her girlhood and young womanhood.

The Juvenile Protective Association record upon Florence Klepka goes back to a complaint received in 1914, that she was incorrigible and running away from home. The parents were of Dutch extraction. The first report is as follows:

"This seventeen-year-old girl is not immoral but has an aggravated habit of lying. Her father [stepfather] is able to take care of her without her working and wants her to stay home and help her mother. Visitor told the girl she must quit her lying, that she should never go anywhere without telling her mother where she was going, and that if she ran away from home again she would be taken into court."

Six years later the social worker's report of a visit to Florence's home was as follows: "Visited Mrs. Klepka. The family are now living in a cottage near the railroad in a very poor location. Mr. Klepka works in a nearby coal yard. The visitor, approaching the house, observed a woman sitting near the window with a parrot on the back of

[1] Adapted from Juvenile Protective Association records.

BACKGROUNDS OF THE TAXI-DANCER 63

her chair. Three dogs were in the room with her. Chickens and another dog, it was discovered, occupied the second floor. The five children of Mrs. Klepka were as dirty as the room."

A later report was as follows: "Talked with Mrs. Klepka and Florence. Florence, like her mother, was very dirty. She seemed shallow and vain. She showed the worker photograph proofs of herself to show her how good-looking she was when she was 'dressed up.' Mrs. Klepka says that they are all 'good-lookers' when they are 'dressed up.' The house was dirty and untidy. Mrs. Klepka this time explained that they had intended cleaning up that morning but had been distracted because of a rat they had unearthed upstairs. However, she said that they were going to get all cleaned up for Easter."

The mother said Florence was working as a counter girl in a Loop restaurant. A visit was paid to Florence in the restaurant: "She filled orders and picked strawberries between times..... She became confidential and told of the entire lack of recreation provided by her home. She can't entertain friends in her home because of the conditions—which the mother won't change. She says she ran away from home because of this."[1]

Conflicts which have their root in the cultural differences between Old World parents and American-reared children are likely to be especially intense. The following document is the record of the childhood experiences, fears, and the religious crisis of a girl of Czecho-Slovakian parents. The conflict centered in the pay envelope, the girl's desire for pretty clothes, and her father's deep conviction that the child's welfare could best be promoted by a frequent use of the cowhide. The constant conflict between Old World patterns and American standards only serves to widen the breach between parents and children, and to give the irate father more apparent justification for the use of his "cat-o'-nine-tails." These experiences lead eventually to a schism with all the dominant groups of the girl's childhood: her home, her

[1] Adapted from Juvenile Protective Association records.

neighborhood chums, the parochial school, and even the Roman Catholic church[1] itself.

My parents were peasants living just a little way out from Vienna. My father came from a Bohemian family; had lived there for many years. We talked Bohemian in our home most of the time. My mother came from a Slovak family. They were married in Austria and came over here when I was just five years old. I was the oldest girl in the family but I had a brother who was older. We came over steerage, and arrived in Ellis Island during the winter of 1913. I still remember how I looked. We came to Chicago because my father had some friends here. We got a house out near West Twenty-sixth Street where other Bohemians live.

When I was seven I started to school. I don't remember just how it was, but at any rate I started to the Catholic school. My father never had much use for religion. He was a Bohemian and always used to associate with free-thinkers and atheists. He hung around the saloon a lot and would often come home drunk. I remember how he used to laugh at all religion and make fun of churchgoers.

When I went to Catholic school I began to see and hear things I never knew before. I learned to read and write and to say the prayers. When I was eight years old I took communion for the first time. . . . . Before long I got to having religious feelings and I decided to be a nun. I began to write religious poetry to Mary, the mother of Jesus.

But somehow I never felt satisfied with the religion they taught me. I now think I was so much influenced by the Sisters because they were more refined than the people I met around home. It seems to me all my life I've been trying to get away from the low drinking and carousing I saw when I was young. Most of those early friends seemed to be satisfied with that life, but never since I started to school have I wanted to live like they did.

I can hardly remember when I didn't know a lot about sex. Where we grew up we heard a lot and most of it wasn't so very good for us.

[1] The writer, in including the following case of a girl's revolt against a part of the system of control of the Roman Catholic church, is interested in the girl's allegations only of course as they reveal the attitudes and rationalizations by which the girl justifies her conduct and prepares herself psychologically for her entrance upon the life in a taxi-dance hall.

BACKGROUNDS OF THE TAXI-DANCER 65

When I started to high school, my mother took me in hand and tried to keep me in closer than ever. I couldn't go out at nights and I had to come right home from school. I never had a date with a boy until I was sixteen years of age. And then I had to get in early.

We children were ruled by fear in our household. I was whipped once or twice almost every day I lived. When I got to going to high school I was ruled by a cat-o'-nine-tails. Each of us kids got it whenever we didn't do just what our parents wanted or whenever my father got drunk. I stood for the whipping until I was sixteen. One night I went to a party and didn't get home until nearly three o'clock. My father got up when I came in and gave me an awful beating. He had been drinking and that made it all the worse. The whipping was the worst I'd ever had. My back was black and blue and sore for months. It bled some at the time. I cried and cried and finally went to sleep right there on the kitchen floor. But the next morning when I woke up I told my folks that if they ever gave me another whipping I'd leave home. They never beat me very hard again.

But my mother and I couldn't get along very well. I wanted more money for clothes than she would give me. So I finally quit school and went to work in an office in the Loop. But we didn't get along any better. We were always fighting over my pay check. Then I wanted to be out late and they wouldn't stand for that. So I finally left home and got a room a little way north of the Loop.

By this time I had lost all interest in becoming a nun and shortly before I left home I had my final break with the priest and the whole Catholic church. We all believed the priest was an impostor. The rest of us would sin if we ate meat on Friday, but he could eat it any time he wanted. It always used to make me hate him to have to go and tell him my sins. When I was sixteen and working downtown I went to him for confession. He became angry because I said I was going with a Protestant boy, and then he asked about kissing and making love. This made me mad. I turned and walked out and haven't been back to a church since.[1]

Cultural conflict may also arise between rural parents and their more mobile children. In the following case the mountaineer father holds standards and values which have been

[1] Case No. 17.

preserved from an early period in the fastnesses of the Kentucky and Tennessee mountains. When his children adopt modern urban standards conflict results.

The Babcocks are a mountaineer family who lived in eastern Kentucky for many generations. In 1916 Henry Babcock, his wife, and their nine children sold their plot of ground in Kentucky and trekked out to a little town in central Iowa where they had inherited a small and heavily mortgaged farm. As the children grew older and went out increasingly with the other young people in the farming community, they found themselves more and more dissatisfied with what they considered the shiftlessness, laziness, and ignorance of their father.

Even during the profitable war years Henry found little time for his farm. Between his various ailments, his whiskey still, and the summer heat, he found it increasingly difficult to raise the staple crops of Iowa. At the same time his older sons proved a disappointment to him. They refused to render to him the years of service—until the time of their marriage—which he had expected of them.

While he had proved unable to control his sons, Mr. Babcock dominated his wife in the new environment. She remained a patient, dutiful wife, according to the mountaineer conception of things. She bore him a large family uncomplainingly, did much of the hard work on the farm, made the clothes for her family, waited upon him at all times. In return she asked nothing except board and lodging.

When the four daughters began to mature, Mr. Babcock had more trouble on his hands. One after another they refused to accept his dictatorship. Sex delinquencies resulted in short order.

At this time—the period of post-war farm depression—Mr. Babcock proved unable to meet his payments on this farm, and the Babcocks found themselves virtually destitute. One by one the girls drifted into Chicago, where subsequently they all entered the taxi-dance halls. The married daughter deserted her husband, and is also employed in a dance hall in Chicago.[1]

Another type of conflict situation which seems to occur in the taxi-dancer's family is the rivalry between children

[1] Compiled from information supplied by persons well acquainted with the girls and their family. To make possible a concise presentation of the family situation the usual quotations from sources have been avoided.

BACKGROUNDS OF THE TAXI-DANCER 67

for the affections of parents. This was the situation in the case of Eleanor Hedman.

Eleanor Hedman, age sixteen, had a brother, age fifteen, who was a cripple, upon whom Mrs. Hedman lavished a great deal of affection. Eleanor, who had always seemed resourceful and capable, received little attention. She left home one day and did not return. The mother's belief was that she had left to enter dancing contests, of which she and Mr. Hedman disapproved. The only recollection which Mrs. Hedman had of her daughter's conduct was that she was noticed to be rather sullen and moody at home. By contrast her whole enthusiasm seemed to be given to the dancing which her parents opposed.

It took some time to locate Eleanor but she was finally found living with a woman who some years before had roomed at their home and of whom the girl had always been fond. Eleanor had entered some dancing contests and had become a taxi-dancer.[1]

In homes where there are step-parents tensions frequently develop. It is especially difficult for the half-grown child and the step-parent to work out a satisfactory adjustment. The result is that many such stepchildren leave home and all too often do not maintain a friendly relationship with it.

The following case is given in some detail, not only because it describes a step-parent situation, but also because it indicates the gradual introduction of the girl into unconventional groups and her acceptance of codes quite contrary to those she had been taught as a child. Cut off from her family and later alienated from the community, she feels no effective control from these sources and tends to follow the code of the group with whom she is associated. In this instance the girl, instead of developing an unconventional philosophy justifying her conduct, rationalizes and defends herself by placing the responsibility upon someone else.

My father died when I was seven years old, and we went to live with my mother's mother. Grandfather had been a minister but

[1] Adapted from Juvenile Protective Association case records.

grandmother now lived on a little farm in Wisconsin. My mother got a job in a silk mill. Soon we children found grandmother almost unbearable. She would give us lard on our bread while her good-for-nothing son could have good butter on his. Then she'd sit there by the hour and tell us how religious she was.

My mother worked regularly until I was about ten years old. Grandmother got tired of caring for us and said she was getting too old. Anyway we wouldn't have put up with her much longer. My brother ran away and joined the navy. Shortly after my oldest sister went off and got married. Mother didn't know what to do with us two younger kids. About that time a German farmer who was a widower came along and wanted to marry mother. I don't think she ever really loved him, but just married him because she didn't see what else to do, and how else to take care of us kids.

I guess my new stepfather wasn't as well off as mother thought he was. He was always complaining about the expenses, and how much we two kids cost. When I was fourteen, he told me to go to work, that I was old enough to help support the family. But we couldn't get any work except helping at housework at some summer resort or somebody's house. So my sister Betty left home when she was just sixteen. She went to South Chicago, where she got a job in a box factory. . . . . It seems to me that ever since I got a stepfather bad luck has just come our way all the time. Finally I also had to leave home, and all because of that stingy, old, ignorant, dirty-minded German stepfather.

About that time I began going out with boys and my stepfather told me I'd have to be in by nine o'clock. Well of course you can't go to a dance and get home at nine o'clock. So we kept having fights back and forth. He even accused me of wanting to do things I'd not even thought of up to that time. One night the auto I was in broke down—it really did—and I didn't get in until after one o'clock. We had a big fight at home and he even tried to whip me.

I left home that fall and went to South Chicago to live with my sister. The next spring I got word from my mother to come home—she thought things would be all right. So I returned. But my stepfather and I got to having quarrels again, and I took to waiting on tables at the resorts. During the next winter I left home and got a job in the silk mills. I got fifteen dollars a week, but my living expenses were low, so I thought I could live well enough in Indianola.

BACKGROUNDS OF THE TAXI-DANCER

I was past fifteen years of age then. That winter I got to going to dance halls with boys. I was with older girls who worked at the mill. These girls did nothing but talk about men. Through them I met some of the boys about town and near by. They took us out to country dances, and for the first time I saw people actually get drunk—both the men and the girls. I was disgusted the first night. But after a while I got used to that and got to like the thrill you always have at places like that.

I was always too frightened to want to do anything wrong but most of the girls did sometimes. I had to walk home twice from auto rides. I went out with a lot of boys but I really wasn't interested in any until I heard of Joe. He was older than I, had a big car, and was very good-looking. But the first thing that attracted me was the way other girls talked about him. They told how he always carried a big knife with him he used to threaten girls. None would go out with him a second time. When I saw Joe I got crazy about him. We went out several times and I had a good time. He said he liked me in a different way than he did the others and I never thought he would treat me the same. That was when I still believed what men told me.

Pretty soon Joe got to going with me all of the time. I liked it because the other girls had said I wasn't the kind boys liked and so I was out to show them. I just seemed to be infatuated with him and couldn't turn him down. Finally, he stopped the car one night, away out in a lonely piece of road, got out his big knife, sharpened it on a whetstone he carried in the car, and said he wanted to brand me. He was a big fellow and I got scared. I finally got that idea out of his head. He really didn't do anything and I got home unharmed; but I had had enough. This fellow had such an infatuation for me I feared to stay there and so I left the town and went to Windsor, ninety miles away, where there was another silk mill.

Before long Joe heard where I was and he came up there in his big car. I was crazy about him and yet I was scared to death. Somehow, I was under his power. He even told me he wanted me to return to Indianola to work, and so I packed up my clothes and drove back with him. I stayed there a few weeks longer, and every once in a while when I was on a date with him, he'd threaten me. He was the queerest fellow I ever knew. He didn't seem to want to make love. He seemed to want to do nothing sometimes but go around hurting girls. Then at other times he was just as safe as a lamb. I decided I'd have to leave for parts where he'd never find me. About that time I got a letter from my sister Betty, telling me that she was married and for me to come to Chicago and live with her. So I slipped out of Indianola one night and came to Chicago and lived with Betty and her husband, on the South Side. I took a job at a box factory. Before long my sister was blaming me for alienating her husband's affections, although I surely never was interested in him in the least. I heard that Joe had joined the marines and so I went back to Windsor to work in the silk mill. I was not quite sixteen years of age then.

Very soon after I reached Windsor I met a short, stocky Dutchman by the name of John. He was good-looking, but one of the meanest men I ever knew. He had a bad temper and a vile tongue—which showed up particularly whenever he got mad. We met at a dance and had a few dates but then had a quarrel and he got white with anger at me for merely dancing with a man he didn't like. So we broke up and I didn't see much of him for a while. But the real reason I did not go back to him was because I got interested in another man—the only man I ever really loved. This man was twenty-eight years old and was married and had two children. I met him at a party where I took him away from a girl.

That was the beginning of a real courtship. He had a date with me almost every night. He sent me flowers and made me presents. Until then I hadn't known what real love was. Suddenly I found myself in love with a married man. But he was desperately in love with me, too. He didn't care, and left his wife and children and came to me. I was foolish and indiscreet, but I wasn't "bad" like the village gossips tried to make out. We quarreled about his drinking and finally separated. Since then I've done all kinds of things, even to getting drunk myself, to try to forget my one love affair, but I can't forget. Since we've broken off I've done all kinds of things I never would have thought of before, just to try to forget him. But it's no use and at bottom I know I still love him, even though I'm now married to another man.

I stayed around Windsor for a time after we broke off, but I couldn't forget. I found that I was being blamed by all the scandal hounds in the town for breaking up Ed's marriage. So I just pulled up and

BACKGROUNDS OF THE TAXI-DANCER

left town. Anyway, I wanted to get away where I could forget everything about Ed.

I finally got a job in Madison as a waitress and had just completed a week there when who should walk into the restaurant but John, the Dutchman from Windsor. We had a date that night and the next night. When he found I couldn't be worked, he got angry. The next day was Saturday and he took me to visit a married couple in their apartment. The married couple walked out and told us to stay and make ourselves at home. That evening I wanted to leave, but John wouldn't let me go, and when I struggled to get free he stabbed me on the hand. Then he was afraid that I'd scream and he began choking me. I was caught and there wasn't anything to do. I got away Monday morning and went to South Chicago.

Even before I had a job, I knew I was pregnant. I never felt so much like committing suicide as then. I think I would have, only I wanted to get even with John. I got a job at the box factory, but all the time I worried about what to do. I couldn't even sleep for worrying. Finally I decided I'd have to do something, but I was so dumb that I nearly killed myself and had to go to the hospital. . . . .

I guess you know by this time that I don't have a very good reputation back home. I really didn't mean anything bad. I just wanted to have a good time. There was a lot of excitement at those dances and I was meeting new men. The neighbors talked about me and accused me of things I hadn't done. That's the way it's always been. No matter where I am, somebody's always saying something bad about me. At Indianola I got in trouble because of Joe, and at Windsor the whole town was talking about Ed, because he came from a well-known family around there. . . . . After I got away from Madison, I knew right away what to do. I must "move on." I've been "moving on" ever since. Sometimes I just seem to get tired of where I am, and just "move on" somewhere else. I held this dance-hall job longer than any other I ever had. I must be a kind of hobo, I guess. That's what I am; I'm a lady hobo.[1]

After leaving the hospital this girl worked for short periods in a restaurant, as a demonstrator of toilet products, as a window demonstrator of fountain pens, as an artist's

[1] Case No. 10.

model, and finally became a taxi-dancer. In each position she found difficulties in continuing, because fellow-employees "framed" her, an employer attempted to make love, or because of illness. Once when ill, with no means of support and no place to go, she married a man she met in the taxi-dance halls, not because she loved him but to have someone to support her.

All the cases given, and particularly the last one, reveal the failure of the home to provide satisfactorily for the girl's needs or to give adequate vocational guidance. Personal and cultural conflicts, often reaching a degree of high intensity, result in the girl's breaking her contacts not only with her family but with other agencies of control, such as the church. At a period when her character is not yet stabilized, she identifies herself with unconventional groups, one of which may be the taxi-dance hall. She builds up a philosophy of life or a system of rationalizations which protects her from self-condemnation.

While not all taxi-dancers have the exact home backgrounds cited here, they undoubtedly come from homes that in some way have failed to provide adequately for them. Often in the interim between the time when they find their home life increasingly dissatisfying and their entrance into taxi-dance halls they have undergone disorganizing experiences which have produced a premature independence and sophistication.

4. HOW TAXI-DANCERS ARE SECURED

Chance is undoubtedly responsible for the initiation of most girls into this life. They happen to meet other girls—often in places where they are working, such as restaurants —who tell them of this easy and thrilling way of making

BACKGROUNDS OF THE TAXI-DANCER

money; or they may meet men—at public ballrooms, or elsewhere—who "tip them off" to the fact that they can make money by dancing instead of paying for the privilege.

I first heard about these halls from a fellow I danced with at the Merry Gardens. I told him I couldn't find a job and was just about broke. He told me I was a good dancer and asked me why I didn't go to a hall where I could earn money by dancing rather than paying for a chance to dance, as you have to in a ballroom. He gave me the address of this place [a taxi-dance hall] and I came here. I liked it and stayed—and here I am![1]

In the case of Lucille Smith, an artist's model colleague introduced her to the taxi-dance hall.

While I was modeling I heard about these dancing schools. One of the girls who was modeling in the daytime was working in one during the evenings. Between the two jobs, she said, she made a pretty good income. So I went with her one night, saw how easy it was, and came back. I would model in the afternoons and go there at night. If I had a regular appointment at modeling, I could make as much as forty or fifty dollars a week. But that wasn't my regular wage, so I found the dance hall a fine place to add to my income.[2]

In some instances, girls may make contacts, quite coincidentally, with the halls themselves, as did the Loren sisters.

One evening we happened to be walking along West Madison Street and we heard dance music. Helene, my older sister, asked me to go up and ask how much the admission was. When I inquired of the manager, he explained that this was not a regular dance hall but a kind of school, and that I could earn money there by dancing. That sounded good to me. He said I would have to dance with Filipinos. I didn't know what they were, but I hurried down to tell the good news to Helene. . . . . About a week later I started to work in the "school," and soon afterward Helene came.[3]

[1] Case No. 12.
[2] Case No. 10. [3] Case No. 19.

Occasionally a girl makes contact with the taxi-dance hall through the direct solicitation by the proprietor or by some lieutenant, as in the case of Alma Heisler.

> I was working as a waitress in a Loop restaurant for about a month. I never worked in a dance hall like this and didn't know about them. One day the "boss" of this hall was eating in the restaurant and told me I could make twice as much money in his "dancing school." I went there one night to try it—and then quit my job at the restaurant. I always liked to dance anyway, so it was really fun.[1]

Probably a less frequent way in which the girl comes to learn of and become employed in a taxi-dance hall is through newspaper advertising. One of the few cases wich reveal this type of contact is that of Jean Barker.

> I had spent two years in New Orleans doing kindergarten-dancing instructing. I was dissatisfied with the money it paid and decided I wanted to do something else. I happened to read a Chicago newspaper and saw an advertisement for girls to teach dancing in a dancing school. I applied for a job, and they replied, telling me to come. The "school" proved to be this place—and I've been working here ever since, even though my girl friend whom I live with thinks it's awful for me to be doing this kind of work.[2]

5. TAXI-DANCER'S ADJUSTMENTS TO HER FAMILY

Once the girl becomes associated with the taxi-dance hall, she usually has to make some adjustment with her family—whether to secure their approval by giving a favorable picture of the hall, to keep them from learning of her new life, or to engage in active conflict with them. For most parents very naturally disapprove of their daughter's being employed in an institution so unconventional as the taxi-dance hall. Except in cases where the parents are too indifferent or too ignorant to realize the possible dangers of the taxi-

---
[1] Case No. 15.   [2] Case No. 16.

BACKGROUNDS OF THE TAXI-DANCER

dance hall, the girls may even suppress all facts except that they are "instructresses" in "dancing schools."

Sophie Zelinski is a sixteen-year-old high-school Senior. Her ambitious Polish parents want her to continue to college, but Sophie has quite different ideas. She is "sick of this school bunk" and wants to see a different kind of life. "My mother tells me that if I gotta go out to dances, I oughta go to the big dance places. But I tell her that I'm not just going to dances—I'm now a dancing teacher, giving private lessons in a dancing school. I tell her: 'You always wanted me to be a teacher, didn't you? Well, I'm already a teacher, making good money.' Then she don't say nothing more. She thinks it's all right because I'm a 'dancing instructress.' Why, she even brags to her friends about me. What'd she do if she knew what kind of a joint this really was?"[1]

It is the policy of some to keep their parents entirely ignorant of their activities in the taxi-dance hall. They develop a "double life" or "dual rôle." Often they pose as being employed in some position involving a night shift, such as that of telephone operator or theater usher. They may live at home and "get by" for some time with this pretense. Indeed, without breaking family ties they may even insist that their work makes it necessary to rent a room miles from home. Further to insure the continuance of the "double life," the girls may adopt aliases in the dance-hall world, thus minimizing the chances that any reports of their activities will reach the ears of their family.

Maintaining a double life is, at best, precarious because of the constant danger of detection. In case the parents learn of the girl's life in the taxi-dance hall, active conflict almost inevitably ensues. This unstable family situation has one of four outcomes: First, the girl may withdraw from the life in the taxi-dance hall. Or, if she refuses to give up taxi-dancing, her parents may put her out of their home and

[1] Records of an investigator.

even disown her. A third outcome is that in which the girl herself may take the initiative and withdraw, psychologically, from the family. This may take place either gradually or through a sudden break. The girl may come more and more to center her interests wholly in the world of the taxi-dance hall—through it acquiring new values and conceptions—and may use her home only for eating, sleeping, and storing her personal possessions. She may withdraw both psychologically and physically. However, it may be noted that rooming elsewhere is less significant than breaking the *rapport* which once existed between herself and her parents.

I don't stay home any more. . . . . Well, you know how it is. Every time I go home somebody always yells about what I'm doing. They don't want me to be down here, you know. They want me to work days at the shirt factory like I was and bring all my money home. . . . . Now, the old woman raises hell every time she sees me with a new dress or even some new silk stockings. Nobody can stand that kind of nagging all the time.

The old lady was worst, but Jack, my big brother, was almost as bad. I'd hardly get into the house before he'd start yelling at me about how much I was making, and what I ought to do to help the old lady and the kids.

One Sunday afternoon about a month ago I came home to see the kids. I'd been out all night, the night before, stayed with my girl friend in her room [rooming-house]. I gave the kids their dime each and then wanted to wash out some clothes. They began raising hell over nothing. It was all about my not coming home Saturday night, and about the money they claimed I ought to give the old woman.

They made me so mad I threw the wash water at them. Then Jack ripped out a dirty name about me and before I knew it I'd landed an uppercut right on his jaw. Boy! Was he mad? I didn't know whether I'd get out of there alive. But finally the old woman stopped him, and I put on my coat and walked out. I've not been back since. But the kids come down to my girl friend's house every Sunday and I give them their dimes just the same.[1]

[1] Case No. 8

BACKGROUNDS OF THE TAXI-DANCER

A fourth form of accommodation is the assumption by the girl of an aggressive rôle in which she successfully dominates the family, subordinating the parental standards to her own requirements and demands. This appears to be especially true in cases of immigrant parents, who, because of language and other cultural handicaps, are virtually subordinate to their children. Immigrant mothers, sensing their incompetence to deal with their daughters when outside the sphere of the home, overlook any misconduct in order to keep their daughters residing in the home with them.

Anna Prasenski first became a taxi-dancer after the death of her father, when she was only fifteen years of age. She easily passed for a girl of seventeen. Her mother, in desperate financial straits, permitted Anna to go to a taxi-dance hall. An allowance from the charity organization as well as a mother's pension subsequently alleviated the family's financial condition. Anna was ordered, accordingly, to leave the dance halls, which, for a time, she did. The excitement and the stimulation of her former life exerted a constant pull upon her, however, and she made a few clandestine visits to her old haunts, finally attending the halls in direct defiance of her mother's commands. When Anna had passed sixteen years of age, the mother's pension was reduced. Simultaneously, Anna was demanding more in the way of clothes than she had before. The solution was the habitual one—more visits to the taxi-dance halls. The mother is said to have been very anxious that Anna have "good times" and "pretty clothes," and her feeble protests were easily overridden. Anna began returning home somewhat irregularly, often telephoning her mother that she was "staying all night with a girl friend." Her mother's remonstrances were "laughed off," or stilled by Anna's threats to leave home entirely.

When Anna later remained away for ten days, she was trailed to a rooming-house where she and several other young taxi-dancers were found to be entertaining Orientals and other men regularly. Anna was found to be not only pregnant but diseased. She was sent to the hospital for treatment. Later the mother and Anna contrived together to secure an abortion.

Eventually Anna returned home—apparently with a gain rather than a loss in status. The mother studiously avoided any mention of Anna's previous experiences, but is reported to have adopted more of a subordinate rôle toward the daughter. She permitted many late-night parties in her home, in which both Orientals and white men were prominent. The younger children saw much of these activities, and according to reports came to consider their big sister Anna an enviable figure.

Anna continued to remain at home, and now is reported to control the household. She decides what clothes the younger children shall have, the age when they may leave school and go to work, and even supervises the family finances. Two of the younger sisters have already followed Anna in a dance-hall career.[1]

The young people of a family, likewise, are enabled to take an aggressive rôle in the family and to dominate it when the parents find themselves economically dependent upon their children, when they have not retained the highest respect of their children, or have proved to be weak in their early efforts to control them. In such cases the parents tend to retreat from ethical issues arising from time to time, and to maintain illusions concerning their children's activities, justifying what is known to be going on in the way most satisfying to themselves. In the case which follows the mother took consolation in her own idealizations of events and in a compensatory form of religious life.

A report came to a social agency that Mrs. Alexander's two daughters, upon whom she is virtually dependent, are insubordinate to her, and, lacking proper control from home, are becoming immoral. It was also reported that the son, age twelve, is permitted unsupervised association with these daughters and their girl friends who come frequently to the house. Bertha, the older daughter, is reported to be separated from her husband and to be employed in a burlesque show.

[1] Adapted from Juvenile Protective Association records and from reports of investigators. To make possible a concise presentation of the family situation the usual quotations from the reports of case-workers and investigators have been avoided.

BACKGROUNDS OF THE TAXI-DANCER

She, it was complained, neglected her baby. Harriet, the younger sister, was reported to be beyond her mother's control, employed in the taxi-dance halls of the city, and to spend the entire night frequently in South Side "black and tan" resorts.

An investigator, familiar with the taxi-dance halls, was instructed to call at the Alexander home to establish the identity of the taxi-dancer daughter and the chorus-girl mother, and to determine, if possible, the moral conditions surrounding the twelve-year-old son. The investigator's report is in part as follows:

The Alexanders live in a deteriorating brick dwelling in the rooming-house section of the Lower North Community. Mrs. Alexander was a middle-aged woman whose dress and manner bespoke "shabby gentility."

"Where did your daughter meet her husband, Mrs. Alexander?" I asked. "Why, she met him at her work," she replied. I persisted. "Where was she employed, Mrs. Alexander?" Again she seemed apprehensive. "Why, they're in theatrical work," she replied with a tone which indicated that she wanted the matter closed. I persisted. "In theatrical work! That's interesting. What sort of work does she do?" She was evasive. "Well, I don't just know," was the reply. "They're on the road very much I suppose," I suggested. "No, they're in theaters here in the city. . . . . No, I don't remember the names, but they're somewhere down near the business district."

Mrs. Alexander veered to another subject. "We are trying to get a divorce for our daughter from this man. He was so abusive that she had to have him put under peace bonds. . . . . He's claimed recently that the baby isn't getting good treatment.

"The girls get home late at night and so sleep late in the morning. I usually take care of the baby in the morning and leave it for my daughters to care for in the afternoon. . . . . You see, I work part-time myself. I work each afternoon. I sell real estate," she said with another touch of finality.

A moment's pause and Mrs. Alexander began again: "Edward is starting to high school next year. He is a good studious boy. . . . . This isn't such a good section of the city, I know. But this apartment is inexpensive. . . . . Edward and I have our membership at ——— Church,[1] and we like to live near by."

[1] Mentioning a fashionable North Side church.

"Do your daughters attend church?" I asked. "No, you see they have to work so late Saturday night that they sleep very late on Sunday morning. They have to be on duty again at night and so they don't have an opportunity to attend church."

Soon a girl whom I had known as "Peggy" Stone in the dance halls and another girl known around the halls as immoral came in. The latter proved to be Harriet, Mrs. Alexander's unmarried daughter, also known by the investigator as a taxi-dancer. The girls came forward, greeting the investigator cordially.

Mrs. Alexander at first seemed stupefied by the turn of events. "Why you must know these girls," she concluded aloud. "But then I suppose you people watch these dance halls, too. These two girls are instructing in dancing. They are both very good dancers and can make much more money in this way than in any other. I hate to have them out late at night, but it seems to be the only thing. Harriet is planning to leave them and get something else this fall. I'm very much worried when they're out so late. Sometime I can't sleep a wink until they get home. Their dancing classes go on until very late and then they always have to go to some café afterward before coming home. But the girls will tell you that every night I say, 'Girls, get home as early as you can.' "

"You see, it's a question of finance," Mrs. Alexander continued. "If we had more to do with, things could be very different, but we never seem to have things the way we want them in this life. . . . . And then, you know, young people are such a trial these days. Sometimes I don't know what the world is coming to with our young people carrying on as they do. There was a time when children were a comfort to one in their old age. But not now. . . . . I do hope and pray Edward will not be the kind of man his father was. I'm trying to keep him close to the church and to church people, but it is so hard when there are so many wicked influences about to drag a young man downward."[1]

It is not known how frequently taxi-dancers can be found who are in a position to dominate the family situation as completely as was true in the Alexander family. Yet the presumption is that such a condition of dependence and ac-

[1] Adapted from special report of boy's case-worker to Juvenile Protective Association.

BACKGROUNDS OF THE TAXI-DANCER

quiescence is found more frequently in the taxi-dancer's family than might at first be thought.

In summary, it may be stated that the majority of Chicago's taxi-dancers are natives of the city, and generally have homes somewhere in the city. There are also girls who have come into the city from smaller towns and rural regions; immigrant girls seeking means of economic and social adjustment in the new world, especially when they break with relatives with whom they first lived after coming to this country; and a few girls from other cities. The native Chicagoans, who constitute the bulk of the taxi-dancer group, come especially from certain areas: first, from certain nationality areas, notably from those predominantly Polish, and practically not at all from Italian communities or from Jewish areas of first settlement. Second, it appears that a culturally heterogeneous neighborhood is most likely to be the home community for the girl who becomes a taxi-dancer. Finally, the addresses of "instructresses" in the taxi-dance hall indicate that the girls seldom know one another as neighbors. Rather the taxi-dancer, in almost every case, even when residing at home, lives, in the world of the taxi-dance hall, a life quite detached from that of her neighborhood.

The taxi-dancer group is essentially a young group, ranging in age from fifteen to twenty-eight years. This is the more striking when one learns the life-experiences of many of them—that at least two-fifths have had matrimonial experiences, almost invariably unfortunate ones. Probably less than a quarter of the girls are from "normal" homes, with considerably over half coming from those broken by death, divorce, or the desertion of a parent. A closer scrutiny of home backgrounds of the girls gives a very good clue to the explanations, both economic and psychological, for their continuance in the life of the taxi-dance hall, once they are brought into touch with it. Family conflicts are quite universal in the homes of taxi-dancers, involving situations at times almost impossible to improve, and which seem to thwart the girl's fundamental desires for status and response. Especially, as the girl comes to have a taste for other types of life than those seen in her home, do conditions within it often seem to become intolerable. Once the girl enters the world of the dance hall, she finds here a substitute for the inadequacy of her home.

Since taxi-dance halls are a type of institution which receives little advertising, the girl's first contacts are usually accidental—frequently through the medium of some girl met while working at another job, or perhaps through some man whom random contact has converted into an acquaintance.

The girl who sets out upon a dance-hall career inevitably has the problem of establishing a satisfactory adjustment to her activities on the part of other members of her family. Often taxi-dancers seek to keep their families entirely ignorant of their activities. This usually results in their living "double lives"—with all of the nervous distraction and uncertainty which it entails. Eventually such efforts at misrepresentation break down and the girl finds herself in severe conflict with her family. This results in one of three courses: Either the girl gives up her dance-hall career, or she becomes rather permanently estranged from the family group, or the family acquiesces to the girl's conduct.

Many of these girls have had neither the family background nor the social and vocational training to enable them to attain satisfactions in conventional ways. Either through family conflicts or the disorganization of an immigrant home they have become detached from the control of any stable group and find it relatively easy to follow vagrant impulses and to ally themselves with the institution which seems to afford an immediate satisfaction of their desires for money, excitement, and affection.

CHAPTER V

THE LIFE-CYCLE OF THE TAXI-DANCER

A generation ago the young girl who broke with her home and neighborhood and set out alone upon the high roads of adventure had little opportunity to do other than sink, almost immediately, into some form of prostitution. But today many legitimate avenues are open to her, and, if she adopts an unconventional mode of life, many intermediate stages precede actual prostitution. The girl may organize her life in terms of an intermediate stage and never become a prostitute. The life of the taxi-dancer is one of these intermediate stages, and, like prostitution, it is an employment which can be of only short duration. The career of a taxi-dancer ends in her late twenties. It is a source of income only for the interim between later adolescence and marriage. Many young women use the taxi-dance hall in this way. Others use it to provide for themselves during the interlude between marital ventures. Still others—married women—use it as a source of additional funds and, not infrequently, as a diversion from monotonous married lives.

All this exists today because, as never before in our mobile cities, it is possible for young people to lead dual lives, with little probability of detection. Thus the young woman may "get in" and "out" of prostitution with a facility and rapidity which renders ineffective the traditional forms of social control. Likewise the taxi-dancer, if she so desires, has a greater opportunity than ever before afforded to such a girl to "come back" and again fit into conventional society.

LIFE-CYCLE OF THE TAXI-DANCER

Many girls, however, do not satisfactorily readjust themselves to conventional life. A part of the explanation may be that they are the more unstable and improvident ones, who naturally would be unable to extricate themselves from any exigency in which they might find themselves. More important, it would seem, is the fact that in this little isolated world of taxi-dance halls, the young woman may very soon come to accept without great resistance the standards of life and the activities of those with whom she is inevitably associated. The impersonal sanction of numbers ("everybody does it") seems quite effective in inducing the immature young woman to change radically the personal standards inculcated by her family.

In the following instance, May Ferguson, a young woman of twenty-four, cut all connections with her relatives and friends in Rogers Park and, for a time, lived intensely the life revolving around the taxi-dance hall. Her reactions to the critical question of "dating" and marrying an Oriental reflect the effectiveness of this social world in making possible a complete change in the activities and personal standards of a young woman of middle-class American society.

It's strange how my attitudes toward the mixing of the races has changed and then changed back again in a little over a year. Two years ago I would have shuddered at the thought of dancing with a Chinaman or a Filipino and hated them just about as much as I did a "nigger." Then I learned that Dick had been unfaithful to me, and I wanted to get away from everything, everybody. For a while I didn't care what happened.

When I first started in the dance hall on the West Side everything was exciting and thrilling. The only thing that bothered me was to have to dance with the Filipinos and the Chinamen. The first time one danced with me it almost made me sick. But after I'd been dancing there two months I even came to think it was all right to go out with

Filipinos. You see, everybody else was doing it, and it seemed all right. But I never got so I would go out with a Chinaman.

I didn't really think of marrying a Filipino until I met Mariano. He seemed different. I thought he was really going to school. He always treated me in a perfectly gentlemanly way, and I thought he was better than other Filipinos. For a time I let myself think seriously of marrying him, but down deep I knew I could never marry a Filipino. One thing I could never get straightened out was the question of the children. What would they be? They'd be neither Filipinos nor Americans.

Soon after, Mariano and I broke up, and I never was serious with any other Filipino. . . . . Then I quit the dance hall, and went back to live my old life on the North Side.

Just a few weeks ago, after I'd been away from the West Side for nearly a year, I was talking with some friends. They were telling about a chop-suey proprietor who had married a white woman. For some reason that made me mad, and I started in telling what I thought of anyone who would marry a "Chink." Then all of a sudden I stopped and bit my lip. . . . . I had just realized that only the year before I was seriously considering marrying a Filipino, who was even darker than a Chinaman. And now, just a few months later, I had all the hatred toward them that I had before I went out on the West Side.[1]

1. THE TAXI-DANCER'S LIFE-CYCLE FUNDAMENTALLY RETROGRESSIVE

For those young women who do not "get out" of the dance-hall life while still relatively new to it there appear to be rather definite and regular stages of regression which eventually lead to some form of prostitution. It may be noted also that the "lower" the level reached by the girl, the more difficult is her re-entrance into conventional society. These stages in their life-cycle appear, on careful inspection, to be so regular and almost inevitable for those who persist in taxi-dancing that in its generalized aspects this life-cycle may be considered valuable for prediction.

[1] Case No. 11.

The hypothesis is here suggested, with a view toward further verification, that the taxi-dancer, starting with an initial dissatisfaction in her home situation, tends to go through a series of cycles of a regressive character, i.e., the latter part of each cycle involving a continual loss of status in a given group, and the initial part of a succeeding cycle indicating a regaining of status in a new but usually lower group than the preceding ones. This cyclical theory of the taxi-dancer's life is simply a graphic way of conceiving of the difficulties of maintaining status over any span of years in a social world of the type found in the taxi-dance hall.

A very important aspect of the hypothesis has to do with the higher status granted the girl by each group during the initial period in each cycle. Finding herself losing favor in one social world, the taxi-dancer "moves on"[1] to the group with which, in the natural course of her life, she has recently been brought most vitally in contact. This may involve a movement from one taxi-dance hall to another, perhaps one of lower standing; and again, it may in the later stages mean a trend toward other social worlds to which the life in the taxi-dance hall is frequently but a threshold. As a "new girl" in a new group, she is accorded a satisfactory status, and in the novelty of the situation she finds new excitement. Thus begins a new cycle in the girl's life. After a time, however, she is no longer a "new girl" and finds herself losing caste in favor of younger and still newer girls. Her decline in any particular social world may be rapid or slow, depending upon the personality, ingenuity, and character of the individual girl, but in any case a gradual decline in status in any such dance hall seems almost inevitable.

[1] See a statement of this type of personal adjustment in the concluding paragraph of the document on p. 71.

Every girl reaches, in time, a point of relative stability. In the ruthless sorting-out process continually going on, the taxi-dancers are certain to find their "level," at which each girl in her own way, and with the personality and techniques she has available, will be able—if she so desires—to maintain herself for at least a few years on a fairly stable equilibrium. In some cases this point may not be reached for some time, and the girl may rush through the earlier stages, eventually reaching an equilibrium at a "low" stage. Others may attain a satisfactory adjustment upon a relatively "high" plane.

The initial position of status accorded the "new girl" in the taxi-dance hall and the later struggle to maintain that status is indicated in the following case of Wanda, a young girl of Polish parentage, who subsequently married a Filipino youth whom she had met in the dance hall. This case also reveals the way in which the girl's scheme of life may be completely altered through a brief sojourn in the world of the taxi-dance hall.

Wanda, American-born but of Polish parents, at fifteen was doing fairly good work at school. But suddenly, with the consent of her parents she secured work in a cigar factory, telling her employer that she was eighteen. Shortly after she left home, and no trace of her was found until four months later, when she was found married to a young Filipino. He said his wife told him that she was nineteen and that he had no reason to doubt her. Wanda met him in the taxi-dance hall in which she had been employed. They had known each other only a month before their marriage.

According to Wanda's story, she left the cigar factory because the work was monotonous. All day long she wrapped cigars until after a month she could endure it no longer. Through a friend in the factory she secured employment in the dance hall, dignified by the name of a "dancing school for men." .... Wanda was rather embarrassed at first at the prospect of dancing with so many strange men, but before the end of the first evening she found herself thoroughly enjoying it and turned in more tickets than any other girl on the floor. She began to look forward to the evenings in the dance hall; she "got a thrill" from meeting so many new people.

Her popularity continued for several evenings, much to the annoyance of the other girl employees. But one night one of her steady partners tried to "get fresh." Wanda left him in the middle of the floor. Her partner complained to the management, and that evening Wanda got a "terrible bawling out." She was made to understand that she was hired for the purpose of entertaining, not insulting the patrons. If she didn't like it, she could leave. But she didn't want to leave. She had been having too good a time, and so she agreed to be more compliant.

But her clientèle began to fall off. She learned that several of the other girls, jealous of her success, were circulating tales that she was a "bad sport" and a prude. To rectify this Wanda resorted to the wiles of the other girls; she rouged heavily, darkened her eyes, and shortened her skirts. Again she achieved popularity, also the other girls grew more tolerant of her.

One evening she danced with Louis, a Filipino. His peculiar accent intrigued her, and she accepted an invitation to supper. Their friendship grew. He told her of his childhood on his native islands, and she confided her growing dislike for the dance hall. They agreed that they would like to "settle down," and so one evening Wanda "resigned" and they drove to Indiana and were married.[1]

In the whole gamut of cycles through which the taxi-dancer tends to go, at least four may be suggested. The first cycle involves the girl's dissatisfaction with the type of life associated with the home and neighborhood. This may come about largely through a growing consciousness of economic lack in the family, through a thwarting of the desire for a type of masculine contacts which the home or the neighborhood fails to offer, through a sense of insufficient prestige in the home and the community, or through a loss of status due to the girl's supposed transgression of the established moral code. At all events, the girl, finding her way

[1] Reported by a Chicago social worker.

sooner or later to the taxi-dance hall, secures therein a satisfaction of certain wishes previously unfulfilled.

Here she at first finds an enhanced prestige accorded her —even though by a world which her family and her neighborhood would adjudge as lower than their own. Thus begins a second cycle for the girl. As a novice in the taxi-dance hall she is at first "rushed," and enjoys the thrill of being very popular. But after a time she ceases to be a novitiate and must make a deliberate effort to maintain her status. If she fails and is no longer able to secure sufficient patronage exclusively from the white group, she comes eventually to accept the romantic attentions of Filipinos and other Orientals.

Thus begins a third cycle for the girl, at the beginning of which she experiences a new prestige accorded her by the Oriental group. Here, again, a girl may continue to "get by" with the group with which she has become associated, being consistently accorded a degree of status which to her is satisfying. But such are the hazards of maintaining standing in this social world that if she accepts the attentions of too many Orientals she is adjudged "common" by them, and thus again loses caste.

A failure to make satisfactory adjustment in the world of Orientals may bring the girl to a fourth cycle, which is begun when she centers her interests upon the social world which in Chicago has been associated with the "black and tan" cabarets. She usually comes into contact with these groups through her association with Orientals. With the Negroes she again achieves temporarily the prestige accorded the novitiate. But here, too, she is doomed to a decline in status, and this seems very frequently to lead to prostitution in the Black Belt.

LIFE-CYCLE OF THE TAXI-DANCER

As has been said, the evidence to support this theory of retrogressive cycles is not conclusive, and the suggestion is offered merely as a hypothesis for further study. Yet the data which are at hand seem to be suggestive. Consider first the case of Florence Klepka,[1] a girl born and raised in Chicago, whose mother and stepfather are of Dutch ancestry. This case has value in that it reveals the conditions under which the girl was reared in her home. It is not a "perfect" case for the reason that in every instance the girl does not gravitate toward a group held in lower esteem. But in no case is there a trend toward a higher social group, and throughout the girl's life there is an unmistakable trend toward a lower estate. It likewise suggests the tendency of the girl to attempt to solve her personal and social problems by "moving on" to a new group and into a new social world.

In the case under consideration dissatisfaction with the home is manifest very early, for at the age of thirteen years the girl has already developed the habit of running away, which the mother seems to have been unable to alter. This no doubt is a way of escaping from an environment which is at least quite unsatisfactory. Lying, too, which came to be chronic with her, was also merely a means for adjusting to a disagreeable situation. Her contacts outside the home very probably caused her to become ashamed of it, and to want to prevent her friends, both boys and girls, from knowing of her home conditions. Such a situation encourages a girl's break with her home, even though, as in this case, she has parents who are willing to support her. She then goes through a cycle of experiences associated with her employment in a South State Street "men only" show. She subsequently passes on to another cycle, centering in the

[1] See document on pp. 62–63.

North Clark Street "Rialto." Finally she gets into the world of the taxi-dance hall, thus starting a new cycle of experiences. These three cycles, while quite distinct one from the other, involving as they do different social worlds in each case, cannot be said arbitrarily to be lower or higher than one another. All can be said, however, to be retrogressive in character, the girl descending as "low" as she permits herself, and subsequently extricating herself and focusing her activities upon a different group. This case, furthermore, reveals very clearly the "white cycle" and the "Filipino cycle" through which the girl retrogressively passes.

Florence Klepka[1] when nineteen years of age was reported by a policewoman to be living at a cheap Loop hotel under the name of Mrs. Bok, and taking part in a "men only" burlesque show on South State Street. She was reported to be hanging around corners at all hours of the night with sailors and recruiting officers, and was seen in restaurants at 2:30 and 3:00 A.M. The mother wanted the girl to return home and keep away from bad company.

Between 1920 and 1924 she is known to have frequented South State Street and for a time to have lived with a man she met there, by whom she had a child. Florence claims to have been involved in several raids of prohibition agents on saloons and cabarets on South State Street and South Wabash Avenue.

Later her center of activities was transferred from the South State Street "main stem" to the North Clark Street "Rialto." Here she entered the cabaret life along the street. She lived in the notorious hotels and rooming-houses of the vicinity, and is reported to have lived at different times by clandestine prostitution and by several unstable alliances.

During the winter of 1925 she entered a taxi-dance hall where she met certain young Italians and Greeks, with whom she associated for a time. She was subsequently discharged by the management when the kind of life she was leading became too well known.

In the fall of 1925 Florence's center of activities shifted to the Near

[1] Detailed record of this family found on pp. 62-63.

West Side, where she continued in a new taxi-dance hall. Her career there was essentially the same as elsewhere. At first she made a very creditable impression, but later became notorious because of her extensive and unguarded promiscuity. Finally she became so notorious that patrons did not want to be seen dancing with her and she was discharged.

She shifted her activities back to a taxi-dance hall on the Lower North Side, where she allied herself wholly with the Filipinos and with the girls associated with them. In 1926 she virtually abandoned all efforts to make a living through taxi-dancing. She had become "common" to the Filipino group as well as to the white. Thence she shifted her activities to the Filipino clubhouse, where she met many men, establishing different relationships with them. Now she has come to be known as a "bum." On some occasions she was reported to have visited the rooming-houses occupied by Filipinos, going from room to room soliciting.[1]

The following case is one in which the girl ran through the whole gamut of experiences until she reached a low level of prostitution. It might be stated here that this case shows, in fact, the steps by which a certain number of girls quickly become prostitutes in the Black Belt.

Tiny was a Polish girl whose parents lived on the Northwest Side. When she was about sixteen she married a young man from the same neighborhood. She later left him, claiming non-support and entered a taxi-dance hall, where she was for a time quite popular. At first she would not dance with Filipinos if she could avoid it. Sometime later, however, when she had come to regard them as a lucrative source for income she became very interested in several. They frequently escorted her to "black and tan" cabarets and in this way she made contacts with young Negroes.

The Filipinos, very conscious of their anomalous racial position in this country, would tolerate no such conduct on the part of any girls with whom they associated. They immediately deserted her, leaving

[1] Compiled from Juvenile Protective Association case records and from information supplied by three men who had known of her activities in three different social worlds.

her in the cabaret. In this way began her activities in the South Side Black Belt, where she subsequently became known as an independent prostitute, carrying on her business chiefly with Negroes and Chinese. Occasionally she seeks to return to the taxi-dance halls and to other Filipino activities, but there are always those who remember her and warn the others that she has already "gone African."[1]

The theory of the retrogressive life-cycles, while only a hypothesis, can perhaps be seen best through a reference to the typical experiences of taxi-dancers before and after entering these resorts. These experiences seem so frequently to have common elements in them and to follow such a regular sequence of typical experiences that they can be conceived as a "behavior sequence." In any event it is clear that a better perspective can be gained by classifying these experiences and arranging them chronologically. Some of the characteristic experiences, fortunate and unfortunate, which befall the taxi-dancer can be seen in the following.

2. DISTRACTING AND DISORGANIZING EXPERIENCES BEFORE ENTERING THE TAXI-DANCE HALL

It is clear both from the discussion in chapter iv on "The Family and Social Backgrounds of the Taxi-Dancer" and from many of the life-history excerpts that the typical taxi-dancer, even though young in point of years, is not inexperienced. Most taxi-dancers have had varied experiences, both occupationally and sexually. They have engaged in a variety of occupations, usually of the unskilled type, such as waitress, factory operative, or salesgirl. Their experiences often include at least one marriage, usually unsuccessful and characterized by considerable infidelity on both sides, resulting in separation or divorce. In most cases there seems to be, in addition, a background of intense family conflict.

[1] Compiled from information supplied by two persons well acquainted with the young woman.

LIFE-CYCLE OF THE TAXI-DANCER

When the girl enters the taxi-dance hall she usually has already broken with many of the stable community groups, such as her family and church. Usually, she also has failed to find conventional ways of satisfying certain dominant interests, such as her need for friendship and affection, for status, and for excitement. Nor does she have a well-defined standard of conduct or a goal in life toward which she may work. The taxi-dancer enters her vocation already somewhat disorganized, often feeling herself in conflict with conventional society.

3. THE INITIAL PERIOD OF UNCERTAINTY AND DISTRUST

The initial experiences of the taxi-dancer are so similar that it is possible to perceive a fundamental sequence in the girl's affiliation with the establishment and its personnel. With few exceptions, the primary factor attracting the girl to the establishment is the possibility of making money in an easier way than she otherwise could. A young taxi-dancer without training of any kind frequently earns as much as thirty-five or forty dollars a week. But the economic interest is paralleled by an interest in the "thrill" and excitement of the dance hall. Yet the strangeness and uncertainty of the situation, coupled with an antagonism or disgust for the conduct of certain taxi-dancers, may cause many new taxi-dancers to remain aloof. Also, detached as she often is from the neighborhood and family groups in which she was reared,[1] she is very slow to confide in other girls whom she meets in the dance hall. Except perhaps for a trusted girl friend, the novice in the dance hall remains for a time a detached figure, associating only casually with the taxi-dancers.

[1] See p. 57.

Many of the young girls who attempt a career in the taxi-dance hall drop out during the first few weeks.[1] Either they are not able to attract sufficient patronage or they are antagonized by the practices seen about the establishment. Likewise, to many taxi-dancers their work in the dance hall is purely a segmental activity, engaged in primarily to supplement an insufficient income earned as clerical office-workers, clerks in department stores, or at light industry and in laundries.

4. THRILLS OF EARLY SUCCESS: THE ROMANTIC PERIOD

The successful novices among the taxi-dancers, however, very soon overcome any hesitancy they may have and throw themselves whole-heartedly into the life revolving about the establishment. Courted intensively and sought after in a manner seldom experienced in more conventional life, the "new girl" comes to enjoy immensely these new thrills and satisfactions. A host of new men, many of them attractive, some of them strange and fascinating, present themselves and bid for her favor. She is escorted to expensive night clubs where she is served in a manner which, according to her conception, befits only the socially elect.

Out of it she very quickly gains an enhanced conception of herself. The Polish girl from "back of the yards" is metamorphosed into a "dancing instructress," and frequently acquires a new name comparable to her new station in life. The following list, while disguised,[2] nevertheless distinguishes in a true manner the characteristic original and

[1] It has been estimated that more than half of the girls who attempt a career in the taxi-dance hall drop out during the first weeks.

[2] All of the real and the "professional" names given below have been carefully altered.

"professional" names, respectively, of certain Chicago taxi-dancers. These new names reveal the girl's new conception of herself and suggest the ideals and aspirations by which her life is ordered.

Real Name	"Professional" Name
Christina Stranski	DeLoris Glenn
Agnes Gretin	Lorine Boyle
Marie Boris	Billye Hart
Florence Klepka	Anita Costello
Louise Lorenz	Bobby LeMann
Sophie Zelinski	Gwendolyn Llewellen
Alma Heisler	Helene de Valle
Pearl Babcock	Melba DeMay
Eleanor Hedman	Gloria Garden
Anna Prasenski	Althea LeMar
Mary Bulonowski	LaBelle Shelley
Gertrude Pressley	Betty Lucrece
Alice Borden	Wanda Wang
Mary Maranowski	Jean Jouette

With this new conception of herself the girl enters a series of romantic experiences, in which every consideration is sacrificed for the free play of the romantic impulse.

I don't know what there is about the dance hall, but I never had so many serious "cases" in such a short time as I had those few months I was on the West Side. I was always getting a flame over this fellow or that one. If it wasn't a Filipino it was a good-looking young Italian or even a Greek. I never have been able to understand what got into me. There was always someone I was crazy about.[1]

When still a "new girl" in the hall, the successful taxi-dancer does not have to give any thought to the problem of inducing patrons to dance with her. She is yet a "new girl"—often with an attractive youthful naïveté—and is sought after by many patrons.

[1] Case No. 11.

5. "GETTING THE DANCES"—THE VETERAN TAXI-DANCER'S PROBLEM

As the taxi-dancer becomes an accepted member of the dance-hall personnel and, unconsciously, has come to acquire in it a certain rôle, the problem of "getting the dances" becomes a more pressing one. While she may remain a popular girl with a certain group of patrons, many others have abandoned her for other new and more interesting taxi-dancers. As her pay check dwindles, she begins deliberately to use certain techniques to attract dance partners. At the same time the girl has become more aware of her standing with her co-workers. They, in turn, demand certain standards of performance from her. In response to their ridicule, jeers, and laughter, she complies with their expectations, changes her mode of dressing, of acting, and of thinking, and gradually becomes accepted into the little group of women who set the mode in the world of the taxi-dance hall. Through these contacts the novitiate gradually learns the techniques for being a successful taxi-dancer.

6. LEARNING THE TAXI-DANCER'S TECHNIQUES

These techniques are often very simple in character. One of the first considerations is the question of the type of dressing and "make-up" most advantageous in the dance hall.

"Say," Lila said to me, "why don't you blondine your hair? You know, all the Filipinos go for blondes.

"I'm afraid you won't go so big. You are too quiet and don't fix yourself up enough. And those earrings! Why the hell, if you're going to wear them, don't you get some that aren't so big and don't look so much like they came from the 10-cent store?

"Of all the goofy ideas of make-up—you have the world beat! You come over to my house tomorrow and I'll fix you up before we go to the dance. One bottle of peroxide will do it. Your hair ain't so dark

LIFE-CYCLE OF THE TAXI DANCER

anyway. And then we'll put a hem in your dress and make it tighter. You aren't such a bad looker. Your shape ain't bad, but you don't know how to show it."[1]

Likewise, another device for interesting patrons is "dancing fast and peppy," and "acting peppy" when waiting for dances.

> It pays to dance close and fast. Act like you're just full of pep. When I'm waiting for dances I walk along the side acting like I'm full of the Old Nick. Sometimes I feel just the opposite, but I couldn't afford to show my real feelings or I wouldn't get the dances.[2]

There is also the ruse by which the girl, who believes that a patron does not recognize her, represents herself to him as a novice with the hope that she will thereby secure more dances with him. The pretended promise of a late night engagement is also used to induce patrons to continue dancing. In this way the patron is kept in a mood for spending money until the dénouement, at the close of the evening's dancing, when the girl informs him that she has made "other arrangements."

A somewhat more complex technique involves the playing of the racial prejudices against each other. Especially with such incompatible groups as Filipinos and race-conscious white Americans, the shrewder taxi-dancer may devise a plan by which she utilizes the racial attitudes of both groups for her own financial advantage.

I noticed a rather attractive young woman of medium build, standing on the side lines beside a Filipino. As she saw me looking at her, her eyes glanced down obliquely toward him in a manner which seemed to indicate that she at least despised the rather dark-skinned youth with whom she had just been conversing. This seemed a new and interesting affection. As she moved away from the Filipino I approached her and began conversation.

[1] Jane Logan, *Chicago Daily Times*, February 1, 1930.   [2] Case No. 15.

"Apparently you don't like your sun-browned friend," I commented. "Well, no!" she replied, hesitatingly. "You see he's a Filipino." "But you should worry about that," I countered. "The Flips [Filipinos] treat a girl better and will spend more money on her than the other fellows." She hesitated a moment and then said in mock concern, "But they're not white!"

Late in the evening, after she had seen me in friendly conversation with several Filipinos, this same girl approached and offered the following explanation of her conduct:

"I don't know whether you know, but I'm engaged to marry the Filipino you saw me talking to. I just acted the way I did about him to get you to dance with me. When I saw you looking at us, I decided I'd have to pretend I didn't like him, so that you would give me some tickets..... Most of the white fellows won't dance with me if they learn I go out all the time with Flips. So I say something against them when I'm with white fellows just so they'll give me more dances.....

"Even if I do go out with Filipinos, it doesn't pay to dance all the time with them. If I dance all the time with Filipinos I've got to dance with many different ones. If a girl dances with too many Flips they think she's common, so they won't keep on coming to her for dances..... I've got to dance with some good-looking white fellows once in a while so the Filipinos will keep on dancing with me."[1]

Other techniques have to do with the exploitation of a patron after the taxi-dancer leaves the dance hall with him. Here again the "sex game"[2] enters the situation. In some instances the devices may be quite simple; in other cases more elaborate.

I've only been in the dance halls a month, but I already know how to be a success. I make $30 a week at the hall and figure on making some on the side.

The first thing in being a successful "gold-digger" is to choose the right fellow. He can be of any age, but he's got to be one who ain't wise. The new ones at the halls are best but sometimes the old ones are all right, too. Some "fish" don't learn very fast, you know. The first impression I have to make is that I'm an innocent little girl in hard circumstances. Then when a fellow asks for a date I tell him how

[1] Report of an investigator. [2] Pp. 46-48.

hard up I am and that I'd like to go but just can't afford to take time away from the hall.

Then I get the idea across that I'll go out if he'll pay me what I'd earn at the dance hall. When he asks how much that is, I make it more than I would earn actually if I stayed. . . . . I always insist on getting the money before I go out. The first thing is to get a fellow to take me to a café, and after I get a good meal off of him, I invent some way of getting away. One way is to ask him to excuse me for a moment, pretending to go to a telephone or to the rest room, and then I slip out the door when he isn't looking.

But if there is only one door and the fellow can see me leaving, I go to the phone and call up an older girl who lives where I do. I tell her where I am and for her to come down and get me. Then she comes in, accidentally like, and pretends she is my aunt who is supposed to take care of me. She threatens to call the police to arrest the man who is trying to make her niece a bad girl. And the fellow is glad enough to let me go. . . . . When she comes down to help me that way I always pay her taxi bill and split with her fifty-fifty on the rake-off.

Of course, I can work that only a few times, but "there's one born every minute" and a lot of them come to these halls. They're such easy "carp" I figure that if they hang around long enough somebody's bound to knock them off. I need the money more than the others, and I might just as well be the one to "fish" them.[1]

7. DISCOVERING A PROFITABLE DANCE-HALL PERSONALITY; TYPES AMONG THE TAXI-DANCERS

Out of the commercial rivalry among the taxi-dancers, certain rather definitely understood "rôles" develop, by which different girls have discovered they can commercialize most efficiently their personal charm. Each of these rôles has its own activities, its own patterns of behavior, its own individual techniques, its own standards, and its own scheme of life.

The highest type among these dance-hall rôles is that of the so-called "nice girl." The "nice girl" is the one who

[1] Case No. 15.

possesses sufficient charm, physical attractiveness, and vivacity to secure dances without transgressing the conventional standards of propriety. She may never accept dates from patrons, or may not even frequent a hall where she is expected to dance with Filipinos and other Orientals. She plays the part of the entirely virtuous girl.

Gwendolyn Costello, as she styles herself, is the "belle" of one of the taxi-dance halls in the Loop, where she has danced for over three years. She is a vivacious girl with a coquettish—almost roguish—manner. She is a graceful dancer, and can follow successfully any kind of dancing. In addition, she has what is called a "good line." Although she looks as though she were eighteen she is probably every bit of twenty-four. She is very popular with the patrons, especially with the men between twenty-five and forty. On busy nights at the establishment she is never inactive except on her own volition. Most of the men—new and old patrons—appear to like her, but she is known never to accept dates from anyone met in the hall. For most of the men who dance with her she remains as much of a mystery at the end of a year's contact as she was the first evening.[1]

While the motive toward exploitation may be found in the case of the "nice girl," it is more prominent in the case of the "smart girl." The girl of this type accepts exploitation as the order of the day and frankly sets out to utilize her attractiveness for all the material gain which can be realized therefrom. "Fishing" and the "sex game" become for these girls the accepted ways of earning a living; and prestige is accorded to the one who is cleverest in gaining the most.

Among the more immoral young women can be distinguished a third type, the "never-miss girl." She is the type who is known by the more initiated patrons to be quite affectionate. Sometimes to other taxi-dancers she may represent herself as successfully "fishing" her men friends. But

[1] Records of an investigator.

LIFE-CYCLE OF THE TAXI-DANCER 103

to her masculine acquaintances she presents an entirely different picture. The girl of this type may occasionally have a little retinue of men who have special "rôles" or functions in her life. Toward each she has a certain romantic interest, though even with her it is sometimes coupled with a unique sense of objectivity and detachment.

> I know men are all deceitful, but still I can't get along without them. It used to be that one man at a time was enough, but now since I'm married I've got to have several..... Now take right now! I have "Frenchy" and "Toughy" and Jimmy, and Buddy, and Al. Now "Frenchy" is a good-looking little Frenchman who knows how to make love. When I'm in low spirits and want somebody to cheer me up, I go to the phone and give him a ring. An hour with him and I'm "sitting on the top of the world." But that's all he's good for. And the worst of it is, I know he doesn't mean it—except for the moment.
>
> Now "Toughy," as I call him, comes from South Chicago. He's a bad boy. He's liable to do almost anything. I guess that's what makes him so interesting. Once in a while "Toughy" comes up and takes me out, but only for one night. Then there is Jimmy. He was my husband's cousin who sometimes interests me; I don't know why. I'm "out" with him now, because of the way he treated me, but he still owes me some money he promised to loan me.
>
> Buddy is the fellow I go to talk things over when I'm in some difficulty. He's a friend to call on when I need help. But that's all. Then there is Al. Al is a tall, slender fellow, good-looking, about twenty-eight years old. He's as safe as the old family horse..... He's got a big car and drives me around wherever I want to go.[1]

Always fearful lest she become notorious and thus no longer able to secure dance patronage, yet desirous of having what she chooses to consider a "good time," the taxi-dancer of this type is torn between the double dilemma of respectability with decreasing income and the greater hazard of becoming notorious and thus unemployable at legitimate dancing in the taxi-dance halls.

[1] Case No. 10.

For the young woman whose character is held in question, or who for some reason cannot measure up to the requirements for the other types, there is yet one opportunity to continue in some taxi-dance halls, if she will but join the fourth class of taxi-dancers—those who engage in sensual dancing. The older, more sophisticated women, the more homely girls, and others not especially superior in beauty, ability in dancing, and who, for one reason or another, do not wish to date patrons, constitute this fourth class.

For the girl who adopts this way of "getting along," financial hazards are considerably reduced. In the other rôles the girl is insecure, always exposed to the vicissitudes of dance-hall popularity, always uncertain of her income. But after once adapting herself to sensual dancing her income becomes more regular and more secure. Every week means that she can earn a certain amount in the dance hall, irrespective of the rise and fall of her personal fortunes outside the establishment. It is also unnecessary for her to engage in coquetry and cajolery to secure patronage.

I used to have to worry about getting my dances. Sometimes I'd make money and sometimes I wouldn't do so well, but the landlady wanted her money just the same. . . . . Now I know if I come up here for so long I'll have so much money when I get through. Before I'd waste all my time looking for dances.

It's a lot easier, too. Before I had to "kid" the fellows along all the time. Now I don't have to worry. The fellows come without being kidded. I've never had to wait long for a dance in months.[1]

The contact of the patrons with the taxi-dancer who practices sensual dancing is almost invariably impersonal and utilitarian. Romance, even of the type found among other taxi-dancers, seldom develops between patron and girl meeting on the basis of sensuality. A cold, impersonal bar-

[1] Case No. 9.

gaining interest identical with prostitution characterizes these contacts. In the dance hall this type of taxi-dancer functions as a utility for her patrons.

While these rôles are rather distinct at any given time, competition among the dancers, as well as the arrival of new girls, makes for continual readjustment among them. The taxi-dancer who formerly was the belle of the dance hall is forced either to work harder for her laurels or to engage in less desirable practices, i.e., accept a new and lower rôle for herself.

8. "MOVING ON": SEEING THE UNITED STATES VIA TAXI-DANCING

When the life and activities in the taxi-dance halls of a certain city begin to pall, the taxi-dancer may travel to another city where she can secure similar employment. She will find in almost every large city[1] taxi-dance halls, all essentially alike. Once adjusted to the life, she can easily make her way in any taxi-dance hall. Another stimulus toward movement from city to city is her constant association with people who are in the habit of moving about frequently. She catches the spirit and also wants to "see the country." Among veteran taxi-dancers it is not uncommon to find girls who have been to both the Pacific and the Atlantic coasts, making their way about the country through their earnings in the taxi-dance halls. Such a story as the following is not at all uncommon.

I've been all over the country because of these halls. My home's Chicago, but I've been in New York, New Orleans, Kansas City, Seattle, and Los Angeles. There are dance halls like this in all these

[1] It is commonly understood among social workers that the taxi-dance hall in some guise is to be found now in most cities of five hundred thousand population or more.

cities—sometimes they work it a little different, but they're the same kind of places.

Everywhere I went, though, I'd meet somebody I'd known somewhere else. In New York I saw some Flips [Filipinos] I used to know here in Chicago. When I was in Los Angeles I met a girl that used to be out on the West Side. The other night I met a Flip here I used to know out in Seattle. It's a small world, after all.[1]

At present there is a tendency for taxi-dancers of the Middle West to migrate eastward toward New York. The stages in this migration often include Kansas City or St. Louis, then Chicago, and finally New York. One Chicago investigator, when visiting a certain taxi-dance hall in New York, discovered in one evening twelve taxi-dancers who were known by him to have been previously in Chicago taxi-dance halls.

The future of this new type of feminine migration is uncertain. These young taxi-dancers, with their good incomes, the relative ease with which they can quickly secure employment in taxi-dance halls in other cities, have become a mobile group of a new variety. They have gained a freedom of movement and a ready source for a legitimate income beyond the conception of any previous generation of girls.

[1] Case No. 6.

PART III
THE PATRON AND HIS PROBLEMS

CHAPTER VI

THE PATRON: WHO HE IS; WHY HE COMES

1. TYPES OF PATRONS

The patrons at a taxi-dance hall are a polyglot crowd. Chinese and Sicilians, Hawaiians and Scandinavians, Mexicans and Russians, Filipinos and Roumanians, Jews and Poles, Greeks and American Indians, Hindus and Anglo-Saxon Nordics all mingle together. There is also a wide diversity in age, culture, and physical fitness. Veterans of sixty years or more take their places alongside youthful swains not out of their "teens." Sleekly groomed city chaps brush elbows with coarsely garbed yokels with calloused hands and lumbering gait. Men of apparently normal physique line up for their social adventures beside those of abnormal size and proportions and beside those with physical disabilities and speech handicaps.

A careful study of this motley assemblage of men, their problems, and the motives which attract them to the taxi-dance hall reveals that they constitute at least nine distinct types. There is, first of all, the group of men who are denied social acceptance elsewhere because they bear an invidious racial mark. Negroes are everywhere excluded, but in Chicago at least a fourth of the patrons of taxi-dance halls are Orientals who are elsewhere ostracized because of color. Of these Orientals nine-tenths are Filipinos,[1] and the Chinese contribute virtually the remainder. Even though with wide-

---

[1] A discussion of the Filipino and the taxi-dance halls will be found in chap. vii.

ly different cultural heritages these two racial groups have confronted the same barrier of racial prejudice in America and are attracted to the taxi-dancer by very much the same motives. For both groups the taxi-dance hall is almost the only opportunity afforded them for free and easy, unconstrained, social contact with American girls.

A second type of patron is the Caucasian immigrant—usually from a European country.[1] These men make up at least one-fifth of the total clientèle in Chicago and represent many nationalities. Italians, Poles, Greeks, and Jews seem to predominate. Except for the fact that they are not handicapped by an ineradicable racial mark, their problem in America is in other respects very much the same as that of the Oriental. It is the problem of the assimilation of an alien culture and language. Many of the immigrant youths make their first adventures in social contacts outside their own nationality by way of the taxi-dance hall. They seem to be attracted to the taxi-dance hall at a time when their own lives, their own rounds of activities, are for some reason dissatisfying. For the immigrant who has naïvely adopted a sensual interpretation of the traits he identifies as distinctly "American"—that is, alien to his own culture—a visit to a taxi-dance hall takes on the character of an illicit excursion. For others the taxi-dance hall appears as a means for making social contacts and for gaining certain desirable knowledge of American customs, standards, and usages. In any event the taxi-dance hall—for good or ill—makes a very strong appeal to many immigrants at a certain stage in their Americanization.

All these points stand out clearly in the following case

[1] Mexicans and South Americans, in addition to the Caucasian immigrants from Europe, are sometimes found in the taxi-dance halls.

THE PATRON

of an Italian immigrant, thirty-one years of age, who because of his professed inability to earn sufficient income was unable to resolve his problem through marriage. He would like to marry a "nice" Italian girl, "a real home girl who never went out much." But he cannot continue in the social circle within his own nationality without being expected to marry. The taxi-dance hall becomes for him an adventure dissociated from the remainder of his life. But all the time, in the non-Italian situation in the taxi-dance hall, he experiences a sense of uncertainty and inferiority because of his language and cultural handicaps.

I've been coming here for a long time and every time I say I'm not coming again. But gee! I can't stay away. You know, a fellow's got to have some fun. . . . . I thought I was going to a real swell dance tonight. I got all shaved and put on my new shoes, but I sorta came down here instead. I don't like to go to swell places alone because you know I don't speak English very good.

I was to two swell dances the last weeks. One was a club dance and I danced almost all night and it only cost me fifty cents, and I had a good time, too. Last week I was at a swell wedding and met a dandy "skirt"—good-lookin' too. I liked her a lot, but she was kinda young. She was seventeen and I'm thirty-one. I'd like to get a wife but I'm afraid I'd have a lot of trouble. But this girl was a real home girl—and never went out much. . . . .

Gee! This is a "gyp" joint! They sure get your money fast. You know, I'd like to dance some more, but I've already spent two and a half dollars. I can't dance more because I got only three dollars left and I won't have enough to take my "skirt" out. You know it costs me about a dollar and a half to get anything to eat, and then cabfare maybe. I can't take a chance. I gotta wait. I gotta wait till two o'clock. That's a long time just to sit around!

See? That's my "skirt" over there! The tall blonde! Don't she look swell? She's kinda skinny maybe, but she's gonna show me a good time. I had her out two times before but both times something crabbed things up. . . . . I came here tonight to bawl her out and she promised she'd treat me better. But gee! I don't know where to go and I don't have a car.

You know it's funny about her. I kinda don't like to see her dancin' around with them other guys since I gotta date with her. Not that I expect to marry her or nothing but, you know, a fellow don't like to see other guys with his girl. .... You know she got jealous, too, when she saw me dancin' around with that other Jane. .....

I don't really care much for the girls here. I could get better-looking girls around my own neighborhood, but they expect me to get married. I'd like to all right—I'm thirty-one now, you know—but I don't make enough money yet. So I come up here.[1]

When the Americanization process has been continuing longer, the immigrant attending a taxi-dance hall usually has undergone a process of individualization. He has forsaken much of his older heritage and has selected from among our contradictory standards and practices those which seem to meet his own immediate needs and his personal desires. Usually this means considerable voluntary detachment from those of his own nationality, and a preference for his scheme of life which he, in almost every case, identifies in his own mind as "American"—to distinguish it from the "old-country ways" he has forsaken.

I was born forty-two years ago in a little village north of Warsaw. My father died when I was a boy. I wanted to go to Warsaw, and I left home for good after I and my grandfather had a big fight. I traveled through Germany, France, and Denmark. The longest I ever stayed in one place was in Germany. I was there four years. .... The rest of my family all wanted to stay in Poland. I have two brothers and three sisters over there. But they've forgotten all about me now. I never hear nothing from them, and I ain't written home for ten years. I don't even know whether my mother's living. I think she is, though. .... Go back? No! Who'd I want to go back to?

I don't live with Polish people. To hell with them, that's what I say. I ain't lived with Polish people for over twelve years. The trouble

[1] From reports of a special investigator.

THE PATRON

with them is they're too nosey—they don't mind their own business like other nationalities do. The Polish figure everything that's my affairs is theirs. It's nobody's business what I do. . . . . No! I don't want to go to no Polish dances. There's too many old people there. You can't have a good time. I don't like the way they dance, some of them. They dance a lot better at these halls!

I can't come up here often—it costs too much. I spent $2.60 already, and I ain't danced much neither. But it's pretty hard to get dances at these big halls. I went up to one on the North Side and stood around all evening and got three dances. When I'd ask a girl to dance she'd take one look at me, stick up her nose, and walk away. Sometimes she wouldn't even shake her head, much less say, "No, thank you." I stayed there an hour and a half and then went home. I been to dance halls all over the city but it's about the same everywheres. The best places to get dances is where the real high-class people goes, but you can't get acquainted so well as you can in these here halls [taxi-dance halls].

I don't go to Polish societies. I only belong to one and all I get out of it is my insurance. . . . . But I'm glad I came over. If I stayed in Poland, look where I'd be. Over here I gotta lotta money and automobile and know more. I'm glad I'm American.

I ain't married. I wanta get married but I don't getta chance to meet the kind of girl I want. You've gotta be careful of these dance-hall girls—some of them is all right, but you can't never tell till you know a girl a long time. When a fellow gets older, he's more particular about the girl's family. I don't think there should be more than five or ten years' difference between them. The only girls from good families I know in Chicago is two daughters of a saloonkeeper. They're American girls and real nice too. They're about thirty and never been married. They just sit around the house with their house dresses on and don't go no place. One of the girls would look real nice if she'd fix up, but she's too lazy, I guess.[1]

When considerably detached in sentiments and personal friendship from the nationality groups with which he once was intimately associated, the immigrant becomes interested in marrying someone whom he considers an "American girl,"

[1] Case No. 2.

not an immigrant girl of his own nationality. Under such circumstances he may become romantically interested in a taxi-dancer who is identified in his own mind as an "American." The cultural barriers between immigrant and native-born are rather difficult to surmount, and the taxi-dancers appear to the detached immigrant as the most accessible.

My brother and I come from Venice five years ago..... When I was first in Chicago I lived in the Venetian neighborhood, but I don't no more. I don't like it out on Grand Avenue—there's too many killings and gang fights there, and I never know what's gonna happen next. I don't like to live wid Italians much. They don't act right. Oh, they's all right but I don't wanta go to old-country parties. There's an Italian dance down to Grand Avenue next Saturday; they want me to go. But I won't. I wanta go to American dances. I'm American, not Italian, and I don't wanta go where I gotta act old-country ways. I'm going to get citizenship papers next spring..... I don't read Italian papers much, only news from Italy.....

I don't go to the big dance halls..... You can't getta girl easy in the big halls, like you can here. This here is the best place in town. I'm gonna get married as soon as I get the work I like. I'm a bricklayer now, but I wanta be an electrical engineer..... Sure I'm gonna marry an American. I don't wanta marry an Italian, do I?[1]

A third type of patron, almost as conspicuous as the immigrant and the Oriental, is the older man—the one well along toward fifty—who often seeks desperately to rival the younger men in courting the girls. These middle-aged habitués of the dance halls are either widowers, divorcés, or deserters. In the big city they usually lead a rather detached life and sometimes give vent to city loneliness by an ardent and sincere wooing of the taxi-dancer, the only woman of marriageable age to whom they may have access. If receiving a good wage, they may even lavish gifts upon their favorite taxi-dancers. The response made by the

[1] Case No. 3.

THE PATRON

girls, if the man so desires, may easily be confused with the evidences of sincere sympathy and affection. In the following case a fifty-four-year-old carpenter and cabinet-worker of German extraction interprets the behavior of his girl friends in a manner most satisfying to his vanity. In this instance the man is obviously eccentric, but the case suggests in bold relief the aspirations, scheme of life, and conception of themselves which motivate the activities of many older men in the dance-hall world.

I've been in Chicago only two years but I've already found it's the most unfriendly city I ever knew. In St. Louis a man can go to any dance hall and get acquainted with some nice, friendly girls who will make a date and not break it. It's nice for these girls that are a little too old to be flappers. They are glad to know an older man who has a good business or a trade and has some money in the bank and owns some property.

I've been married twice, and since my second wife died I've kept a housekeeper most of the time. But since coming to Chicago I haven't had one, and I've not had anybody to take care of my things, mend my socks, and cook my meals for me like I like them. One of my daughters is married and living here in Chicago; I live across the street from them. But she don't take care of me like a paid housekeeper would. It's been a lot more lonesome since I came here to live.

One evening, soon after I came to Chicago, I was walking along this street and saw the sign and heard the music from this place. I came up to see what kind it was, and "got in" right away with four girls. They liked me from the start. Afterward I took them out and showed them a real good time. I went back here often after that. It was handy to where I was living. I got in real well with some of the other girls, too. There was one Jewish girl I liked a lot and for a time I thought of marrying her. But one night I went home with her, and found whiskey bottles all around her room, so I quit her. . . . .

About that time I started going to another hall. When they found out I was attending there, six girls left the other hall and came there. Wherever I go the girls "fall" for me. One girl I met out on the West

Side I liked right away. I could tell as soon as I saw her she was German and told her so. She was pleased, and told me her mother's people were German. I guess I liked her because she had just come from a small town. I decided long ago that a country girl is better because she's not acquainted with the extravagant ways of the city.

I soon discovered she wasn't trying to get money from me. One of the first nights I danced with her, she gave me three dances free. I offered her the tickets but she said she liked me and didn't want me to spend too much money on her. That's the way she's always been. This summer I went to the dance hall and spent about $8.00 dancing with her. I usually spend no more than $4.00 and $5.00 an evening. But I spend more when I dance with her. I know she needs the money, and anyway I like the way she dances. Then the next night she said she'd rather I'd give her just a part of what I'd spend if we came to the hall and then we'd do something else. So I gave her $5.00—about what she'd make in one night here—and then we would go to a movie instead. Then the next afternoon we would go for a walk in the parks, and at night take a boat trip. . . . . Of course I knew she was sacrificing a good deal so I'd often go to the hall and dance all evening with her— or sometimes I'd give her a few extra dollars in cash at the hall. But more often she wouldn't take it, but would ask me to keep it and buy her something with it. I've bought her a good many dresses, and some jewelry, too.

Soon after we got acquainted I told her about how much I needed a housekeeper. . . . . Then I got to thinking about it more and more, and decided I wanted to marry her. So I proposed and just recently she accepted me. I'm giving her my most precious ring. She's the only girl in Chicago I've liked well enough to want to give that ring to. . . . . The time of the wedding isn't set yet, but I tell her any time she gets tired of her job, just to let me know and I'll marry her. Not so long ago she came to me and said she would have to have her tonsils taken out. She asked me if I'd give her the money and I told her I would if she'd promise to marry me next spring. She said: "Why, of course I will."

I'm figuring on having a son after we're married. One reason I want a boy is to have somebody to leave my tools to. I've got over four hundred dollars' worth of carpentry tools, and I don't want to throw them away. . . . . My relatives say my girl is only fooling me, and just taking away my money. They say they've got a girl for me to marry, but I don't want her. I want to pick my own girl.[1]

In other cases, the older man has no interest in the taxi-dancers other than the satisfaction and flattery of receiving romantic attentions from young girls.

I happened to go to the New American one night last fall and met two pretty nice little girls. At first I thought things must be pretty bad because of the kind of dancing, but after a while I learned that these two girls were pretty nice. I don't take them home afterward. Even though I've known them for months I don't think they'd let me. Not that they're afraid. They know me too well for that. But they say it would look bad, and would make it hard to turn down somebody else.

But I go up there every Sunday afternoon and dance with them and then I take them out to dinner, probably at the Canton Tea Garden, and then take them back to the dance hall. . . . . Sometimes they come downtown early during the week and if I'm not working that day I take them out to dinner.

It's funny why I like these girls. I'm not interested in them except to dance with and take them out. It's better in the end not to let yourself get involved with women at all, because they'll "hook" you if they can. I just like to be around pretty little girls and dance with them. . . . . Some people say: "If you want to dance, why don't you go down to the Lonesome Club or the big halls?" But there ain't the pretty girls down at them places. And who wants to dance with old women anyway?

There's something about old women that makes me tired before I start. The people where I live are good to me and always invite me to the parties they have. But they're always dragging in some old woman for me. If there's anything I hate it's to spend a whole evening with one. Just last night they had a party and invited me. But the old women were there and so I finally broke away and went down to the Park instead. They've got some nice little girls down there.[2]

A fourth type, closely associated with that of the older detached man—yet nevertheless distinguished from him—

[1] Case No. 5.   [2] Case No. 28.

is the married man, either young or middle-aged, whose matrimonial venture has ended disastrously. Especially when the causes for his marital unhappiness seem to be beyond his understanding or control, or when the wife has been viewed as the aggressor in bringing about the rupture, the husband's distraction and disorganization may become a serious problem. The man is no longer able, by his own efforts, to build his domestic life as he would like. Yet his whole emotional nature is so bound up with the old order of things that he cannot begin immediately to rebuild his life rationally about some new personality or interest. Associated often with these feelings is a painful sense of inadequacy and inferiority. He feels bitterly his inability to measure up to what has been expected of him; and in this maelstrom of self-abasement frequently turns for relief to orgiastic behavior of one form or another. When such an individual drifts toward the taxi-dance hall, as quite often happens, his interest is shaped very definitely by these experiences.

I've learned my lesson. I know now that beauty is only "skin deep." Three years ago I was married to the prettiest girl you ever saw. But the trouble was she wasn't satisfied with me, and I couldn't do anything to help it. I don't know why she ever married me..... About a year ago she got interested in a big tall fellow and wouldn't forget him.

He had money, and an auto, and was a bigger fellow than I was, and of course I couldn't stand up to that kind of competition. So finally I just had to get out of the picture. There isn't much a fellow can do in a case like that but blow the fellow's brains out. And I wasn't much of a hand at that.

It's been two months now since we broke up and I haven't been near a woman since. I vowed I'd never get mixed up with another. I've gone on a drunk every week-end since we broke up, but it doesn't seem to do much good. I guess after all I'll have to get me a girl.

.... See that little blonde over there? She's a girl who looks a lot like my wife—blonde, you know—same size, wears her hair in the same way—and almost as pretty..... I wonder if I could get acquainted with her?[1]

The following case represents very much the same type of marital situation, but from the cultural level of a highly trained professional man. In this instance, however, there is the development of a scheme of life which is believed by him to compensate, in part, for his unhappy marriage. It suggests some of the possible accommodations for such men which may sometimes be found through the taxi-dance hall.

My wife seemed to be much in love with me until the time our first baby arrived..... She began complaining of her living accommodations—though they were better than when I had married her—and accused me of being too selfish to want to provide her with a better home.

It came to a place where we were always quarreling about something. Finally, she began accusing me of not loving her, of not wanting to make her happy, of being a brute, of being selfish, and all the rest. For a while I thought it was her nervous condition, and I did my best to humor her.

Finally, I began to see that this new attitude was likely to be permanent. I did everything I could, one way and another, to reawaken her old love for me. You see, she didn't want to have a baby, and in some way or another blamed me for the child. No matter what I did, nothing seemed to please her. Everything she interpreted in a wrong way.

To please her, we moved into a better house and went into debt for furniture. Then we took in a roomer to help pay expenses. But that was the worst step of all, because he was the one who later broke up my home.

Then we moved to another town, where I secured a better job, paying more money, and I thought she would surely be happy now. We leased a pretty little home, up on the hillside, in the very best section of town, the nicest home we'd ever had. But it wasn't long before she was fretful and moody. Our second baby was born then.

[1] Case No. 34.

It wasn't long before she began talking about going to school to finish her college course and to take some special training. I couldn't see so very much need for it, but she had her heart set on it, and so two years after moving to this town, she left to come to Chicago, while I took another position a thousand miles away—in which, however, I would be making more money. It was agreed that I was to support her and the two children in Chicago, while she was going to school.

For a time her letters came regularly. They were newsy letters, and I was glad to get them. But they gradually became less and less definite, until after six months or so, I knew very little of what she was doing in school. There were few letters in those days, too! I'd been planning to come to Chicago for a visit, but she'd been discouraging it, and had said that we couldn't afford to spend the money.

I became worried, and came to Chicago anyway. I found that she was not living at the address she had given me, but had made arrangemens to have my mail held for her at that address until she called for it. They didn't know where she was. I hired a detective and finally traced her to an apartment on the North Side where she was living with that young and handsome roomer we had taken in some years before. There she was, supporting him with my money! . . . .

For five years I've been working pretty steadily and had little to do with women. But through a friend of mine I've learned a lot I never knew while I was married. When we moved to Chicago recently he and I began coming to these dance halls. He's good-looking, has a car, and knows the ropes pretty well.[1]

A fifth type of patron is the lonely, isolated stranger in the city. Usually from a smaller city or a rural community, the young man is unfamiliar with the ways of the big city. He lacks the knowledge of how to make contacts with young women in the metropolis; and, in any case, feels a diffidence and uncertainty in approaching city-bred flappers. Driven by sheer loneliness, however, he may find his way to the taxi-dance hall, where he at least will be accorded a cordial reception—even though money-bought.

[1] Case No. 27.

THE PATRON

I've been in Chicago for over two months and I don't know nobody. I come from down in southern Illinois. My father and I were coal miners. I went into the mines five years ago when I was sixteen. But when things was slack in the mines down there, my father went to the Texas oil fields. I didn't want to go there and so I came to Chicago. I'm a spot-welder now.

I don't like the big city—I'll take the small town any time for mine. A big city is no place to get acquainted. Right now I don't know nobody except the fellows I work with and the girls up at this place.

When I first come to Chicago I went to these big dance halls. But I couldn't get acquainted easy. The only girls that would dance with me were poor dancers, and I couldn't get a break with the girls who looked good..... But up at this place I'm sure of getting a good dancer. The same girls are always here, and you get to know them pretty well. I like it except it costs too much.

Once a fellow gets started it's hard to quit. After you get acquainted with the girls you have so much better time here that you just keep coming back all the time. I know it costs too much, but it's too slow trying to break into the big halls.[1]

Fully a fifth of the total clientèle of the taxi-dance hall may be classified as unprepossessing men, living a lonely life in the furnished-room sections of the city, who find considerable pleasure in the taxi-dancer's money-bought hospitality.

A sixth type, closely affiliated with that of the lonely stranger in the city, yet distinguished from it, is the footloose globe-trotter. In distinction from the lonely stranger in the city, the globe-trotter very probably is quite adjusted to a life of high mobility and anonymous contacts. His scheme of life is, in fact, organized upon just such transient associations. For him a changing panorama is the chief stimulus in life.

I was born in Australia and grew up in Melbourne. I'm what you call a globe-trotter. I've been on the move ever since I was a lad in my "teens" in Melbourne. I've just gotten back from spending seven

[1] Case No. 37.

years going around the world. I left the States in 1919 and took ship to England. After about a year I went on to the Continent, stopping a short spell at Marseilles in Southern France. Then I took ship to Italy.

My one regret is that I didn't see Paris this trip. I was anxious to get on farther east. Some time I think I'll go back to the Continent and pass some time in Paris. It's a good city to know.

After I left France I stopped at Rome a short spell and then took ship for Egypt and the Suez Canal. I stopped a good many times from there on but I finally came to port at Sydney. I came back by way of Japan and Shanghai, and got to see a little of the Orient.

I'm an advertising man. I learned copy-writing when I was still a young lad in Melbourne and have worked at it ever since. I made my way around the world by it.

I've been going too fast to stop and get married. But I'm about ready to, if I find the right girl. Other times, I think I'll have to spend another year on the Continent before I can settle down. I haven't seen Paris and Germany yet.

This is only the second time I've attended this dance hall. I've been to many of them out on the West Coast. They're all about alike. I just drift in once in a while to dance a few dances. But I don't take out the girls. They're not interested in a fellow of my age, and when I want a prostitute there are surer ways than these girls.[1]

Many of these transients are men who possess the rudiments of some standardized craft, such as barbering, molding, structural ironwork, or bricklaying. They are able to secure immediate employment at lucrative wages in almost any city. Thus they can "see the country," traveling from city to city "on their trade." To these young men a special problem in social contacts with young women presents itself. If they are to enjoy feminine society at all, the normal process of "getting acquainted" must sometimes be speeded up. The taxi-dance hall is one place which facilitates the rapid establishment of contacts with young women.

[1] Case No. 4.

THE PATRON

I've been out on the road ever since I was fourteen years old. I've been all through the West and up in Alaska. I was a newsboy even before leaving home. Then I got a job as telegraph boy, and while loafing around the office I learned something about telegraphy. When I took to the road I'd work as a telegraph boy and finally got to be a telegrapher.

Then I worked in the harvest fields of North Dakota and Minnesota. I also worked in some of the mines out West and even tried gold-mining in Alaska. I thought I could make money prospecting but I lost everything. Then I took up salmon fishing and was able to make a living at it. But it was too cold up there, so after three years I came back to the States. I worked for a time in Seattle, and then came East. I worked awhile in Minneapolis, then in Milwaukee. Then I came down to Chicago. I'm thinking about staying here. I'm a structural ironworker now.

My "buddy" and I are up here tonight looking for a couple of good "skirts." He's not so good-looking, but he has a way of getting acquainted with the girls wherever we happen to be. I've seen that boy in a strange town and thirty minutes after he's arrived he's got six girls on the string. I don't know how he does it. He's so fast at it, I let him go out and fix up the dates for us. It's pretty handy to have a "buddy" like that when you're moving around—it's more interesting if you can get acquainted with the "skirts" when you first hit a town and not when you're getting ready to "blow" it.[1]

A seventh type of patron is the "slummer." He comes from a wide variety of social groups in the city and offers many different reasons for his presence. In some instances it is simply the novelty of the experience that attracts him. He desires merely to "see how the other half lives." But in a majority of the cases it is because of a desire to do what he considers unconventional that the "slummer" seeks out a more notorious taxi-dance hall for his private adventures. Many of these young men who come expecting to be "shocked" are so disgusted by the experience that they do not return.

[1] Case No. 7.

A friend of mine told me about this place and I thought I'd come up here to see what it was like. Gosh, this is awful; it's disgusting! .... It's a joke to see that sign up there, "No Improper Dancing Allowed." This is no place for me. I wouldn't hang around a dump like this for anything. .... Once is enough![1]

Occasionally the "slummer" is a person of older years and of considerable cultural attainments and social position. Either because of idle curiosity or a desire for social helpfulness he may visit the dance hall. His first reaction is always unfavorable and ordinarily he never returns.

Near the corner at one end of the dance floor stood a middle-aged man whose dress and bearing indicated that he did not belong to the dance-hall crowd. He was found to be a banker from a small city in Iowa who was spending a few days in Chicago. His hotel was within walking distance of the dance hall, and while strolling in the evening he had happened upon this establishment.

"This is a terrible place for young people," he said vehemently. "Here you have these young girls being exposed to Chinese and Japs, and Filipinos, and to those even worse among the white race. Some of the girls look pretty tough already. On the other hand, the little girl I just danced with seems to be a sweet little thing. She told me she hadn't been here long, and didn't like it. Yet, there is no question what her fate will be if she stays here. This is a terrible place. . . . . You won't know how one feels about a thing of this kind until you have a daughter growing up in your home. . . . . I'd rather see my daughter dead than in a place like this."

He left without using all of the tickets supplied him upon admission, and was never seen again.[2]

However, there are some "slummers" who are not displeased by their experiences in the taxi-dance hall. Under the cloak of anonymity in the taxi-dance hall they may seek to experience something of the thrill and fascination of unconventional life in the city. Certain married men find here

[1] Special conversation reported by an investigator.
[2] Report of an investigator.

an opportunity to enjoy clandestinely a certain amount of diversion from the continuous attachment to wife and family. More often single men are attracted to the taxi-dance hall because of the opportunity for new and stimulating experiences.

Three other fellows and I "took in" a taxi-dance hall last Saturday night. One of the fellows was in the city only over the week-end, and he wanted us to show him the town. He was a married man and didn't want to go in too deep, but still wanted to have a big time.

We first got a quart of whiskey and two gallons of wine. By midnight we were feeling pretty good and somebody suggested we go to a taxi-dance hall. Only one of the bunch had ever been to one but he knew the way and took us.

It was an exciting night. When we got there a fight was going on. A Jap or a Filipino had stabbed some white fellow. His arm was cut up pretty badly. The cops spirited the Jap away. Police were around everywhere and they surely needed them. Five minutes after the stabbing the dancing was going on again, just as though nothing had happened. There were several other fights started, but the police stopped them before any serious damage was done. They'd pick up the fellows who were fighting—often they were little Italian fellows—and hold them by the back of their coat collars and drag them to the front door.

The girls were all good dancers and knew how to show the fellows a good time. The dances were short. We danced until 3:30 in the morning, when the place closed. One of our bunch got stuck on one of the girls and spent over twelve dollars and the rest of us averaged about nine dollars each. It's an expensive place, but it was worth it. . . . .

I almost had a fight myself. The friend who got interested in the girl ran out of tickets along toward the end and she started to leave him for somebody else. I ran over and grabbed her from this new fellow and he got sore, but only took one "pass" at me. I told her to stay with our bunch, or that there would be another fight that night. She didn't say anything, but stuck with us. She finally began giving us free dances.

We could have had some dates, I guess, but we didn't care about it.

After the place closed we went to a cabaret until five in the morning, and then came home. It was a big night.

We had such a good time there, we decided we'd have to go back some time. But not just yet. There are some other things in Chicago we haven't seen. We haven't been to one of Capone's places yet, and I want to see the Dill Pickle Club and some of those other places in the Bohemian section. . . . .

I think I'd get a "kick" out of that dance hall for about two or three times. Then I'd get tired of it. If I kept on going, I'd get interested in some of the girls. That's the one thing I don't want. I'm through with girls for a while. All they seem to want to do is to get married.[1]

The remaining two types of patrons are, from the standpoint of numbers, of lesser importance. Yet they are distinct types with individual problems and interests. The eighth type is the man suffering from physical abnormality or disability. He is a misfit socially, as well as physically, and turns toward the taxi-dance hall for his social activities. In it he can secure the society of a young woman without feeling that he has taken advantage of friends or relatives or has forced himself upon groups where, because of his abnormality or handicap, he is not wanted. Whether it is an instance of those who are unusually short or unusually tall, corpulent or slender, pock-marked or crippled, the taxi-dance hall is a haven of refuge in a world none too kindly toward the afflicted. For many it is their only opportunity for informal and intimate association with young women.

The following case suggests the plight of the young man who is abnormally tall and has no redeeming graces.

Jack was a twenty-four-year-old youth who saw the world from a height of seven feet, one and one-half inches. A gaunt, angular chap, he apparently had no claim to distinction except his height. For a time he had been employed in a circus side-show and was ballyhooed as the "World's Tallest Man." He carried pictures taken of himself

[1] Case No. 1.

while on these trips. Afterward he was reported to have engaged in petty racketeering along West Madison Street.

Jack is a regular attendant at the taxi-dance halls. Here he invariably selects the youngest and shortest of the girls, and proceeds to execute an awkward shuffle, much to the amusement of the others in the hall, and to the dismay of his dancing partner, who frequently retires into hiding after a circuit about the room.

But get Jack away from the little group of admiring boys, which frequently gathers about him, and he is a very different person. In a reflective mood he will soliloquize in some such manner as this: "I like the little skirts in this place. They're nice little kids. But they don't seem to like me," he adds regretfully. "I guess it's because I'm too tall." And with that observation he shrugs his shoulders and goes on about the business of chartering another taxi-dancer.[1]

The man who is dwarfed in size has a problem greater than that of the very tall individual. With small stature there is often associated a sense of timidity or feeling of inferiority. For such an individual the taxi-dance hall holds definite attractions.

He appeared to be a meek little man, not over five feet in height, and seemed preoccupied with nothing but the problem of keeping out of everyone's way. He always stood alone, several feet away from the nearest person. His complexion was of a pale, sickly color and he wore heavy eyeglasses mounted on a high-bridged aquiline nose. Upon establishing acquaintance his conversation was as follows:

"I don't really care so much for dancing, but it's a pleasant way to pass an evening, and to enjoy the girls. . . . . I've never been out to any of the big halls. I've often thought I'd go, but I'm pretty timid about meeting people—I always have been—and I probably wouldn't enjoy myself. I hear it's hard to get dances at those big halls; anyway, the girls don't like a little fellow like me. Then the young fellows always get the pick of the girls anyway.

"If I'd been of a different temperament, I might have gotten farther, even though I was a runt. I'm a born musician and never had any taste for business. My health broke down in dentistry and I got a

[1] From the report of a special investigator.

cataract on one eye, but my wife wanted me to keep on bringing her the money I was making, and didn't want me to go into music at less money. We broke up, and I got a job with a jazz orchestra. . . . .

"When I found I could get acquainted easily with the girls in these halls, I started coming more or less regularly. I like it here. The girls at least can't refuse me dances. I think I'll dance once more with that short girl in blue over there and then go home."[1]

Finally, there is the type of patron who is a fugitive from justice or from local condemnation of his conduct. In some cases he is a bootlegger or gangster.[2] More frequently, however, he is a lesser offender. For such a person the taxi-dance hall holds out definite attractions. Through its protective cloak of anonymity he is enabled to enjoy some social life without revealing his identity.

Harry was a large fellow, perhaps thirty years of age, who danced much of the time. He used better English than many of the patrons. He said he was the son of a prominent minister and social worker in an Indiana city, had become involved with a young girl in his home city and had left hastily. Even though virtually a college graduate he was employed as a day laborer in a construction gang, working on a Chicago skyscraper, and living under an assumed name in an inexpensive hotel in the Loop.

"The girl was a pretty little blond kid but her family was no good. Her mother was dead and her father a drunkard. She had a brother who was a burglar and another who was an extortionist.

"This one learned about us and I guess decided he'd scare some money out of me. He threatened to give the whole story to the newspapers and to sue me on the Mann Act. Since my father is prominent in the community I decided the only thing to do was to marry her.

"After we were married I found that she had lied about her age and was only sixteen, and not eighteen, as she had said. That let her out of the contract but not me. She can marry again, but I can't. I

[1] Records of an investigator.

[2] An Associated Press news story of May 3, 1931, carried an account of the arrest of an alleged Capone aide in the Club Floridan, a taxi-dance hall located on the Near West Side.

THE PATRON

started divorce proceedings two weeks ago, just before coming to Chicago.

"I had a regular girl back home, a daughter of one of the college professors. She's a school-teacher and already has a good-sized bank account. The scandal didn't get into the papers but her father learned of it and was pretty 'sore.' He hasn't forgiven me but she still loves me.

"I tore out two weeks ago and decided to spend the summer in Chicago, waiting for everything to blow over. Then I want to go back and marry my girl. I'm sorry for the whole thing, especially because of her and my mother. The whispers are going around now, of course."[1]

Other instances of this type would include racketeers, gamblers, and petty criminals. But patrons of this type are few in number—not over three cases in a hundred.

2. INTEREST OF PATRONS

A study of these nine types of patrons and of the attractions which the taxi-dance hall has for them reveals that the patron's interest in it may be either utilitarian or romantic. In the case of the utilitarian interest the motive may be a desire for instruction in dancing, for physical exercise, for the physical exhilaration of the dance but without the personal responsibilities entailed in other social gatherings, or for sensuality. The taxi-dance hall is for such patrons a commercial situation in which they are enabled to use the taxi-dancers for any one of several purposes. On the other hand, many of the romantically inclined patrons crave affection and feminine society to such an extent that they accept willingly the illusion of romance offered in the taxi-dance hall.

The patrons whose initial interests are romantic are almost invariably those who elsewhere encounter difficult or insurmountable social barriers, either because of race prejudice, language and cultural handicaps, age discrepancies,

[1] Case No. 40.

physical disabilities, or because of the isolation of the stranger in the big city. The taxi-dance hall is a welcomed institution which grants such a man social acceptance upon an equality with all others. He embraces it, attends frequently, and seeks to make the most of his new freedom. But at the same time he is conscious of his social limitations. He aspires to venture farther up the social ladder but is restrained by a feeling of inferiority and a baffling sense of inadequacy. Even though he may make the effort he often has unpleasant experiences and returns to the more comfortable environment of the taxi-dance hall.

I've been up to some of the big halls, but I like this place best. It's more friendly up here and everybody has a better time. I was to one of the big halls not long ago, where the highbrows go. I have a friend, a civil engineer. We went there to meet some girls. I had the car and he was to get the girls.

But he got in with some high-class "Janes" and when he brought them out to the car I was nearly tongue-tied. I couldn't say nothing all evening. . . . . I have a cousin who married a rich fellow. They live at a "ritzy" North Side hotel. I was up there one night for dinner. It was a swell place. But before we got through we was supposed to use sixteen different knives and forks and spoons. I didn't know what they was all for, and when I got up from the table I was just as hungry as when I sat down. I'm just a workingman and don't go in for all that high-class stuff.[1]

The sense of personal inadequacy may lead to attempts to overcome these handicaps. But these schemes sometimes fail and the man drifts back again to the taxi-dance hall.

It's hard for a man of my age to get acquainted with the girls in these big dance halls. After they get to know me, the girls like me. But the trouble is to get the first dances. If I had a young fellow who would go with me to these big halls, I could break in, because he could get acquainted with the girls and then introduce me to them. One night I went to a dance hall up north on Broadway, and met a young fellow I

[1] Case No. 49.

used to know. He introduced me to some of his girl friends and I had a real nice time. But he wouldn't go out with me again and pretty soon I lost track of the girls. . . . . Up at these places I have a chance to work things alone. The girls have to dance with everybody, and in that way we get acquainted.[1]

Although the patrons who from the outset have turned to the taxi-dance hall for romance quite generally are those who have found other avenues closed to them, it does not necessarily follow that all patrons who experience social restrictions are necessarily romantic in their attitudes toward the taxi-dancer. Quite often the older man frankly admits that "these girls aren't interested in a man of my age." The globe-trotter may insist that he "can't be bothered" with them. Even some immigrants as well as those who are the objects of racial prejudice may use the taxi-dancer for instruction in dancing and in American customs, or for sensual stimulation. Yet, it is nevertheless true that these same individuals will, in most cases, become romantically interested when they believe an opportunity is presented them. In this way the romantic motive is in the taxi-dance hall interwoven with the various utilitarian interests of the patrons to create a complex design of contradictory impulses and desires.

The first type embodying distinctly utilitarian interests, which suggests itself, is that of the man who attends the taxi-dance hall naïvely expecting to receive instruction in dancing. In Chicago these establishments in their official name invariably represent themselves as "dancing academies," and so occasionally attract a few men who are really in search of dancing instruction.

It's getting so a fellow can't get acquainted unless he can dance. Out in Colorado, where I come from, they all dance different from

[1] Case No. 5.

what they do here. They dance the old square dances and things like that. I've been around Chicago for over two weeks now, and haven't gotten acquainted with anyone. So I came to this place to learn the new steps. I saw the sign coming home from work today and decided I'd come up here.

But I see right now I'll never learn to dance in this place. I've got to have slow music and all they give you here is fast, jazzy stuff. It looks like they really don't want to teach anyway. Why, the last girl I danced with acted like she was sore because I didn't dance better. But I came up here to be instructed. Then another girl danced too close. She got in my way. Do you know some place where a fellow can go and take some private lessons with some girls who really want to teach?[1]

Most of the men in the furnished-room areas of the city are sufficiently well acquainted with Chicago and with the system of the taxi-dance hall to distinguish between such an establishment and a bona fide dancing school. And in any event one visit is sufficient to make the difference apparent.

On the other hand, there are some patrons who find in the taxi-dance hall an opportunity to gain practice in dancing after the initial stages in learning have been completed.

I never danced until last December. I was going around with a bunch of people who were dancers. They wanted me to try to dance but I couldn't. That meant that I had to sit out the dances with the girls I was paired off with and I had to depend on the other fellows to give my girl a chance to dance. I finally decided the best thing to do was to learn.

I went to a real dancing school on North Clark Street, and paid a dollar and a half an hour for instruction. That's a place where they really teach a fellow to dance. You go in there and the manager selects a girl to be your "teacher." She's picked because she's a good dancer and can teach.

The instructor I got the first time I went up there wasn't so good-looking, but she was a good teacher..... But after I learned the

[1] Case No. 46.

steps I decided I wouldn't go back and then got to coming to this place. It's more expensive, but I can pick the girls I want. These girls don't teach anything, most of them don't have enough brains to know how to teach, but just dancing around helps. Now I can dance with any woman that comes along.[1]

A second type of utilitarian interest can be seen in the patron who is attracted by the opportunity the dance hall affords for an enjoyable form of physical exercise. Though patrons of this type are few in number, they nevertheless suggest the variety of uses to which the taxi-dance hall can be put.

I'm fifty-nine years old next month. I don't look my age except for my weight. When I started dancing six months ago I weighed over two hundred pounds. Now I weigh less than one-hundred and eighty-five and feel better. My doctor suggested dancing as a pleasant way to reduce. So last spring I decided to learn. I went to a dancing academy and took some lessons. It was slow for a time, but they had good teachers, and finally I learned.

Dancing is my chief sport now. I eat only one meal a day now and expect to reduce my waist line still more. There was a time when I couldn't sleep at night. Now after an evening here I go home all tired out and can get a sound night's sleep.

Personally, I'm not interested in the girls. They seem like a pretty nice bunch, at this place, as far as I can tell. I'm not interested in taking them out! I'm too old for that sort of thing. I'm already a grandfather. My wife tells me to come up here. She thinks it will help keep me in better health, although she doesn't know how much it costs. She's too old to enjoy dancing herself, she says.[2]

A third kind of impersonal interest found occasionally is that of the patron who regards dancing as a form of art in which he finds satisfying self-expression. He is concerned primarily with the rhythmic execution of the dance and views the taxi-dancer merely as a necessary accessory to

[1] Case No. 43.   [2] Case No. 33.

his art. His chief concern in selecting his partner is in her ability to interpret properly his art.

He presented a striking picture as he danced gracefully about the floor. A man apparently about thirty-five years of age, of slender build and average height, he wore his hair quite long and frequently brushed it back over his head after the manner of a virtuoso. His dark hair and eyes, his abbreviated mustache, his brunette complexion, his immaculate dress, and his almost effeminate manners made him an outstanding figure in the dance hall.

There were but two or three girls with whom he would dance. He never seemed to converse with the girls, and during the dance seemed completely absorbed in its artistic execution. At the end he left his partner as abruptly as he had presented himself.

On several occasions I sought to make conversation with him. But usually after a few noncommittal remarks he withdrew. Once, however, he seemed more communicative. In response to guarded though honest praise of his dancing he replied eagerly, as follows: "Dancing is the one great universal art. It can express love, happiness, sorrow, hate, everything. But it is debased here. Here it means just one thing. . . . . Love is all right. But they forget everything else dancing can be. . . . . These girls! All they know is to keep time to the music or to wiggle, wiggle, wiggle! They don't know music. Dancing is an art interpreting music. How can they interpret it if they can't understand it?"[1]

Others less eccentric might be cited. For there are at least a few men who attend the taxi-dance hall primarily because of their love for dancing and because it provides them with young women partners who are able to adapt themselves to any style of dancing.

A more common form of utilitarian interest, however, is found in the patrons who—though not especially concerned in dancing as a form of aesthetic expression—find much satisfaction in it and in the exhilarating association with young women. Patrons of this type, whether old or young, have

[1] Records of an investigator.

THE PATRON

an individualistic and rather egocentric scheme of life. Because it provides many of the satisfactions of more normal social life, but without its responsibilities, the taxi-dance hall attracts them. The following case reveals graphically the problem of the older man in the taxi-dance hall, and suggests an individualistic scheme of life.

I'm in and out of the city quite a good deal. I usually spend about two weeks a month in Chicago, and when I'm in the city I often come here. This hall has the finest girls of any in the city. Many of them are very nice girls and some are positively beautiful.

I don't believe I'd enjoy the Lonesome Club. There aren't any attractive young girls over there. Much of my enjoyment in dancing comes from being near a beautiful young girl who is graceful in her movements and is a good dancer. I really enjoy being among young people and these are about the only ones I have a chance to meet and know. Associating with them helps to keep me young. Just to associate with these hopeful and enthusiastic young people a few hours a week is better than any tonic. . . . . No, I don't attempt to secure dates with the girls. They aren't interested in a man of my age. However, that doesn't keep me from enjoying them here.

The dancing itself is very beneficial. I come here about ten o'clock, after I've spent most of the day in reading and study, and am ready for relaxation and exercise. I pick out a girl who is a good dancer, dance several times with her, rest for a few moments, and then dance again. After several hours here, I go directly to my hotel, get into a Turkish bath, and then go to bed. . . . .

I don't feel especially out of place here. As a matter of fact, I really enjoy my dancing here more than I would at some important social gathering. When I was operating my clothing factory in New York City, and my wife was living, I used to go out in society quite a little. But there were always some restraints. At a social function I had to dance with certain women, not because they were good dancers or were attractive women, but because they were the wives of some friends of mine or of someone else who was influential. But at this establishment I don't have to dance with a girl unless she is attractive to me, and I can stop dancing whenever I want—and there are no further obligations. A man is absolutely free here.

I never go to the big halls. In the first place, I don't have a girl. I'm too old for that sort of thing, but even if I did I don't believe I'd want to take her to a ballroom for a whole evening. It is seldom that I find a girl who is such an excellent dancer that I don't want to change off before the evening is over. Besides, there are so few girls who are interesting enough mentally to want to spend a whole evening with them.

I'm not so sure I'd want the responsibility of escorting a girl to a public ballroom. Before I could dance with anyone else I'd have to see that she had other dances, and in a strange crowd that would be impossible. It's impossible unless several couples go together to a dancing party. I don't know anyone here in the city who would be interested in doing that. Most of my friends in Chicago are older people who have given up dancing years ago. But even if I could arrange it, I'm not certain I would want to. It would involve some social responsibilities I might not want to assume.[1]

Associated with this absence of certain social responsibilities is a sense of personal freedom in conduct felt by the patron in the taxi-dance hall. In a social situation where he is unknown and where—unless desiring after-dance dates—he is not greatly concerned about his taxi-dancer's opinion of him, he experiences a sense of freedom from restraint not found in other social gatherings.

I don't know why, but I always feel at ease up here. This group isn't like the crowd I travel with most of the time. With them I always feel that I must be on my dignity. There is always a sense of suspense because I'm always trying to make the very best impression I can.

But at these dance halls it's different. Here I can do what I please with these girls. If I want to dance close, it's all right. If I want to dance otherwise, that's all right, too. It doesn't make any difference to these girls. I'm not indebted to them for anything and really don't care much what they think of me. . . . . Not that I want to get mixed up with them! I've never taken out a girl from these places and don't expect to. I know what they are. But just the same I always get a kick out of dancing here that I don't with other crowds.[2]

[1] Case No. 42. [2] Case No. 35.

THE PATRON

This same satisfaction in the absence of certain social responsibilities and restraints is seen in the following case of a Jewish youth, a law student, who expresses these feelings quite effectively though in the vernacular of his own community.

Did you think I was drunk last night? Naw! I was just actin' crazy. The other fellow was getting me sore with naggin' to go home. Such a quiet guy he is! . . . . I come up here and let loose. . . . . You wouldn't know me in the daytime—I'm a different guy altogether. I've got a peach of a job in a law office. . . . . I work for some swell lawyers. . . . .

I come up to this joint to raise hell. I've been coming up here since I was on the outs with my girl friend. I was goofy about her. Boy, she was great, a wonderful kid! But her old man wouldn't let me go around with her because I was Jewish, and my folks didn't like it none.

What's a fellow goin' to do when he can't go around with a Jewish girl without bein' figured on for a husband, and when other girls won't have him? I want to forget this gentile girl but I can't. . . . . I can come up to this place and have a wild time anyway. I told my father that it's bad enough that I'll have to marry a Jewish girl—so he lets me have my fling now.[1]

Closely associated with the desire to evade social responsibilities is a fifth and final utilitarian consideration—the desire for sensual stimulation, either inside or outside the dance hall. The taxi-dance hall is one of several institutions which make it possible for patrons to mingle intimately in groups where they are not personally known and where an unusual opportunity for freedom in conduct is afforded them. They may, if the management and taxi-dancer permit, engage in sensual dancing upon the floor. One visit to such an establishment is enough to make it apparent that some find in this activity considerable sensual gratification.

[1] Adapted from record of a case reported by a special investigator.

Others spurn this as a perversion; and, instead, find in the institution an opportunity for establishing illicit relations. But, in either case, these men visit the taxi-dance hall with very much the same interest they would have in frequenting a house of prostitution.

A unique development in the taxi-dance hall is the growth of a form of immediate sensual gratification in the dance itself. In these days of social reforms, with the segregated district abolished, the prostitute often made immediately inaccessible, and clandestine visits to houses of prostitution frowned upon as never before, some men have discovered in the taxi-dance hall a substitute. Certain patrons are so habituated to these practices that it has become a regular function in their lives, around which has developed among the men participants a certain amount of social life and conviviality.

> My two buddies and I make it a regular thing to visit the hall every Thursday and Sunday night. We are all printers and work at places near each other in the Loop. On Thursday evening we eat together in a restaurant downtown and then go to the "Opera" as we call it [burlesque show]. After the show we usually drop into a restaurant for another bite to eat and then come here to finish out the evening.[1]

These practices, while engaged in by less than one-fifth of the patrons, are nevertheless very significant in the lives of those indulging regularly in them. Even though tolerated by only a few of the establishments, these activities reveal in the extreme the possible avenues which utilitarian interests may take in the unsupervised taxi-dance hall.

Many patrons desiring sensual stimulation, however, seek instead late night engagements with taxi-dancers. "Picking up," as this is called, is in fact the chief interest of certain patrons.

[1] Case No. 38.

THE PATRON

He was a short, heavy-set fellow who sat alone for a long time, occasionally puffing at the stump of a cigar he was smoking. He had little to say to anyone, but merely sat, eyeing the taxi-dancers. He never danced. I used this for a cue, and approaching him, asked, "Ain'tcha dancin' tonight?"

He turned, eyed me for a moment, his face still expressionless. "Naw!" he drawled. "I don't dance much. I'm 'picking up.' " He lapsed into silence. We sat near each other for several minutes without further conversation.

I tried again. "Gotta dame yet?" I asked. Again he roused himself and began his drawling, imperfect English: "Naw, not yet! Lotsa time yet. My buddy, he's dancin' an' pickin' two 'broads' for us. He getsa 'broads'; I hava car," he concluded.

Another lapse of time, and I began again. "I ain't gotta girl yet. Where you take 'em?" This time his face betrayed a slight smile. "Out in country ten mile or so," he replied. And then with a cynical grin he continued: "We tell 'em to walk home if they like. They no walk home," he concluded, laughing dryly at his own joke.[1]

On a higher plane there is also the patron who is angling for a girl to enter a more permanent alliance.

But the dance hall is not a situation where everything is conducive to the desires of the patrons. Schooled in the practices of exploitation, the seasoned taxi-dancer uses the techniques of the "sex game" for all the returns which they will net her. Many times the patron finds that his taxi-dancer has availed herself of his special interest in her and has "played" him for as many tickets as he would buy. And, having once proved himself gullible, he loses his suit with the girl as well. The following case suggests the attitudes and behavior characteristics of the chronically "unsuccessful" patron.

I've spent three and a half dollars already and I've been sittin' around most of the night. There are too many fellows here. The "skirts" are too independent; they give me a pain. I've been dancin'

[1] Record of an investigator.

around with one girl all the time. She tells me I can take her home. But like as not she's just stringin' me along to get some tickets.

You know a fellow's better off if he goes to a regular dance hall. You can dance all night for six bits or a dollar and you have just as much chance of making a date as you do at this dump. You hang around here all night, spending all kinds of dough, and don't know what your chances are.

I just got through working a sixteen-hour stretch. I run an elevator downtown. I worked for somebody else today. That's how I worked so long. I'm gonna sleep all day tomorrow, but I wanta have a date tonight. I think I'll look up my woman and remind her I'm still waiting—here goes another dollar.

[*Later:*] Well, I'm not goin' to stick around this "dump" any longer. First, she told me she'd go out with me at two o'clock, and now she wants me to wait till three. I think she's just stalling. It's all right for you younger fellows to stay up all night, but I'm going. So long, kid.[1]

The "sex game" may be played by the men as well as by the women. There are a few patrons who, out of their experience, have developed certain rules of strategy. Instead of plunging about blindly they follow set plans. Their rules of strategy vary, but usually a definite technique for securing a date is employed.

It's lots easier to get acquainted with one of the younger girls in the hall than it is with some of the old-timers. The old-timers are hard-boiled about everything. But the new girls are usually younger, don't know so much, and are likely to "fall harder" for a fellow.

But I don't even try for these girls on Saturday or Sunday nights. I figure there's not enough chance. I have a friend who runs a restaurant in the Loop who figures it like this: He says every fellow when he get his pay check on Saturday goes out for a big spree and takes his bank roll with him. But by Monday he's spent most of his week's pay and has to "go light" until the next Saturday. Then he's all ready again for another big time.

[1] From records of an investiagtor.

THE PATRON

On Saturday night there are ten fellows for every girl on the floor. There isn't a chance unless you are willing to throw away your whole bank roll. But by Tuesday or Wednesday these girls don't have so many after them, and it's easier to get a date with any girl you want.[1]

These rules of strategy also include some judgments as to successful methods in courting the taxi-dancer.

I've found that the main thing to remember in trying to interest these girls is that they are not hard-boiled prostitutes. They don't want to make money that way. But they do like presents, and—most of all—attention.

Even though they may know it's mostly make-believe, they still expect the man to court them. They expect him to show them a lot of attention on the dance floor, to compliment them, and give them presents.

They are great on expecting presents. But I soon found that an inexpensive present would do just as well as an expensive one. What they are interested in is its sentimental value. They want presents, not for their money value, but as keepsakes to remind them of their good times and their men friends.[2]

In conclusion, it is possible to state certain generalizations concerning the patrons. In the first place, they come from the occupational groups of the skilled and semiskilled craftsmen and from commercial employments involving relatively little special training or skill. Only occasionally are professional people and business executives found in these establishments. The patrons represent, in the main, the great "lower middle class." A census of a sample group of one hundred patrons reveals the accompanying occupational classification.[3]

[1] Case No. 38.   [2] Case No. 27.

[3] The classification was based upon the statements made by these men in the dance hall. Though in most cases, no doubt, these are their true occupations, no means for further verification was available.

Advertising copy-writer	1	Landscape-worker	1
Auto mechanic	1	Law-office assistant	1
Bakery assistant	1	Locomotive engineer	1
Barbers	3	Locomotive firemen	3
Bell hops	4	Machinists	2
Bookkeeper	1	Musician	1
Bootleggers	2	Novelty-store proprietors and clerks	3
Bus boys	2		
Candy salesmen and confectioners	3	Office boy	1
		Plasterer	1
Carpenters and cabinet-makers	4	Plumber's assistant	1
		Postal clerks	2
Clerks and office assistants	2	Prohibition-enforcement officer	1
Clothier (retired)	1		
Collector	1	Racketeers, petty	2
Dentist (retired)	1	Sailors and soldiers	3
Elevator operators	4	Salesmen, traveling	2
Factory workers	10	Shoe-store clerk	1
Radio factories	3	Spot-welder	1
Stock Yards	2	Steam-fitter	1
Others	5	Stockroom clerk	1
Freight-handler	1	Students, college and high school	5
Fruit-store proprietor	1		
Furniture-dealer	1	Surveyor	1
Household-canvasser	1	Taxi-drivers	2
Iceman	1	Terra-cotta worker	1
Inventor	1	Truck-driver	1
Ironworkers, structural	2	Waiters	3
Ironworkers, molders	2		
Laborers, unskilled	4		

A second generalization deserving restatement here is that the patrons tend to be those who experience elsewhere certain social barriers and restrictions of a serious character. A third conclusion is that, with the possible exception of the globe-trotter and the slummer, the patrons are recruited from among those men who, when facing serious obstacles, have experienced a bitter feeling of inferiority and a sense of inability to measure up to the necessities of the situation. Hence, instead of facing the issues to the best of their ability, they have sought the taxi-dance hall where they could gain temporarily a sense of equality or even superiority.

These social restrictions and obstacles, and the inability to overcome them satisfactorily, naturally aggravate even further a fourth characteristic of the patron—his social and psychological maladjustment. He finds himself unable, under the existing conditions, to direct his efforts intelligently toward satisfying his basic needs and interests. The patron's maladjustment usually revolves around his fundamental wish for response and affection, and his desire for recognition and a favorable status in the eyes of his fellows.[1] He feels unable to gain satisfying response from those whose affection he covets and feels incapable also of attaining the status in the eyes of others which he has come to consider necessary. He becomes restless, erratic in his behavior, or even psychopathic. This is, in fact, so characteristically the result that the patron's restlessness and contradictory behavior may be considered symptomatic of his basic psychological maladjustment. In turn, the universality of this restlessness among patrons reflects incontestably the extent to which they find their lives fundamentally unsatisfying.

In the fifth place the regular patron is, with few exceptions, definitely egocentric. Unable to satisfy his basic desires for response and prestige in a world where he is socially ostracized, he is thrown back upon himself, and becomes increasingly self-centered. For him the world comes to revolve

[1] See W. I. Thomas' statement of the "Four Wishes" in *The Unadjusted Girl*, chap. i.

largely about himself, his wishes, his tastes, his ambitions, his conception of things. This trait is so universally a characteristic of the patrons that, in their own way, even the taxi-dancers perceive it. It is their common complaint that the patrons are "all so conceited," that they seem to "want to do nothing but talk about themselves all the time."

Finally, the regular patron is, in his own life-organization, conspicuously unconventional and individualized. In frequent conflict with others, and often at variance with some of the standards of conventional society, the typical patron has adopted some chance adjustment or compromise which seems for the time, at least, to be satisfactory. These individualized schemes of life are not at all in agreement. Yet they are all accommodations of different individuals to the difficulties they have experienced in social life. Moreover, these adjustments instead of being products of group effort almost invariably are the result of individual experimentation. It is significant to note in this connection that the more regular patron is seldom a member of a gang. In Chicago, the city of gangs, the matured gangster is in the taxi-dance hall conspicuous by his absence. Seldom, if ever, does a gang, or a Caucasian youth dominated by his gang affiliations, become other than a transient part of the clientèle of the taxi-dance hall. Instead, the institution serves chiefly the distraught, the individualized, and the egocentric.

CHAPTER VII

THE FILIPINO AND THE TAXI-DANCE HALL

At least a fifth of the total patronage of the taxi-dance halls in Chicago has come from the Filipino group. These young men, more than half of them under twenty-five years of age when entering America[1] and very few married,[2] are quickly attracted to these halls. Alone in a foreign land, far from the rather simple family and community life in the Philippines to which they have been accustomed, and with very few young women of their own race in the United States,[3] it is not surprising that many have been drawn to these resorts. Also, the all-important factor of race prejudice must not be overlooked. The Filipino finds himself in a racially hostile society where not only his occupational and professional opportunities are restricted but where he is denied the usual social contacts with young women.

The situation is made more difficult by complications arising from the fact that he is a very new racial element in the United States. In 1920 there were but 5,603 Filipinos in the entire country. In 1931, only eleven years later, the total

[1] Bruno Lasker, *Filipino Immigration* (University of Chicago Press, 1931), pp. 23-24.

[2] *Ibid.*, p. 25.

[3] Of 31,092 Filipinos admitted to the United States through San Francisco and Los Angeles in the ten years 1920-29, 93.3 per cent were males and only 6.7 per cent females (*Facts about Filipino Immigration into California*, California Department of Industrial Relations, Special Bull. 3 [April, 1930], p. 32), and the ratio of female to male migrants admitted through these two California ports has decreased from 13.9 per cent in 1922 to 3.2 per cent in 1929 (*ibid.*, p. 33). See Lasker, *op. cit.*, p. 23.

number had been increased to an estimated 56,000.[1] This phenomenal growth is going on with little abatement;[2] and with no legal restriction upon the Filipino's migration to this continent it can be expected that the influx will continue. At the same time the Filipino's legal and social status in the United States is very uncertain. He is a national of the United States, yet because he is neither white nor "of African descent" he cannot become a citizen.[3] As a non-citizen he in many states is denied certain occupational opportunities, especially the practice of law.[4] And, because he is not a voter and cannot become one, politicians turn a deaf ear to his agitation for better opportunities and better living conditions in the United States. Other civic-minded Americans tend to regard him only as a transient in this country and see no need for establishing more certainly his legal and social position here.

Even the Filipinos coming to this country think of themselves as transients. Hence they do not concern themselves with the ultimate welfare of the Filipino group in this country, as they would were they planning to remain here. Many ties hold them to the Philippines. A closely knit family life, their devotion to the wishes of parents and older relatives, the business or professional careers which have been held open until their return, the prestige in the Philippines of having studied or traveled in the United States, and

[1] Lasker, *op. cit.*, p. 21.

[2] *Ibid.*, pp. 22–23.

[3] American citizenship appears to be impossible except through service for three years with the American navy. See E. S. Bogardus, *The Filipino Immigrant Situation*, Council on International Relations, Los Angeles, 1929.

[4] Eliot G. Mears, *Resident Orientals on the Pacific Coast*, p. 318; see also Lasker, *op. cit.*, pp. 63–64.

THE FILIPINO 147

the absence of population pressure or economic stringency in their homeland all cause them to plan ultimately to return to the Philippine Islands. Filipinos in the United States, even though they may remain for as long as five or ten years, are thus handicapped by this common assumption that they are merely transients.

Filipinos in the United States are also embarrassed by restrictions upon their freedom to marry and by uncertainties as to their racial classification. When considered a "Mongolian" the Filipino is deprived of the right to marry a white woman in California, Arizona, Idaho, Nevada, and Oregon.[1] On the other hand, there are places even in these states where officials disregard the racial restrictions. Says Bruno Lasker:

.... There has been much uncertainty concerning the Filipino's "official" race in states that impose restrictions upon marriage between Mongolians and whites. Marriages between Filipinos and white women are frequent; and it was left, apparently, to the discretion of county clerks in issuing licenses to decide on the racial membership of applicants. Sometimes the Filipino's status in a California county changed over-night as new county clerks were appointed whose anthropological ideas differed from those of their predecessors. .... The majority of officials seem, without any recourse to science at all, to have married Filipinos indiscriminately with white and with Japanese and Chinese girls. .... [In a recent] case at Los Angeles evidence as to the Filipino's race .... ranged over the whole of anthropological literature, from Linnaeus and Cuvier in the eighteenth century down to recognized textbook writers of today.[2]

The racial and marital status of many Filipinos and their families is yet unsettled. In other parts of the country this same feeling of racial uncertainty, with its resulting marital instability, can often be observed even though it is without

[1] Lasker, *op. cit.*, pp. 117-18.
[2] *Ibid.*, pp. 118-19.

an immediate basis in legal issues such as found in these western states.

1. FILIPINO CULTURAL HERITAGES

The most surprising and significant fact, perhaps, regarding the Filipino is that culturally he is an Occidental. Though an Oriental from the point of view of geography and in physical appearance, much of the Filipino's present-day culture can be traced to the Western world. Other of his cultural traits often cannot be considered either Occidental or Oriental, but are characteristic of an isolated and stable plantation society everywhere. To be sure, his respect for his elders, his sense of filial duty, the acceptance of his economic obligations to all of his relatives—to the large family group or clan—and his great emphasis upon courtesy and decorum all suggest the Orient.

On the other hand, the Filipino through the conquests of the Spanish and the efforts of Catholic missionaries has been exposed to Western culture for four hundred years. When most of the Orient was still closed to the Western "barbarians" the Filipinos were already "Christianized." Their simple, primitive culture had been quickly overcome by the more complex culture imposed by the Spaniards. With Christianization came also Latin-European customs and institutions, Latin mores, and the acceptance of the Spanish language as the language of refinement and culture.[1] Today the native Filipino's love of the music of the Occident—not of the Orient, his Western dances, the village fiesta, his romantic conception of the rôle of the lover, and the strict surveillance customarily given young women—all bear testimony

[1] For a more extensive discussion of Filipino cultural heritages and Filipino adaptations to American city life see forthcoming monograph by the writer.

THE FILIPINO 149

to the fact that the Filipino has gained many of his cultural traits from Western sources.

America in recent years has also made important contributions to Filipino life. The compulsory public school and the almost universal knowledge of English by the young people throughout the Philippine Islands have been two of the most significant. Through these new instruments American ideas and ideals have made rapid headway with the young people. And with these increased contacts, and the present political prestige of the United States in the Philippine Islands,[1] the younger Filipino of today is most anxious to acquire American ways. Instead of being difficult to assimilate, the young Filipino in this country is, from the point of view of some people, too readily Americanized. In contrast to the earlier complaint of Pacific Coast whites to the other Oriental groups—that the Chinese and Japanese did not assimilate fast enough—the fault which many have found with the Filipinos is that they assimilated all too rapidly.

With a greater knowledge of the United States certain misconceptions have become prevalent among Filipinos. One deals with the easy success possible in America and the possibilities for securing an education through self-help. Especially to the young men of the traditional "upper class" who must partially support themselves while in college, yet cannot think of "lowering themselves" to physical labor while in the Philippines, the opportunity for self-help offered them in American colleges has seemed very attractive. Often the obstacles to success in America have been found

[1] This prestige of the United States and of American practices is due largely, no doubt, to the political relationship of this government to the Philippines.

to be much greater than at first conceived. Also American motion pictures and popular magazines, designed chiefly for people in the United States but circulated extensively in the Philippine Islands, have been the basis for naïve misconceptions of American life. In the words of one Filipino confidant, "I got the idea for a time that every wife in the United States had an extra lover hidden away in the clothes closet."

The young Filipino, accustomed to very close supervision in courtship, finds most appealing the freedom with which young men and women associate in the United States. Demonstrations of affection, even between husband and wife, are considered an impropriety in the refined Filipino home, and unchaperoned dates are impossible except in the larger cities.

Most of the Filipino fellows have never had a date before coming to this country. They have never been allowed to be alone with a girl. Except in Manila there isn't such a thing. One can meet a girl at a dance where she is escorted by her brother or her father, or sometimes after school a group of girls will walk together to a corner store, where the fellows can talk to them, but that is all. I had only one date before coming to the United States. That was in Manila with a girl I had known for a long time. She thought it was a very daring thing to do.[1]

To be kissed or embraced by her lover means for the Filipina girl a loss of virtue, purity, and girlhood. As a matter of fact, a girl who has once had a sweetheart whom she did not marry practically loses her chance to marry a young man from the same town, although nothing has happened in the love affair. She is usually looked upon as "cheap" and "common" and has to leave her home town to find a suitable husband.[2]

Through the tales which the young Filipino in the Philippine Islands has heard from those who have returned from the United States, he has a rather definite attitude toward the American girl. He has come to regard her as one who,

[1] Case No. 57.   [2] Case No. 56.

though beautiful and fascinating, is—in the Filipino conception of things—certainly not modest and lady-like. At best she is thought to be "bold" and "forward," and at the worst she is regarded as definitely immoral. In any case, however, she appears to many young Filipinos as mysterious, fascinating, and alluring.

After the Filipino reaches the United States a "date" becomes a goal to be achieved. He has heard other Filipinos back home tell alluring stories of their adventures with American girls, and so very naturally has come to covet such experiences for himself. Not only does the novelty of an unchaperoned date attract him, but he feels that he will enhance his standing among his fellows by having an American girl. In a social situation in which only a few of the Filipinos are able to secure sweethearts, those who can exhibit them regularly to their fellows and can talk familiarly regarding them enjoy a satisfying status in their own eyes as well as in the eyes of many others of their group.

Even though I'm not interested in the girls at the clubhouse dances I always get a big "kick" out of going. There are always three or four times as many Filipino boys there as girls, and every fellow is fighting hard to win favor with some one or two. . . . . These boys are so interested they'll fight over a girl with their best chums.

What I like to do is to stand around for a while, pick out some girl I want, and then take her away from her fellow. There's something about my personality that makes me able to do that. I'm not as good-looking as the other fellows but somehow I always can win from another Filipino any girl I want. For that reason I'm a "dangerous man" and they all respect me.[1]

Filipinos who have become more closely associated with American life discriminate more carefully in the women sought, but the same sense of status and intense rivalry is found.

[1] Case No. 44.

2. CHICAGO FILIPINO SETTLEMENTS

The early Filipino migration to the United States was almost entirely of students who lived close to their colleges and universities and who usually had some financial resources. More recently, as the number of Filipinos migrating to this country has increased the proportion of bona fide students has decreased. Also, many who come planning to study find that they must turn all their energies toward self-support. Consequently in Chicago there has been a drifting-away from university neighborhoods to the Near West Side, the Lower North Side, and the Near South Side, where rents are lower. In the polyglot rooming-house population of these areas there is also less discrimination against Filipinos. The West Side colony has included a clubhouse that has served as a center for the social life of many young men. In the North Side colony Filipinos have opened restaurants, pool and billiard parlors, and barber shops, and have organized an athletic association. Aside from these efforts on the part of the Filipinos themselves, the taxi-dance halls furnish most of the social life. The halls are easily accessible, for the same disorganized communities which most readily tolerate the Filipino are also the ones which shelter the taxi-dance hall.

3. THE APPEAL MADE BY THE TAXI-DANCE HALL

With such a background and with the Filipino's characteristic attitudes, the taxi-dance hall has a definite function in his adjustment to American life. It provides him his first opportunity for social contacts with American young women. Even though still diffident and uncertain of himself, he may, with his tickets, buy an unchallenged claim to a young woman's society and attention for at least a brief period. It is, in a sense, a "school" by which he gains self-confidence and a certain degree of social ease when among white Americans. It likewise provides him all the thrills and novelties which he anticipates. And—oddly enough—the girl employed in the taxi-dance hall is more likely to conform to his own rather naïve moral conception of the American girl than those met in any other setting.

The Filipino gravitates to the taxi-dance hall the more readily because he is already familiar with the taxi-dance halls. Under the name of "cabarets" taxi-dance halls are now to be found in the larger cities of the Philippines. They are run on much the same plan as the American taxi-dance halls.[1] Thus the taxi-dance hall, instead of being a strange sort of public dance establishment, may be the one kind with which a Filipino is most familiar.

The young Filipino making his first venture into the American taxi-dance hall is interested chiefly in the excitement and thrill of these new experiences. He may not at first think seriously of marrying a taxi-dancer, any more than the Filipino of a "good family" would consider marriage to a *bailarina* [Filipina taxi-dancer] in the Philippines. He is, however, excited by the new and stimulating contacts with white girls. And although he professes to be romantically indifferent, he nevertheless courts them ardently and lavishes gifts upon them. At first he seems to be actuated primarily by the novelty of the situation and by his conception of himself in the racial situation.

Just to have a date with an American girl, and to be alone with her in a taxicab, and perhaps to kiss her, is enough for a time for most

[1] From information supplied by Filipinos. See also the description of the "Santa Anna" in Manila, "the largest dance hall in the world," apparently a taxi-dance hall, in "The Peace Rôle of Our Asiatic Fleet," *New York Times Magazine*, March 6, 1932.

Filipinos. I'll always remember my first date with an American girl. She was a dance-hall girl, but I thought she was wonderful. We were alone together in a taxicab and later I took her to a chop-suey restaurant. I didn't dare to do more than hold her hand, but I had a wonderful time.[1]

Even when he talks glibly of love and marriage, he may not be seriously considering matrimony. It is merely the way most familiar to him by which he seeks to please his lady.

Some newly arrived Filipinos, with their typical attitudes toward American life and the American girl, conceive of the "date" in terms of immorality. Unable as yet to make effective contacts with Americans, they are forced to depend for their insight into American social life upon newspapers and magazines and upon the accounts of adventures with American girls retailed to them by other Filipinos. Occasionally young men who have been in this country several years have shown an inability to distinguish between a "date" and immorality.

Mr. F. T., a rather dark Filipino, lived in the West Side colony exclusively and was attending evening-school classes in a downtown branch of a university. As we became better acquainted it was apparent that he made no distinction in his mind between the conventional date and immorality. To him the unchaperoned "date" seemed to be the institution by which the presumed profligacy of American life was made possible. Even though he had lived in the United States for nearly two years, he apparently had not discovered that there was any different conception in the minds of Americans.[2]

Not all newly arrived Filipinos, to be sure, hold this attitude. But these earlier impressions color their first contacts with American young women. A majority of the young men are deterred, no doubt, by a sense of personal inferiority and uncertainty. But the more adventurous youths may seek

[1] Case No. 44.
[2] Records of an investigator.

THE FILIPINO 155

to put their interpretation of the American girl and the "date" to the test of experience,[1] though always with manifestations of Filipino courtesy and the ever present fear of arousing racial animosity.[2]

4. TECHNIQUES OF COURTSHIP

Thus arises among the more adventurous Filipinos an unusual emphasis upon the techniques of courtship. In a hostile racial situation, in which the young Filipino is forced to break down the age-long barriers of race, as well as the natural feminine reserve, courtship becomes a problem challenging intellectual effort. Schemes and techniques may even be studied out, discussed, and evaluated. Lavish expenditures of money, dinner dances, beauty contests, extreme courtesy and politeness, and proposals of marriage may all come to be regarded as effective means for gaining favor.

[1] It would certainly be a grievous error for anyone to infer from this discussion that Filipinos as a group can justly be considered more irregular in their conduct than any other group of young men similarly isolated in America. The emphasis given by the writer to this aspect of Filipino life in the United States is necessary, unfortunately, because it is upon these activities that the taxi-dance hall has the most direct bearing.

[2] It should always be borne in mind that even the most innocent efforts to make the acquaintance of young women of the dominant racial element by men of a minority racial group will usually be wrongly construed by the public. The Filipino's interest in meeting a young woman is not different fundamentally from that of any other young man, except very probably that his desire and need are more intense. The Filipino's conduct, even in the taxi-dance hall, is one to which he can point with pride. He is seldom guilty of sensual dancing, and is much more the pursued than the pursuer in his contacts with taxi-dancers.

Bruno Lasker, after a careful survey of the evidence, has this to say of the essential morality of the Filipino: ". . . . The consensus of opinion among those best informed seems to be that in their attitude toward members of the other sex the Filipinos do not differ much from any other group of young men finding itself in a foreign country, far from the control of family life or of older persons of its own nationality" (*op. cit.*, pp. 330–31).

Successes are accepted as laurels of victory. Failures are attributed to racial prejudice—a handicap which the more resourceful Filipinos believe must be circumvented by still more effective techniques for gaining preference. Their devices may be objectively conceived but usually, no doubt, do not include as elaborate a system as that suggested in the following account by a somewhat sophisticated Filipino in Chicago.

The musical comedy was nice, with pretty music and scenery and we became sentimental. We didn't say much, but just held hands. You know you can say a lot through touch that you can't say by talking. By the time the show was over we both wanted to be alone so we took a taxi. I kissed her a good deal in the taxicab, but not too much or too frequently. Just enough! Then I kept telling her how much I loved her and that I couldn't be away from her.

We drove to a chop-suey restaurant in Chinatown. . . . . We ate a big meal together—off in one corner where we could be alone. I kept holding her hand and kissing her and telling her how I never saw her looking so pretty as tonight. I knew she was responding, and of course the warm food was having its effect. If you want to win a girl's love you must first get her in the most favorable frame of mind. Buy her pretty things, and give her a nice warm meal. Girls always love you more after a big meal.

Of course we didn't say very much except that I kept telling her how much she meant to me. That's where most American fellows fall down. They think they've got to keep talking to their girls. But talking, unless it's concentrated on the love you have for the girl, will distract her mind to other subjects. That means that you have lost all you gain by your efforts up to that time.[1]

Success does not always crown the Filipino's efforts. More often than not, when he picks upon a scheming and worldly wise taxi-dancer he finds that he has met more than his match. She is not only fully capable of taking care of herself but, in her own way, she is seeking to exploit the

[1] Case No. 57.

Filipino. The following document reveals both the objectively conceived techniques used by the more sophisticated Filipinos and, in this instance, the unskilfully handled devices of the taxi-dancers.

"Another Filipino and I attended a dance given in a downtown hotel. We saw a dance-hall girl who looked pretty good to us. We danced with her several times and she seemed clever. Then she asked me why she'd never met us before at Filipino affairs and I explained that we had our own life around the campus and didn't come to these dances often. Pacito took the cue and began bragging me up to her. He told her that I was a very rich fellow, that I had my own automobile and bought a car just because I didn't know what else to do with my money. Then he told her that I had several college girls who were crazy about me and that I didn't have to come to the dance halls. She became interested and invited me to come to the dance hall and see her.

"But I didn't go right away. I figured on disappointing her for a while so she'd be even more anxious when I did show up. About a week later my friend and I went around to the dance hall. She said she had a sister named Hazel and introduced us to her. So we decided to give the girls a rush. We laid our plans carefully, though. The only trouble was that they were too smart for us.

"He and I planned to 'talk up' each other to our girl, especially about the other's wealth, with the knowledge that each would tell the other what she heard, so we'd both profit. I guess our scheme worked because they surely began working on the principle that we had lots of money.

"After we left the dance hall, we drove to Chinatown. . . . . The girls told us they'd get kicked out of their home if they were seen with a Filipino. That made us all the more interested because of course we thought they must come from a pretty good family if that were true. The next night my girl recalled that she was to have a birthday the following Friday. I told her I'd get her a present, even though I knew well enough she probably didn't have a birthday at all. The next day she called me to remind me of her birthday.

"I asked her for a date for a dance to be given the following week. But she said she already had a date with another Flip [Filipino]. She said she liked me better but that the other fellow was going to give her a dress. The implication was, of course, that if I'd buy her a dress she'd break her date and go with me. I told her that since she had already made this date with the other fellow that it wouldn't be right to break it. She seemed kind of nonplused by that but finally intimated that I must not love her much or I wouldn't want her to go out with other fellows when she was already halfway engaged to me. I replied that I was liberal that way, that I always wanted my fiancée to have a good time.

"Then later in the week she phoned and asked if I wanted to go to a Filipino picnic. She said she'd go with me if I'd buy her a dress. Then she threatened to go with somebody else. I told her to go ahead, that I was broadminded that way. She wasn't satisfied; said she wanted to go with me and that the dress would be my birthday present to her."

For some time the Filipino and the girl fenced verbally over the dress, the Filipino defending himself by implying that his refusal to buy it was due to the crass way in which the girl had asked for it, the girl refusing to make any dates with him unless a dress was bought. As soon as the girl was convinced that she was not to receive a present she lost interest in the Filipino. He, on the other hand, disgusted by the turn of events and by the girl's lack of finesse, took comfort in the new and—presumably—higher impression of Filipinos he created by his refusal.

"I was sore but didn't want to give the impression of being a tightwad. So I fixed up a story. I called her into a side room and said: 'It isn't because I don't want to give you a dress or because I don't want to spend the money. I don't like your principles. . . . . You don't give me a chance to offer to make a present.' She was dumb with amazement. She probably didn't think a Filipino could talk like that. She just stood there with a blank look on her face for a minute or so and then turned and walked away."[1]

But whether he is imbued merely with a desire for the novelty of associating with American girls, or with more definite interests, the Filipino who continues his activities sooner or later becomes sincerely attached to some American girl.

[1] Case No. 44.

Alone in the city, with little opportunity for feminine society, he comes gradually to idealize some one of the girls whom he can meet, very probably a taxi-dancer. In true romantic fashion he makes an "exception" of his lady friend. While other American girls, and especially other taxi-dancers, are considered unworthy, his girl is "different." He thinks seriously of marriage to an American girl—and to a "common" taxi-dancer as well. He dreams of taking her back to his native village as his wife and paints to her a roseate picture of the life she would lead in the Philippine Islands. Violating all the solemn instructions from his parents and family, he prepares to marry an American girl.

Were the girl whole-heartedly in earnest, and were the problems of interracial marriages less difficult, it is very probable that such romances might flourish satisfactorily. But to the veteran taxi-dancer, the Filipino youth is at best merely a passing interest; and at the worst a "fish" to be exploited for all the financial returns that can be realized. These maladjustments are painful, distracting experiences.

Philip said he was just nineteen years of age, had been in this country less than a year and in Chicago only three months. He said that he had never courted any other girl but Betty. Soon after coming to Chicago he had accompanied several Filipinos to the dancing school, where he had met Betty, and fallen in love with her.

"Betty was a nice girl, I thought, and so I went out with her," Philip continued. "The boys at the house said I was a fool to spend all my money on her, but I didn't care because I loved her. Sometimes I dreamed of taking her back to my home town as my wife, and showing her off to the people in my town.

"She always acted nice when I was out with her. She didn't act tough and drink like some of the other [dance-hall] girls. I bought her a watch, a necklace, and a ring, and she said she loved me.

"I told her she was too nice to be in the dance hall and for her to leave it, but she said she needed the money. Then I asked her to marry me and she said she would, but not yet. Then last week she said she wanted me to marry her at once, and so we got married.

"But now she won't live with me. She says she won't live with a Filipino. She says her big brother will kill her if she lives with me, and that he'll kill me if I ever come around her home. She says she won't live in the apartment I selected and wants a bigger one, but I can't afford it. She knew I was making only twenty-five dollars a week when she married me.

"Then I tell her to stay home, not to come to the dance hall, that I don't want my wife in a dance hall, but she stayed home only two nights and then came back. She said she got tired doing nothing all the time..... But I tell her to come live with me, but she won't. .... Now, what can I do?'

Subsequently the wife's parents succeeded in having the marriage annulled, but Philip was never satisfied. He threw himself into affairs with other taxi-dancers, but he didn't permit himself to become enamored again. "I don't trust these girls any more!" he later explained.[1]

When such a young man as this comes into touch with a scheming or disorganized taxi-dancer, his morale frequently suffers. Having once been "fished," he less readily capitulates again.

But every week new faces appear among the Filipino group. Many of the newcomers still have some of their own and their family savings brought with them from the Philippine Islands, and they are often easy and willing prey for designing taxi-dancers. Many girls practice their craft upon young Filipinos whom they meet in the taxi-dance halls. Others are former taxi-dancers who have learned the trick of exploiting the newly arrived Filipinos. They frequent many of the special social gatherings and dances sponsored by Filipino groups, where they single out new quarry for their game.

[1] Report of a Chicago social worker regarding a West Side Filipino.

THE FILIPINO

5. THE "VAGABONDS"

Such disillusioning experiences leave their impress upon the youthful Filipino. From unrequited affection he turns to cynicism and exploitation—the competitive motive to romanticism running throughout life in a taxi-dance hall. He frequently throws himself into the life with more abandon, shifting alternately between impulses toward exploitation and toward sincere affection. Preoccupied with this almost unsolvable problem of meeting desirable young women —a riddle which because of our racial prejudices is most difficult—he often loses step in the educational or occupational advance which very probably was his ambition in coming to this country. These social maladjustments, far more than any economic handicaps themselves, serve to defeat the best-laid plans of many ambitious Filipinos each year.

Many young men, dissatisfied with this life, yet unwilling or unable to change it, protect themselves by gradually breaking old ties with relatives and friends in the Philippine Islands and in America, who recall for them their old ambitions for themselves. In some cases the relatives in the Philippines lose trace of them and appeal to the United States government to locate the wayward ones. Thus arises the phenomenon of the "lost Filipino," concerning whom such notices as the following frequently appear in Filipino magazines published in this country.

The Bureau of Insular Affairs has received requests for information regarding the whereabouts of Esteban Rueda, native of Labores, Pandacan, Manila; Pablo Capulong of Paombong, Bulacan; Lucas Agapito, employed sometime ago at San Francisco Workshop; and José L. Gutierrez, pharmacy student of New York University. Also requests for information have been received regarding Fermin Debelin y Dantis. When last heard from, in 1921, he was in Buffalo, New York. His mother, who lives in San Miguel, Bulacan, is anxious to hear from him.

Antonio V. Amat, Dalases, Tayabas, left the Philippines about 22 years ago. The last place he was heard from was Santa Maria, California. His relatives at home are anxious to hear from him.

Kindly send any information you may have about these persons to the Bureau of Insular Affairs, Washington, D.C. . . . .[1]

The manner in which the Filipino may become "lost" in this country is revealed in the following case of two young men coming from the same community and the same type of family in the Philippines, who had entirely different experiences in the United States.

Miguel Ocampo and I came to America together. We used to spend the evenings in our crowded quarters in the boat visualizing far into the future and in the earnestness of our imagination often forgot about the opium-eating coolies whose laughter and unintelligent noise thickened the air. We sped past Hongkong and Japan, and as we neared the coast of our "promised land" our air castles soared into insurmountable heights.

Four years passed, during which time Ocampo's letters became fewer and fewer. He was in New York City, "doing fine," and I was struggling my way through a western university—this was the last we heard from each other. His letters not only became fewer and farther between; one after another they became more vague and indefinite.

I soon learned that Ocampo had not only forgotten me, but he had also neglected to write to his worried folks, who soon wrote to me inquiring about him. It was a complicated affair to locate Miguel in little old New York, and when I did succeed, the alibi came: "I stopped writing because there is no longer anything in my life of which my friends and my relatives can be proud. This damnable city has made of me a failure. I have lost my ideals, and no one knows it better than I do. I have fallen by the wayside. If you are still on your feet you are

[1] Published in the *Philippine-American* in 1925.

THE FILIPINO 163

a lucky dog. Keep on and forget about me." A pathetic figure, you say, but let him who is without sin throw stones at him. He is a typical case among many Filipinos in this country.[1]

These young men become "drifters"—they enjoy from day to day the excitement and stimulation which is afforded, with no thought for the future, and with little sense of direction or purpose. In the vocabulary of the Filipinos, they become "vagabonds." Ashamed to return to the Philippines admitting defeat, these young men continue indefinitely in this country and so make for a piling-up of the Filipino driftwood in the rooming-house sections of our cities.

6. THE "OPPORTUNISTS"

There are, in addition, those young men who can best be described by the term "opportunists." Out of the conflicting interests of life as discovered in the taxi-dance halls, the schools, and their places of employment, these youths have developed a scheme of life satisfactory to themselves which, in all probability, is entirely at variance with their own Filipino heritage and with our dominant American standards. While not identical, these schemes are similar in that they are all "American made," the result of the efforts of Filipinos to adjust to American life as they have found it. This "Americanized Filipino," as he is sometimes called, is the unique product of American city life and the American taxi-dance hall, and is so recognized in the name given him by his compatriots. While the term "Pinoy," of island origin, describes the young Filipino new to America, the word "Flip"[2] is more clearly the "Americanized Filipino's" name for himself. It is the "Pinoy" who enters the life of the taxi-

[1] *Ibid.*
[2] It has been claimed that this term originated among Chicago taxi-dancers, who first applied it to their Filipino suitors.

dance hall in America. It is the "Flip" who successfully graduates from it.

The fundamental characteristics of the "Flip" or Filipino opportunist are very real, though not easily described. Occupationally he has adapted himself to business or professional opportunities as he has found them in American cities. Instead of wasting his energies in combating race prejudice he has adapted his plans to it. Thus the Filipino trained in American business methods and with a good knowledge of the Spanish language specializes in developing on a commission basis an export trade with Spanish-speaking countries. Another becomes a labor manager supplying the radio industry with trustworthy Filipino youths to work in its factories. Similarly, a practicing physician successfully specializes on a Mexican clientèle because of his knowledge of Spanish and because of his Spanish name.

In personal conduct the "opportunist" is likewise adaptive—though certain characteristics are always present. In the first place, he is certain to be "dapper" in his dressing. In his manner he is courteous and suave. The opportunist has usually attained a certain financial success in an honorific occupation, and has the self-confidence arising from this achievement. Interesting and significant is his attitude toward the taxi-dance hall and the taxi-dancer. Toward her his attitude is at best utilitarian and sometimes one of exploitation. Coupled with this is an individualistic impulse —a curious indifference to the welfare of his newly arrived countrymen.

> My attitude toward these dance-hall girls is changing. Last year I used to get a big "kick" out of these girls even if I didn't take them out. But now I don't even get interested. Sometimes I go out to the

West Side just to pass the time and to meet the other Filipinos, but I never get interested in the girls. But I get a big "kick" out of watching the newcomers get enamored over them. Pascal is like that. He doesn't get infatuated with the girls. Doesn't even dance much with them. But is just interested in watching the girls "fish" the newcomers. He gets a big "kick" out of it, too. But he's adjusted to life here. He knows enough not to get married to these American girls, yet also knows how to reach them clandestinely. He comes from a good family in the Islands and with his education and business experience he could go home and get a good position. But he can make more money here, and besides he likes his white girls too well. After being in this country for ten years he knows he could never be content with Filipina girls, and so he stays on in this country.[1]

The Filipino opportunist is a supreme individualist in practices, standards, and in his philosophy of life. Yet his schemes of life may differ radically. While some Filipinos of this type conform rather closely to our conventional standards—especially in business activities—others have schemes of life quite contradictory to the prevailing mores. Nevertheless, these standards and practices are all individual adaptations to the racially hostile society in which the Filipino seeks to make his way. They are all adjustments by which certain young men have been able to make some occupational and social advance. Yet in almost every instance this advance has been made only at the sacrifice of some of the Filipino's earlier ideals and standards. He has been forced to change his practices and personal ambitions to suit the situation, and often in doing so has acquired a distorted view of American life. This misconception is seen most strikingly in a perversion of moral standards, and reflects the immorality which for some Filipinos has been "American society."

[1] Case No. 57.

I'll admit there are some things in which American customs are better than in the Philippines. Now take the sex freedom here, for instance. If a fellow goes out with a girl from here [taxi-dance hall] and perhaps they take a few drinks too many, the girl doesn't expect the fellow to marry her. In fact, she probably doesn't even want him and won't marry him, especially if he's a Filipino and she has some race prejudice. That's the way things ought to be. Why should a couple have to get married because of what happened a long time ago? . . . . When we go back to the Philippines we'll have to change things to the American way.[1]

7. OTHER TYPES

It is only just to point out that there are many Filipinos for whom American life is anything but demoralizing. It cannot be denied that there are Filipinos—"vagabonds" in America—who lose all effective ambition or sense of achievement; and that there are "opportunists" who, in acquiring a reorganized scheme of life, sometimes become "Americanized" in the worst sense of the term. Nevertheless, it is also true that there are many Filipinos in America who find here an opportunity for study, inspiration, and personal advancement, and who, in spite of great obstacles, make an enviable record for themselves. These young men, in contrast to the others, remain true to their earlier ideals, and refuse to permit other interests to crowd in. These goals, however, are attained most certainly only when the Filipino deliberately renounces all opportunity for feminine society while in this country. Thus a loss of the normal opportunity during young manhood for the society of young women is the price most Filipinos pay for scholastic achievement in this country.

There are those who pay this price, and as a result many

[1] Case No. 47.

young men return to the Philippines well prepared to lead in the advancement of their country. Such successful young men are impelled almost invariably by the devotion to a great cause, larger than themselves. Thus arises the "political zealot," the type to whom Philippine independence would seem to be the all-important consideration, and the "social welfare type," for whom broader interests of human welfare is the real dynamic.

8. INTERMARRIAGE

In Chicago, with the entrance of Filipino young men into the life of the taxi-dance hall the number of intermarriages has greatly increased. While many of them were soon annulled, usually at the insistence of the parents of the young women, a considerable number have been established. Rumors are current that at least 125 Filipinos in Chicago are married to American girls. A survey made in 1927 revealed that at that time at least 55 married couples were living together in the city. Of this number 46 were legal marriages, and in addition there were at least 9 others that may be considered common-law marriages. All the common-law marriages and certainly more than three-fourths of the others were with former taxi-dancers. The other young wives, often quite superior to the taxi-dancers in character and in cultural attainments, were met in their places of employment, in the schools or colleges which they attended, or through church affiliations. Many of these Filipino unions are companionate, and a considerable number do not last beyond a two-year period. There are, however, at least 30 instances in Chicago in which the marriage is apparently on a more stable basis. Already in Chicago there are at least 10 children of these intermarriages. These "American mestizos," as they are called, are the beginning of a new racial group.

Ill advised as these marriages may seem to some to be, they are often contracted with the highest romantic idealism. The young Filipino, who in the past has had his marriage made for him by his parents, adopts completely our extreme American romanticism and gallantly weds an American girl. While these marriages are more often hasty affairs, they occasionally may be made with considerable deliberation, and even with some effort on the part of the young man to acquaint the girl with the difficulties of the racial situation into which she is entering. The following case represents the highest type of romantic marriage in which the parties were very much in love.

When I was in college I hadn't allowed myself to get interested in American girls. . . . . By the time I had been working two years after graduating from college I had accumulated nearly $2,000, part of which was invested in my business.

One evening I saw a girl I liked a lot. She was very pretty and had a good personality. I danced with her again and again, but she didn't seem to care for me. She was going with another Filipino then. . . . . She wouldn't give me a date, but I decided I'd make her pay attention to me.

Finally, one night when the Filipino organization in Chicago was having a special dance at a big Loop hotel she attended with a Filipino. They always finance these things by having beauty contests in which the fellows buy votes at twenty-five cents each. Someone started to run her. I decided to make her beauty queen. But there were other girls being pushed and it cost me seventy-eight dollars. After that she had to pay attention to me, and it wasn't long before we were going together all the time. I bought a Cadillac car and began taking her around to cabarets and theaters. I had to sell my business to get money to keep going with her.

My parents heard about us. They wanted me to come home at once. Father wrote offering me the management of another store he was opening. I wrote back and told them about my girl.

THE FILIPINO

Then I received a ticket for my passage home. You see my folks were in earnest. I noticed that the ticket was good for two weeks and that if it wasn't used it could be turned back. The more I thought of it, the more I couldn't think of leaving her. So I finally proposed to Hazel.

I showed her the ticket, told her I loved her; that I'd stay in this country, do anything she wanted me to—if she'd marry me. Otherwise I'd use the ticket and go back home and start things over again in the Islands. I said that if we got married it wasn't to be one of those "fly by night" marriages like some of the Filipinos were having, but that we were going to make it a permanent thing, or not at all. I told her I was willing to change all my plans for life if she would marry me.

But I told her I loved her so much I wanted her to know ahead of time the difficulties we would have. In addition to the usual difficulties I said there would be special ones in our case because of race.

In the first place, her parents might feel "disgraced" because their daughter married a Filipino. Then she would have special difficulties because she married a Filipino. Some people wouldn't have anything to do with her. Then I said that if we went back to the Philippines to live, there would be difficulties. I said that even though my mother and grandmother would respect her and come to love her and accept her into the family, they would be so different they might not always get along well together. . . . . I told her of the difficulties she'd have talking to my parents and grandparents because she didn't talk Spanish and they didn't speak English.

Then I let her know some of my troubles if I married her. . . . . If I stayed in this country I couldn't have a big business opportunity. Also, if I went back there with an American wife there might be some other handicaps. . . . .

Of course I didn't tell her all this at once, but gradually I let her see the whole situation. I said that I loved her enough to make the sacrifice and asked her if she was. . . . . But I said I didn't want her to make a hasty decision, and wanted her to think it over carefully. Her folks were nice about it, but they didn't want her to marry me. But at the end of two weeks her parents were won over and said that since Hazel seemed to be so set on it they wouldn't oppose any longer, and so we were married.[1]

[1] Case No. 53.

Yet even with the most careful preparation an interracial marriage may not prove successful. The explanation can be found in part in the widely divergent cultural heritages. The Filipino husband, probably a man of some college training and with certain rather definite conceptions of propriety and family life, may find himself in complete disagreement with the standards and interests of his ex-taxi-dancer wife.

For a time the young married couple were quite happy. But before many months their entirely different interests and desires began to be seen. At the end of a busy day in the office José wanted nothing more than an opportunity to sit at home, reading the daily newspaper, a magazine, a book, and perhaps listening to the radio. She desired thrilling social contacts. She wanted to attend theatres, dances, cabarets, and to entertain at home.

This was not what he wanted his wife to do. But he was discreet. He bought her books, magazines, cultivated her interest in poetry and philosophy. He sought to arrange parties at his apartment where she might entertain. But this was not entirely satisfactory, for those whom they could invite to their home were not always the type of people most interesting to her. Their marriage idealism, however, helped them to preserve the relation for over a year and a half, at which time it had become intolerable to both.[1]

Contradictory standards and conceptions of life, while frequently elements in marriage discord, are especially significant in the case of interracial marriages, because of the identification of certain distinct traits with each racial group.

A more significant factor, no doubt, is the loss of status which the parties to an interracial marriage experience, owing to racial prejudice. In the well-ordered community etiquette and the accepted social conventions tend to encourage a married couple to draw more closely toward each other. But in the case of an interracial marriage, all the

[1] Report of an investigator.

forces of the community seem to be organized to break down the *rapport* existing between husband and wife. While either party alone may be acceptable in his own circle within the community, as a couple they can never be admitted. A few intimate friends may make an exception and admit them to their society, but the community as a whole will not. Thus arises the pathetic isolation of the interracial couple.

In the large city where anonymous transient contacts are most frequent, the antagonism of the community is seen most clearly in the conspicuousness of a mixed couple and the immediate hostility evidenced by the public.

During the first three months of our married life we went out frequently together. Sometimes my wife and I thought that we couldn't stand the staring of those ignorant people. At times my wife was almost on the verge of "flaring up" but by careful handling. . . . everything turned out satisfactorily.

When we walked along the sidewalk and my wife took hold of my arm I felt uneasy most of the time for fear I might hear some remarks from the passers-by. So far, we have not been insulted even by the most prudish persons.[1]

Some couples, however, are not so fortunate. The following newspaper story suggests the possible consequences of "being insulted," i.e., overhearing a chance remark from others. Many incidents similar to the following, some of them fatal, could be cited.

John Cruz, 27 years old, a Filipino, was shot and seriously wounded following a quarrel in the new Sunset Café at South Parkway and Thirty-fifth Street early today. The shooting occurred in the alley in the rear of the resort, and followed a quarrel between Cruz, seated at a table with his white wife, and three men and a woman at a nearby table. One of them was overheard to remark, "There is a Filipino with a white woman."

[1] From an unpublished monograph on Filipino intermarriage, by Aproniano A. Basa.

Cruz, according to his wife, walked over to their table and said: "I don't like that remark."

"If you don't like it, come on outside," one of the men said. Cruz accepted the invitation, and both men went out into the alley. Several of the diners followed them. As Cruz was removing his coat, the other man suddenly drew a pistol and fired twice at Cruz, witnesses said. He and his companions, including the woman, fled. Cruz was taken to the hospital, where his condition was said to be serious.[1]

Some of the more discerning Filipinos recognize that the hostile public attitude toward any American girl seen associating with men of other races will for a long time be a serious difficulty in making an interracial marriage permanently satisfying to the wife.

Whenever I took Marjorie anywhere we were always being stared at. So I always take a cab rather than travel in a street car. . . . . Of course, she noticed that we were being stared at, but she didn't think anything of it. But I knew that they all thought she couldn't be very much or she wouldn't go out with a "Chinaman," as they probably thought I was. But sometime she would come to understand what people meant by that stare and then she would be very unhappy.[2]

In matters pertaining to the children there are likewise difficulties. For a typical young girl in our racially conscious society, it requires considerable mother-love to admit, before a hostile public, that the "brown baby" is her own. Others, while willing to accept certain Filipinos as their husbands and perhaps even willing to endure the isolation and hostility which such marriages invite, do not feel that their conscience permits their bringing into the world children with such an anomalous racial heritage and with so uncertain a future in our racially hostile society.

Should the interracial couple return to the Philippine Islands with their children a new problem presents itself—

[1] *Chicago Journal*, September 8, 1928. Name of Filipino is here altered.
[2] Case No. 44.

the isolation of the American wife. While she may have the respect of her husband's kinfolk and the community she may yet find it difficult to establish *rapport* with them. Language handicaps and wide cultural differences play a part; and, in addition, it is naturally very difficult for the husband's family to forget that she is, "first of all, an American and only secondarily their son's wife."[1] Associated in the attitude of the older generation toward her is very likely a slight animus born of the fact that she was not their choice for a daughter-in-law. In recent days a diffidence toward the American wife has developed, owing to the common knowledge that some of them were of questionable character, or "did not come from a good family" in the United States. In the words of one discerning Filipino, "If I took an American wife back to the Philippines . . . . I'd always be obliged to prove that my wife was a nice educated girl and came from a good family in the States. We'd have to frame her college diploma and hang it in the parlor."[2]

The American wife's opportunity for contact with other Americans in the Philippines is also very unsatisfactory. As the wife of a native she finds herself rather completely ostracized by those of her own complexion. Out of contact with others of her own race in the Philippines, a month in time-distance from America, she leads an isolated life in her new home. While occasionally she may be treated as the "queen" of the village, she in most cases very probably lives, until well assimilated, a lonely and rather uneventful life.

Thus, although the taxi-dance hall functions as a means of acquainting the Filipino with American life and gives him contacts with American girls, it also may be a means for

[1] Case No. 57.   [2] Case No. 44.

disorganizing these young men. Filipinos with well-defined goals who bend every effort toward achieving success in their educational or vocational career do not readily become a part of this unstable dance-hall life. But for others the drawing-power of the dance hall, the thrill of dates with American girls, and the material demands made upon them by these girls are sufficient to induce them to abandon their life-ambitions. Contacts with taxi-dancers, likewise, rarely promise entrance into more stable American groups or the establishment of permanent marriages and family life. The taxi-dancers themselves are too thoroughly detached from stable community groups to bring the Filipino completely into American life, and too transient in their affections to accomplish the difficult adjustments of an interracial marriage.

PART IV

THE NATURAL HISTORY AND ECOLOGY OF THE TAXI-DANCE HALL

CHAPTER VIII

THE ORIGINS OF THE TAXI-DANCE HALL

The taxi-dance hall, like every other institution, has had a natural history. Its rise and evolution have been the product of certain natural forces, and in its evolutionary development it has followed a sequence of steps or "stages," each the natural product of the previous one and yet preparing the way for that which was to follow. From this point of view the origins and evolution of the institution come to the foreground and the personalities themselves become of lesser significance. And this is in conformity with the facts. For the rise of the taxi-dance hall is not the result of the perverse machinations of a little group of wilful men; but is rather the natural commercial response to a more or less inarticulate and undiscovered economic demand. Many personalities have played a part in its history, but for the most part they participated without knowing the tendencies of the institution itself and in many cases without even perceiving that a new institution was in the making. Unplanned and uncontrolled, the institution followed a definite line of development probably not entirely in keeping with the wishes of any single person participating in its growth.

Even in its short existence the taxi-dance hall has passed through three distinct stages in development. There was, first, the threshold movement, in an informal and largely unrecognized responsiveness of certain dancing institutions to new economic demands. The second stage is that of institutional consciousness, in which many proprietors became aware that they were bringing into existence a new type of establishment and so set about developing acceptable patterns for it, as well as perfecting and standardizing their methods of management. A third stage represents the period of intense competition and subsequent specialization among different establishments.

It is significant that the taxi-dance hall had its inception approximately during the World War years when we as a nation were engaged in the greatest period of social reform in our history. Perhaps more than a mere coincidence is the fact that the first steps in the evolution toward the taxi-dance hall pattern occurred soon after the nation-wide movement to wipe out the segregated vice areas in our cities, and were contemporary with the local-option campaign against the saloon and the enactment of national prohibition. Whether these reform measures, coupled with the disturbing influences of the World War, actually prepared the way for the taxi-dance hall cannot be proved. Nevertheless, it would seem probable that closing the saloon and the segregated vice district would very naturally favor the rise of new enterprises as substitutes. It is a fact, certainly, that the taxi-dance hall emerged as a new institution during the post-war period, as did also the "night club" and the present-day roadhouse.

The taxi-dance hall had its roots, apparently, in the accommodations and adaptations of three entirely different types of dance institutions of the pre-war period. These were: first, the Barbary Coast dance hall; second, the gradual adoption of the taxi-dance system by certain dancing schools; and third, the degeneration of the public dance hall into the taxi-dance hall.

1. THE BARBARY COAST OR "FORTY-NINE" DANCE HALL

In the Far West, the "Barbary Coast dance hall," or the "forty-nine ['49] dance hall," as it is sometimes called, was the direct ancestor to the taxi-dance hall. In these establishments dancing was incidental to drinking, and the women dancers earned their official income by a commission upon the drinks which they could induce patrons to buy. Of the notorious Barbary Coast in San Francisco, Will Irwin writes as follows:

> The Barbary Coast was a loud bit of hell. No one knows who coined the name. The place was simply three blocks of solid dance halls, there for the delight of the sailors of the world. On a fine busy night every door blared loud dance music from orchestras, steam pianos, and gramophones, and the cumulative effect of the sound which reached the streets was chaos and pandemonium. Almost anything might be happening behind the swinging doors. For a fine and picturesque bundle of names characteristic of the place, a police story of three or four years ago is typical. Hell broke out in the Eye Wink Dance Hall. The trouble was started by a sailor known as Kanaka Pete, who lived at the What Cheer House, over a woman known as Iodoform Kate. Kanaka Pete chased the man he had marked to the Little Silver Dollar, where he halted and punctured him. The by-product of his gun made holes in the front of the Eye Wink, which were proudly kept as souvenirs, and were probably there until it went out in the fire. This was low life, and the lowest of the low.[1]

In its heyday the Barbary Coast of San Francisco was a thriving place, frequented by sailors, gold prospectors, and wayfarers from all parts of the world.

For years the Barbary Coast, known from one end of the country to another, rivaled the most infamous resorts of Europe in abandon

[1] *The City That Was*, pp. 21–22.

and picturesque vice. Dancing was one of the chief attractions in the hundred-odd halls, in which at one time over 2,000 girls were employed.[1]

During the later history of the Barbary Coast all kinds and conditions of men found a place for themselves in its dance halls, and their conduct was strikingly like that of the patrons of the taxi-dance hall of a later day.

In the Barbary Coast halls everybody—fishermen, scavengers, dishwashers, cooks, waiters, seamen—came in working clothes, just "washed up" some. Everybody ate, smoked, chewed gum, while they danced with their hats on. Spanish men in cowboy suits and sombreros, red kerchief and sash, were among the crowd. In one hall vendors frequently appeared. One supervisor recalls fowls being sold in the hall, also a monkey.

The girls were Portuguese, Italians, French, and Americans, the Portuguese and Italians predominating. The orchestras included the manager as one of the players, and usually consisted of an accordion, horn, drum, and piano. There were no seats for the men, as they danced more without them; so they stood about, and the result was long lines that formed human walls. Behind this wall crap-shooting was a pastime. There was no special police officer, as he was always beaten up when an attempt was made to employ one.[2]

At the time of its final abolition in 1913, owing to continued public demand, the "Coast" was patronized largely by local "slummers" and by tourists.[3] This fact was used at this time as an argument for its extermination.

As a result of the closing of the Barbary Coast there sprang up in the sections adjoining an institution in which the liquor-drinking was divorced from dancing and wherein the girls secured their legitimate revenue from dancing.

[1] *Report of Public Dance Hall Committee of San Francisco Center*, p. 7.

[2] Special report of Mrs. M. Alice Barrows, chief supervisor of public dance halls, San Francisco Center to Juvenile Protective Association of Chicago.

[3] *Report of the Dance Hall Investigation Committee of the Commonwealth Club of California.*

ORIGINS OF TAXI-DANCE HALL

In September, 1913, the Police Commissioner prohibited dancing in any café, restaurant, or saloon where liquor was sold. This resolution wiped out dancing on the "Coast" and resulted in the appearance of the so-called "closed" hall in the districts adjoining. There the girls were employed to dance with men patrons on a commission basis and salary. These halls had continuous dancing with practically no rest periods, and made large profits. Patrons paid ten cents for each dance, lasting less than two minutes. About six hundred girls were employed in these "closed" dance halls.[1]

These new establishments, the "closed," or—as they were later called—taxi-dance halls, were somewhat more select in both clientèle and deportment.

In the halls in the district outside of the Barbary Coast, the music was by a regularly organized orchestra of professional players. Girls employed here were Italians, Portuguese, French, and Irish-Americans, and here the French and Irish-Americans predominated. They were expected to be more careful in appearance than in the Barbary Coast halls, and the Mexicans, Filipinos, Chinese, and Japanese men were not so freely admitted, the attendance of very dark-skinned patrons being regulated. Also patrons were expected to be less carelessly dressed than in the Barbary Coast.[2]

These new halls were designed to serve very largely the same groups as were served by the old Barbary Coast halls, and were in reality direct successors to them. Yet the method of organization and control was entirely different. The shortened dance number and the ticket-a-dance system, by which the girl received her pay on the basis of the number of tickets she could collect, were first introduced in these establishments of San Francisco.[3] There was little effort on the part

[1] *Report of Public Dance Hall Committee of San Francisco Center of California Civic League of Women Voters*, p. 14.

[2] Barrows, *op. cit.*

[3] *Report of Public Dance Hall Committee of San Francisco Center of California Civic League of Women Voters*, p. 15.

of the managers of these places to camouflage them as "dancing schools";[1] and in this frank admission of the special character of their establishments as well as in the flagrant abuses existing therein, those opposing them found increasing justification for their hostility. Later, under a slight disguise as dancing schools they were permitted to continue legally until 1921 when the police commissioners ruled definitely against the employment of women as taxi-dancers.[2] The taxi-dance hall, legally at least, became for San Francisco a thing of the past. Today, through efficient dance-hall supervision,[3] there is a constant check upon the tendency for "dancing academies" to merge into taxi-dance halls.

In Seattle the transition from the "forty-nine" or Barbary Coast dance hall to the taxi-dance hall was not entirely completed, and in many cases establishments remain which still pay a commission on both drinks and taxi-dancing.

The older police officers state that very early in Seattle's history, especially during the Alaska Gold Rush, many dance halls were in existence in connection with bars. The girls in attendance there worked on commission, receiving their money from the drinks sold, not as taxi-dancers. About 1910 a number of dance halls were opened that combined the two ideas of commission on dancing and on drinks. They were called at that time in our newspapers as a term of condemnation " '49 Dance Halls." They were never entirely closed, but

[1] "You will assume from what I have said above that the closed dance hall in San Francisco never made any pretense of being a dancing school. That pretense is a later step in the evolution. As a matter of fact the pretense is very slight in San Francisco today, but it is carried out in great detail in New York" (personal letter of Maria Ward Lambin, formerly director of San Francisco Dance Hall Study for the San Francisco Center).

[2] See *Report of Public Dance Hall Committee of San Francisco Center.*

[3] "In these 'academies' we require at least the outward signs of actual teaching; i.e., step drill and practice dancing. This of course acts as a check upon any flagrant departure from the instruction idea" (Barrows, *op. cit.*).

after Prohibition became much modified and exist until this time with girls working on commission on drinks and dancing.[1]

The taxi-dance hall, in its characteristic form, is also to be found in Seattle and other cities along the Pacific Coast.

2. ADOPTION OF TAXI-DANCE HALL METHODS BY DANCING SCHOOLS

In other parts of the country the taxi-dance hall had its local development from two other dance institutions—the dancing school and the public ballroom. In the first instance the organization of the taxi-dance hall was introduced as a by-product incidental to the intense struggle for survival among dancing schools themselves. In the second case, the competitive struggle between the public ballrooms forced those less favorably located and equipped to turn to the taxi-dance hall plan as a means of forestalling business failure.

The record of the process of diffusion from the West Coast throws much light upon the forces favoring and opposing the introduction, in whole cloth, of such an institutional pattern as the taxi-dance hall. The first introduction into Chicago of the ticket-a-dance system, a requisite feature of the taxi-dance hall, was an importation, not from the West Coast, but from New York City. This ticket-a-dance plan was devised—as far as the available information indicates—by a former dance-hall proprietor of San Francisco who in his New York ballroom combined the line-up system, common to dancing schools, with the ticket-a-dance plan of San Francisco with which he was familiar.[2] It is interesting

[1] Mrs. E. W. Harris, superintendent, Woman's Division, Seattle Police Department, in a personal letter to the writer.

[2] From information supplied by Maria Ward Lambin, director of the dance-hall studies of San Francisco and New York.

to note the social resistance to the introduction of a new system. This man did not introduce the taxi-dance hall system *in toto* to New York, but selected only one essential feature and combined with it that with which the city was quite familiar, i.e., the line-up system of the conventional dancing school.

It was this hybrid which was imported by a reputable dancing master of Chicago.

In my dancing school here in Chicago, we had had trouble holding our pupils after they had learned to dance a little. With the simplified dancing steps that were becoming popular, people could take a few lessons and be able to "get by" on the dance floor. I was in New York during the summer of 1919, and while there visited a new studio opened by Mr. W—— W—— of San Francisco, where he had introduced a ten-cent-ticket-a-dance plan. When I got home I kept thinking of that plan as a way to get my advanced students to come back more often and to have experience dancing with different instructors.

So I decided to put in a ten-cent-a-lesson system in the big hall on the third floor of my building. I hired a good orchestra, and placed a very competent middle-aged couple in charge, and thought I would have no more trouble. But I soon noticed that it wasn't my former pupils who were coming up to dance, but a rough hoodlum element from Clark Street. .... Things went from bad to worse; I did the best I could to keep the hoodlums in check. But we were always afraid of fights and disturbances and at last I abandoned the plan.[1]

But a proprietor of another reputable Chicago dancing school had observed the system and incorporated it into his own dancing academy in the Loop. The line-up plan was still maintained. This first attempt in Chicago to combine the line-up system and the ticket-a-lesson plan is described in the Juvenile Protective Association records as follows:

At 9 o'clock announcement was made that everyone who wanted tickets for single dances could purchase the same from the desk where

[1] From an interview with Mr. Godfrey Johnson, Mader-Johnson Studios.

two young men were seated..... The price of these single tickets was ten cents each. All the young men were then put in seats at the left of the hall and the girls marshalled into line, and at a flare of the drum they were marched forward, being thus paired off for the dance.[1]

The new proprietor, although conscious of the new elements in the plan of organization, still conceived of his establishment as a "dancing school."

When I took over the ten-cent-a-lesson idea from Johnson I just thought of it as a new way of running a dancing school which would make it possible for the students to dance with different instructors. I figured that the men would probably pay out more in an evening at ten cents a dance than they would if they had to lay down a dollar or a dollar and a half at one time, as they had had to do before. I always made the girls line up at the beginning of each dance and made the men take the girl at the head of the line just as Johnson had managed it.

Before long I began noticing that many men who came were good dancers. When I first realized that these fellows were coming back all the time just to get somebody to dance with, I laughed out loud. Up to that time I wouldn't have believed that there were fellows who would be willing to pay as much as they did—just to get a chance to dance..... Sometimes I noticed that certain fellows always wanted to dance with certain girls, but I wouldn't allow that, except as they took an instructor at the hour rate..... I only ran the hall a year, but all the time I thought of it as a dancing school—not a place to rent a dance partner.[2]

Even though the proprietors recognized a changing clientèle after the introduction of the ten-cents-a-lesson ticket system, there was still a resistance to be broken down. Themselves dancing masters with status in the profession, and with years of experience behind them, they either did not perceive fully the economic possibilities of the new clientèle or were unwilling to undertake the new venture.

[1] See Juvenile Protective Association records.
[2] Interview with a former proprietor of the Colonial Dancing Academy.

It remained for an "outsider," a "stranger,"[1] with little professional status in the city, to perceive the full economic opportunities of the new system and to undertake to put it into operation. A Greek immigrant, himself a detached person in the city, and unhampered by some of the customs and by the restricted perspective of the established dancing-school proprietors, was the first to undertake the venture. The earliest record of this enterprise, in the files of the Juvenile Protective Association, under date of May 10, 1921, is as follows:

> Officer visited this dance hall and school of instruction at 10:00 P.M. Five young men, Greeks and Italians, were hanging around the door, and the hall itself is about as large as the interior of a street car, located on the third floor of the Haymarket Burlesque Building on West Madison Street. This place is run by a Greek. Patrons pay ten cents a dance, a ticket being issued, and the girl gets five cents on each ticket. A player-piano furnished the music, and seven girls were present, so-called instructors.[2]

In this humble fashion the taxi-dance hall in Chicago got its start.[3]

The significant alteration of the system of management made by this proprietor, Mr. Nicholas Philocrates,[4] was the elimination of the old "line-up" routine, by which the patron was forced to accept the dance partner directly opposite him in a double line, and the introduction of a plan by

[1] See discussion of the economic and sociological significance of the "stranger," in Werner Sombart, *Quintessence of Capitalism*, pp. 292–307.

[2] Adapted from Juvenile Protective Association records.

[3] See account of small taxi-dance hall, operated as a "private club" for Greeks only and antedating the Athenian Dancing School by several months. The Apolon Dancing Club went out of existence on February 22, 1922 (Juvenile Protective Association case records).

[4] This and all succeeding names of taxi-dance hall proprietors have been disguised.

ORIGINS OF TAXI-DANCE HALL

which patrons were permitted to select their dance partners. Thus, another decisive step was taken in the direction of the taxi-dance hall. Mr. Philocrates' own story is as follows:

When I returned to Chicago in 1920 after a trip to the West Coast I decided to open a school of my own. I first visited different schools and found that Mr. Swanson at the Colonial Dancing Academy was the only one conducting one on the lesson-ticket plan.

But I found that Mr. Swanson didn't allow the pupils to choose their own instructors. He used the old "line-up" system, which meant that the pupil's success in getting a suitable partner was just a matter of luck. Sometimes he drew a good dancer suitable to his height and his taste who could dance the kind of dances he wanted; but most of the time he didn't have such good luck. He spent most of his money on girls he didn't want to dance with at all.....

Then there was another trouble with the "line-up" plan. It always takes time to line them up and get them paired off. The people weren't dancing more than half the time but the expenses were going on just the same. It would be better, I said, to get a plan that wouldn't waste so much time.

I knew of the ticket-a-lesson plan as it was used on the Pacific Coast—I visited some of the halls out there—and so I knew that the idea of having the pupils select their own instructors would work all right, when people got used to it. So I started in a small way and it was a success.[1]

The guiding principle of management followed by Mr. Philocrates—that the patron should be allowed to select his own dance partner—came directly from his observations of the taxi-dance halls on the Pacific Coast. Yet in Chicago the taxi-dance halls have been more definitely associated in the proprietors' and patrons' minds with the dancing-school concept than was true in San Francisco. This difference was due in part, at least, to the fact that the early proprietors aspired to operate bona fide dance schools and firmly be-

[1] From an interview with the proprietor.

lieved that the ticket-a-dance plan could be incorporated into a legitimate dancing-school organization.

However, the intensely competitive struggle for existence with other more firmly intrenched dancing schools made necessary an almost blind accommodation of the institution to a new clientèle which, though inarticulate, was nevertheless making itself felt at the box office. The foot-loose Greek-Americans who were the first proprietors of Chicago taxi-dance halls, while handicapped in other branches of the public dance-hall business, combined within themselves the primary requisites for success with the taxi-dance hall. First, they were already in daily contact with a host of potential patrons of such an establishment: rooming-house dwellers, who, like themselves, were somewhat out of place in the ordinary public ballroom. In the second place, because of their own free movement about the country, several of these Greek-Americans had become acquainted with the taxi-dance hall of other cities and could easily conceive of its application to Chicago. Finally, all of them were new in the dance-hall business and had achieved no professional status. They had everything to gain and little to lose in a venture with a dubious form of public dance hall. These enterprisers had few personal, professional, or cultural ties binding them to Chicago and to the traditional American standards of propriety. Thus they could see certain human relationships with greater clarity and objectivity and could push more vigorously any type of enterprise in which there was an opportunity for profit.

Even though some of these first Greek-American proprietors were sincerely interested in developing a legitimate dancing school by the lesson-ticket plan, the system itself, making possible frequent changing of couples, inevitably at-

MAP III

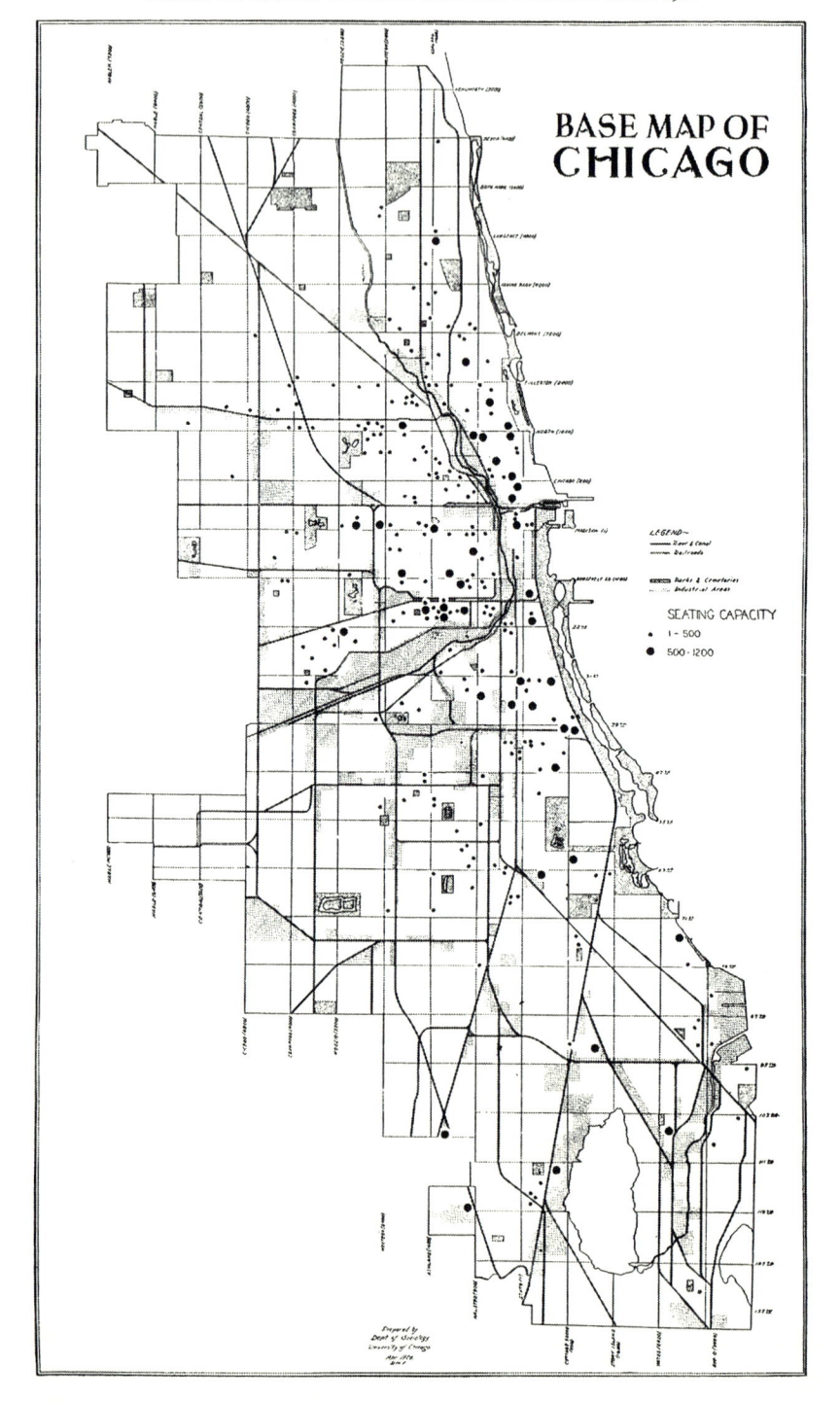

SHOWING THE LOCATION OF CHICAGO DANCE HALLS LICENSED DURING 1910

tracted those seeking dance partners rather than those desiring bona fide dancing instruction. In this way the new enterprise, designed originally as a "dancing school," by gradual and almost imperceptible degrees adjusted itself to the patronage offering immediate support. Features such as practice-rooms for private lessons, and graded classes, both of which had been thought of in the original plans, were dispensed with as unprofitable, and the business persisted in its attenuated form, still calling itself a "dancing academy."

3. TRANSFORMATION OF THE PUBLIC BALLROOM INTO THE TAXI-DANCE HALL

Public ballrooms at a disadvantage in competing with other dance halls may also be a beginning for the development of the taxi-dance hall. When a public dance hall finds itself unfavorably located for competition with other more favorably located and better-equipped dance halls, it may be forced either to reorganize as a taxi-dance hall or to go out of business.

Especially during the last decade when there has been such a change in the character and location of the better public dance halls the struggle for survival of the older halls has become acute. In Chicago there has been a striking trend toward the large and ornately equipped public ballroom patronized by both men and women and located at "bright-light" centers several miles in each direction from the Loop. This significant change can be seen clearly in Maps III and IV, which locate the licensed dance halls in Chicago for 1910 and 1927, respectively. It will be noticed that between 1910 and 1927 the number of small dance halls has been greatly reduced but that new and much larger ballrooms have sprung up at new "bright-light" centers at considerable distance from the center of the city. It is with these new "million-dollar" or "wonder" ballrooms that the small, poorly located halls are now forced to compete.

With the rapid expansion of the city at the center and the pushing outward still farther of the adjoining areas of deterioration these older halls, more centrally located, are forced frequently to adapt themselves to an entirely new clientèle if they are to survive. These changes take the form either of lowered standards of supervision and conduct in the establishment or of a change in the institutional organization to attract a different patronage.

The first of these alternatives is seen in the history of the Vista Dance Hall, located on East Forty-seventh Street, in an area of transition just east of the "Black Belt." The efforts of the management to meet new competition by a lowering of standards, but without the introduction of a different structure such as the taxi-dance hall, is shown graphically in a Juvenile Protective Association case record.[1] The earliest report indicates a small public dance hall with a fair patronage, with little formal supervision, but in which the dancing was conservative.

May 15, 1920.—At 8:30 there were about 300 persons present but the crowd increased with the maximum number of 500 at 11 o'clock. Most of the girls were about eighteen or over. . . . . The dancing was modern, fox-trot, one-step, and only mild shimmying on the part of a few couples. As compared with many other dance halls the dancing was rather conservative. Music while jazzy was not violently syncopated. No supervision exercised on floor by management.

During the following six months patronage decreased noticeably, though a great increase in sensual dancing was re-

[1] The succeeding excerpts are taken directly from one Juvenile Protective Association case record.

MAP IV

SHOWING THE LOCATION OF CHICAGO DANCE HALLS LICENSED DURING 1927

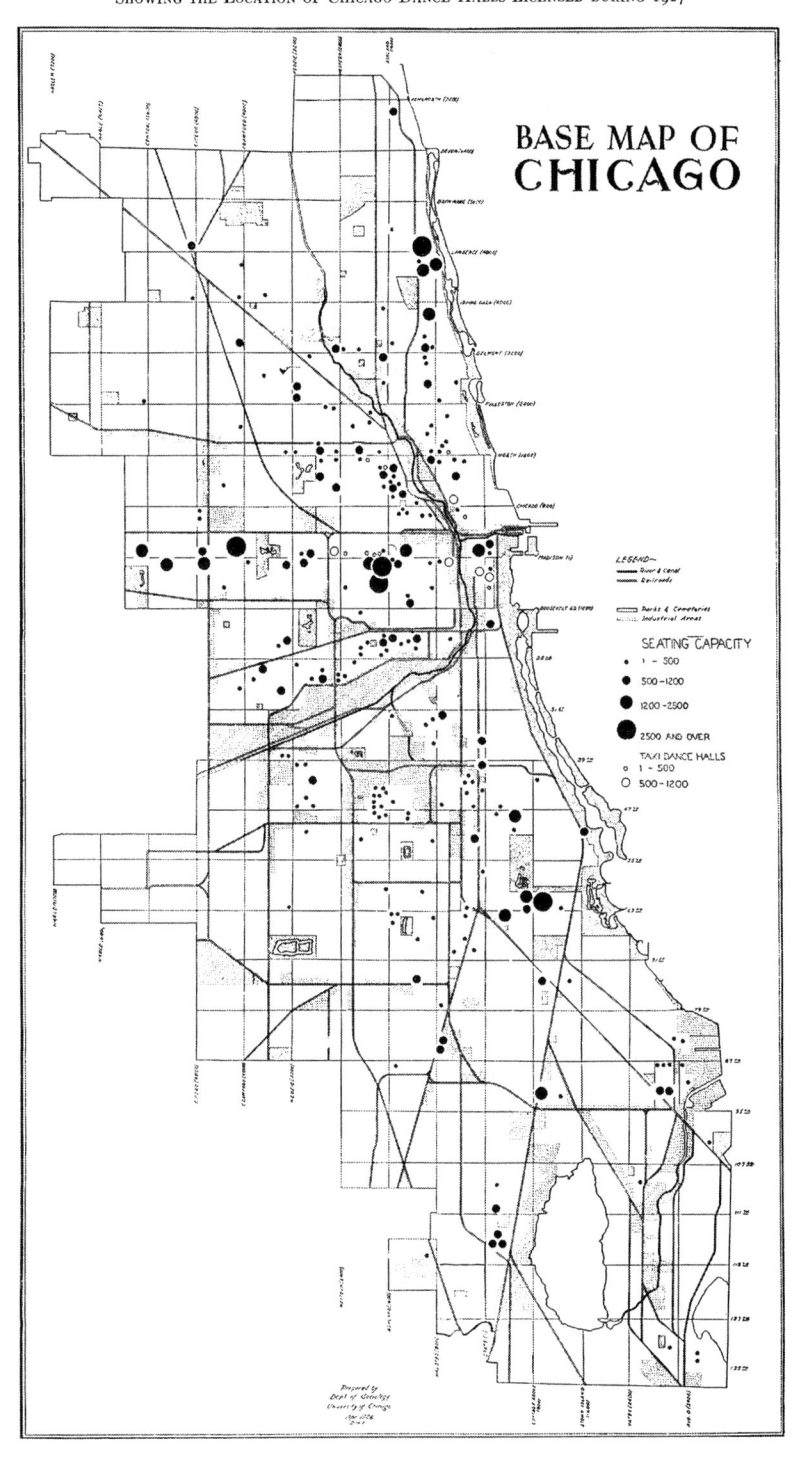

corded. The first reaction of the management to this condition was an attempt at formal supervision.

January 15, 1921.—The proprietors seemed to be making an honest effort to put on clean dancing and were partly successful. They had two men walking up and down the middle of the floor during the whole evening and any immoral conduct immediately attracted their notice. Most of the people who came seemed to belong to the better class and there didn't seem to be any desire to make trouble.

Conditions, however, did not improve. A different clientèle became noticeable. Still more improper dancing and sensuous music were reported. Supervision was abandoned. A bid to secure sufficient feminine patronage is apparent in the offer of free admission to ladies on certain nights of the week.

April 10, 1921.—Hall very dimly lighted and no attempt at supervision. Much indecent dancing noticed. During intermission girls sat on men's laps. Orchestra fairly good. Several waltzes and two-steps were played but the dancing to this music was as indecent as when fox-trots and one-steps were played. Manager announced that in future Tuesday and Thursday nights would be free for ladies.

In the succeeding three months conditions at the hall became even worse. Only a small crowd of young people now attended. These resented all efforts at supervision. The management, now realizing its dependence upon this small group of patrons, permitted almost any kind of conduct.

July 14, 1921.—At 10:30 P.M. 50 people were dancing to Victrola music. The girls nearly all wore extremely short dresses and had their stockings rolled down. The dancing was as indecent as worker has witnessed any place and no effort was made apparently to control the dancing. Told manager that we had several bad reports about the hall. He said he was willing to clean up if the other South Side halls would do the same. He said that whenever they have tried to make people stop shimmying they have told him that they could go to the Crystal and dance any way they wanted, and they threatened to take a crowd of friends away from this hall.

This pictures the plight of the small dance hall in a declining area, with inferior equipment and in competition with a "dance palace" in a nearby bright-light center. Already losing money, it, by seeking to be respectable, could only lose more money.

> *January 8, 1922.*—Visited at 10:00 P.M. A small crowd present. Music good and dancing only fair. Miss K. stated that they were losing money every night that they operated—that the Midway Gardens [about thirteen blocks away, a new and ornate "dance palace"] had ruined their business.

The dancing was now admitted by the manager to be improper, but business, according to his statement, was so bad one had to be a "little easy on them." The management changed hands and finally, after continued failure as a ballroom, the building was converted into a pool and billiard parlor.

The cycle of degeneration of a dance hall with a good reputation is here seen. Under adverse competition the management makes various adaptations in an effort to preserve the establishment. In the end, however, the dance hall capitulates to these unseen ecological forces, and goes the way of all other enterprises not suitably located to serve their clientèle.

A change in organization to attract a different clientèle is another means by which a dance hall may preserve itself in spite of an increasingly unfavorable location. The taxi-dance hall is one form of reorganization which has proved effective in Chicago in protecting an enterprise against unfavorable ecological changes. This type of adjustment to meet new conditions is shown in the history of the Victoria Hall in an unfavorable location on the West Side at the intersection of Western Avenue and Madison Street. For many years it was the headquarters of Mr. J. Louis Guyon, who gave private dancing lessons and conducted public dances in the hall. His record as an exponent of "clean dancing," even in spite of the character of the immediate neighborhood, has been noteworthy. The Juvenile Protective Association report for December, 1912, reveals the propriety insisted upon in this public dance hall.

This is a good, well-regulated hall. Professor Guyon, dancing master, was on the floor all evening. Many of the crowd seemed to be his pupils and danced very well. *Men did not ask women they had not met to dance.*[1]

In spite of the rapidly declining neighborhood, Mr. Guyon maintained a dance hall of high standards all the time he was in this location. His own story is as follows:

I first went into the dance-hall business in 1909 at Victoria Hall. The first week I kicked out about a hundred and fifty toughs each night, until I let them know what kind of place I intended to run. I lost money for a while, but soon began getting a good crowd. I began giving dancing lessons as well. I stayed there until 1914 when my crowds got too big for Victoria Hall; and I went over and leased the Dreamland Ballroom. I again had to clean up conditions. In 1916 I built the Paradise Ballroom and have been there ever since.[2]

When Mr. Guyon left Victoria Hall and subsequently moved into his beautiful and spacious Paradise Ballroom he took with him much of the patronage which had been his for years. Victoria Hall, less favorably located, now had to compete for patronage with the newer, more beautiful, and more spacious appointments of Mr. Guyon's new establishment—and others of the "wonder dance palaces."

The old Victoria Hall, after being vacated by Mr. Guyon,

[1] Juvenile Protective Association records. Italics are the writer's.

[2] From an interview with Mr. J. Louis Guyon. Quoted with his permission.

passed into the hands of several different proprietors, none of whom was able to attract a permanent patronage. For a time it was rented for special dances, but eventually it was leased with the expectation that it would be reopened as a public dance hall. The proprietor's story reveals the inability of a new proprietor without prestige to build up a public dance-hall patronage—especially when he had to compete with the former proprietor in a much more attractive dance establishment. His deliberate efforts to overcome the handicaps of insufficient patronage from young women shows graphically the manner in which the organization of a taxi-dance hall may be developed.

I used to run Victoria Hall before the Greeks got it. I rented the hall for three nights a week and figures I could get a crowd to come to the hall. That was after Guyon moved out to his big place. I got a lot of the boys to come up to my hall because the prices was lower. But all the dames wanted to go to the new places.

So I decides to cut the admission for the girls so they'd come to my place. But the only ones that come was dames that looked like they was so poor they didn't have a nickel. So I says to myself, I got to get some good-looking dames for these here fellows or they won't come no more. Then I took to payin' the dames something on the side to come to my place. But that didn't work so well because the girls wouldn't dance with a lot of the fellows that was coming to my hall. Sometimes the girls would want to dance with one another instead of the boys.

So finally I starts a dime-a-dance hall like the Greeks had on North Clark Street and paid the girls a nickel a dance. I thought it was going to work but I never got a big-enough crowd to pay the rent and the girls and the orchestra. So I finally had to quit and sell out to the Greeks. That's how they got started there.[1]

The dance establishment by the very exigencies of the situation was forced either to revise its system of organization or to go out of existence.

[1] From an interview with a former proprietor.

ORIGINS OF TAXI-DANCE HALL

The first period in the natural history of the taxi-dance hall is thus seen to include the responsiveness of three different types of dancing establishments to the potential clientèle of the taxi-dance hall. In the West the "forty-nine dance hall" or "Barbary Coast dance hall" responded to changing public sentiment, and developed into a taxi-dance hall. In other parts of the country the bona fide dancing school, in response to decreased box-office returns, gradually became a taxi-dance hall, taking with it some of the dancing school's claims to respectability. A third institutional adaptation was the change from a conventional public dance hall to a taxi-dance hall, made necessary by new competition and by the changing character of the community.

In these three ways[1] arose a new institution with its own distinctive structure to meet the demands of a group of transient, non-family, and socially isolated men for whom no adequate provisions for public dancing had been made. As in the case of other new institutions, the taxi-dance hall has been forced to adjust to the possible reactions of public opinion and to adapt itself to the various groups within its own clientèle.

[1] It is interesting to observe that these three lines of development conform rather closely to some of the outstanding conceptions and points of view of present-day sociology and anthropology. The spread of the " '49 dance hall" throughout the country may be seen as diffusion; the second development as institutional accommodation and adaption, and the third as an ecological process.

CHAPTER IX

THE TAXI-DANCE HALL MEETS THE PUBLIC

Shortly after the establishment of the first taxi-dance halls in Chicago[1] the more discerning proprietors recognized that a big problem confronting the institution was its relationship to the larger public outside which—though only imperfectly conceived—was nevertheless acknowledged to be all important. Thus arose the second stage in the natural history of the taxi-dance hall, the period of institutional consciousness. During this time considerable effort was expended in trying to give to the taxi-dance hall at least a specious respectability by emphasizing the claim that it was in reality, as well as in name, a dancing school.

Even in such minor points as the printing upon the dance tickets there was an early effort on the part of the more cautious proprietors to maintain consistency with their dancing-school claims.

I had feared from the start that if some other men opened dancing schools run on the lesson-ticket plan like my own that some of them would not be very strict and so they'd give us all a bad reputation. I saw that once the thing would get started with no one to stop it, the river would carry us all along. I was responsible for having one of the new proprietors change his plans. He had his tickets printed, "One

[1] It should be noted that the data upon which this chapter is based have to do with Chicago taxi-dance halls exclusively. While the problem of meeting the public necessarily would have had to have been faced by proprietors in other cities, there is no certainty that developments in Chicago were typical in detail of other cities.

Dance Ticket, 10 Cents." I told him that they should read, "One Dance Lesson, 10 Cents."[1]

In one way or another the effort of leading proprietors to give a satisfying representation of themselves and their institution to the public, to officials, and to all law-enforcement agencies was a dominant interest during this period.

An immediate problem confronting early pioneers in the business of the taxi-dance hall in Chicago was securing and retaining a dependable patronage. While detached men of Greek, Polish, and Italian nativity were admitted without question, the acceptance of Filipinos in considerable numbers became a matter of special concern. Their subsequent welcome to the first permanent taxi-dance hall in Chicago was partly because one of the proprietors was acquainted with certain Filipinos, and with the interests and preferences of these young men.

I became acquainted with Filipinos first when I still lived in Detroit. We had two Filipinos room with us for a time and I knew they were nice fellows. Most of them are college students, you know. I told my partner we ought to let them come to our dancing school, but he didn't want to have them. I fought for them and told my partner they were nice, quiet fellows and wanted to dance and would spend a lot of money. But before we opened the B—— I went to see some aldermen about letting in the Filipinos, and they even went to —————[2] to make sure that everything would be all right.[3]

The special solicitation of Filipino patronage, early in the history of Chicago's taxi-dance halls, may be considered a matter of chance peculiar to Chicago, yet it is inevitable that in the competitive struggle for a foothold some of the new establishments would seek Filipino patronage.

[1] Comment of a proprietor of a taxi-dance hall to an investigator.

[2] Naming the chief of a political faction which was then in control of the city government.

[3] Interview with a former proprietor.

THE TAXI-DANCE HALL

To retain a dependable patronage, however, it was recognized that the taxi-dance hall must meet, as completely as possible, the preferences of the patrons themselves. A major consideration was to secure the type of girl most attractive to those whose patronage was desired.

The big difficulty in this dancing-school business is to get just the right kind of girls for the men. Get the kind of girls the boys want and you get the boys. That's my idea! You've got to get the kind of girls the men will pay out cold cash to dance with, or you don't have a crowd. . . . . The girl that makes a success here has to be pretty, and young, and well built. She's got to be able to dance all the different ways and to follow anybody. She's got to know how to show a fellow a good time while he's dancing with her. But the girls have to have a good reputation. Once a girl gets a bad reputation in this business you've got to get rid of her quick. She'll give your place a bad name in no time.[1]

During this period in Chicago it was generally believed that, even though privately she might not be so impeccable, the most valuable young woman to the taxi-dance hall was the one who commanded the respect of the patrons, i.e., "had a good reputation."

Likewise it became a common belief that while very young girls were desirable as a lure for trade, their employment involved so many hazards that it was not considered a good business practice.

There are too many risky things about having girls below sixteen. You're likely to "get it in the neck" if they find you've got phoney working papers [certificates]. But even if you can get by with fake papers it don't pay. Most of these young kids never had much experience and once they get a little they go wild. They can soon get the hall in trouble.[2]

[1] Comments of an early organizer of taxi-dance halls in New York and Chicago to an investigator.

[2] From the conversation of a dance-hall attendant with an investigator.

Even though sufficiently old to "get by" the laws, the most desirable girl was considered one who looked petite and youthful, yet who could be trusted to be discreet at all times.

The management, it was thought, must be ever watchful lest any incidental activity of patrons or taxi-dancers, associated with the hall, bring the individual establishment into public disrepute or within the toils of the law. Unless the enterprise was financially very profitable such activities were to be drastically rooted out. Any invidious court record of people associated with an establishment either gave additional evidence for those demanding that the hall be closed, or at least was thought to make it possible for politicians and police to exact higher fees for "protection."

It don't pay to let nothing "get by." If you let your place get a reputation as a "shimmy" joint, you think you're making a lot of money but you don't—because before long the grafters will come and take it away from you, and you're back where you were before. . . . . If a girl in your hall gets a record in the Juvenile Court she gets away easy, but it will cost you a lot before you can open again. If you let the grafters get anything on you, they "hook" you for some more cash.[1]

Exorbitant charges for "protection," more than the fear of being closed, it was thought, made flagrant violations of conventional dancing standards unprofitable. Thus, under the influence of a system of petty grafting the observable conduct of taxi-dancers in and near the halls was for a time kept well within the bounds of conventional public dance-hall standards.

One of the first public policies of dance-hall proprietors to receive formulation was regarding the supervision of conduct in the hall. Closely allied to this was the employing and

[1] Comment of a former dance-hall proprietor reported by an investigator.

supervising of the taxi-dancers themselves. On this very critical matter of supervision early proprietors in Chicago indicated a desire to maintain every evidence of respectability.

In contrast to the first complaints received concerning this hall the record of the Juvenile Protective Association for May 12, 1921, indicated a desire on the part of the proprietors to conform to prevailing standards of dancing. The proprietor asked the officer to secure for him a copy of the dance-hall regulations such as are used in Sioux City, Iowa. He said he would supervise at all times. Other policies were in the process of developing. He said that he would make it a rule that any girl who made a date with a patron or gave the patron her name or address would be discharged, and that the girls would not be allowed to leave the hall under any circumstance until closing time.[1]

Subsequently the policy of the taxi-dance hall concerning the supervision and employment of taxi-dancers became even more rigorous.

Men will not be allowed to congregate at the foot of the stairs at closing time. Nor will girls be allowed to meet men—even though they are known to be husbands or brothers—on the street at the foot of the stairs. Instead they are forced to meet them at some prearranged meeting place—such as a nearby street corner or restaurant. The proprietors say it is necessary because otherwise their hall gets a bad reputation. The girls are threatened with discharge if caught disobeying the rule.

The proprietor states that he interviews each applicant personally and does not employ her until he is satisfied that she is not under age, is not lying concerning herself or her means of livelihood, and is not a runaway. In many cases he requires a baptismal certificate or working certificate when he is in doubt. He keeps a complete record of his girls, including name, age, address, and length of time in employment.[2]

This vigorous supervision began early in the history of the taxi-dance halls and was persisted in by all pioneers in the

[1] Adapted from Juvenile Protective Association records.
[2] *Ibid.*

business. The supervision extended itself to such matters as the portion of the hall where unchartered taxi-dancers were to station themselves, the conduct of the taxi-dancers toward prospective clients, and the supervision of the dancing of both patron and taxi-dancer.

> The dancing at the B―― was very strictly supervised. There was a husky Greek with a special deputy's badge who was busy on the floor all the time. He always had a weather eye out for any questionable dancing and was continually "bouncing out" boys who looked as though they were going to start a fight. The man in the ticket booth not only sold tickets but watched the goings-on on the floor. He could spot a ticket cheater faster than anybody I ever saw. The girls who were not dancing were forced to stand in one corner of the room only. They could not sit for very long at a time but if they wanted to rest had to go into the restroom. The girls were not allowed to carry on conversations with young men except when dancing with them, and sometimes the girls were fired for very slight infractions of the rules.[1]

It is quite probable that, in addition to the economic advantages of conducting a well-supervised establishment,[2] the rather arbitrary restrictions upon the taxi-dancer's freedom in dating and conversing with patrons had other advantages to the proprietors. They, of course, served to give the establishment an additional claim to "respectability," and to protect it somewhat from blame for incidental de-

[1] From an interview with Daniel Russell, Department of Sociology, Texas Agricultural and Mechanical College, formerly a special investigator for the Juvenile Protective Association of Chicago.

[2] Frequently proprietors have insisted that in the long run the well-supervised place is more profitable. One ballroom proprietor recently sought to explain this assertion in the following way: "It's like this. If one man gets drunk in your place, he's happy. But nobody else is, and he spoils the evening for the others and so you lose patronage. If you let one drink you've got to let them all get drunk and then your place gets a bad name. Then sooner or later somebody comes along and closes it up and you've lost your business and everything."

linquencies for which the business might otherwise be held accountable. Even more, these restrictions were sometimes considered an economic boon to the proprietors as well. One man, closely associated with the development of the taxi-dance hall in Chicago, has this to say of an early competitor:

> When you go to see him he will tell you of his very strict rules concerning his girls. And he's right! They are strict. If he ever finds that one of his girls is going out with the men he fires her immediately, even though he believes there's nothing wrong. He says that his is a dancing school and not a matrimonial bureau. But there's more to it than that. He figures that every fellow who comes to his hall has just about so much money to spend, and if he spends his money on the girl outside the dancing school she's taking just that much business away from his school.[1]

Toward the politicians and the police, with whom the dance-hall proprietors early came in contact, a more or less definite policy seems to have been developed. Politicians were apparently regarded as "friends" to whom to go when in doubt as to what policy to pursue or when in need of influence. Some looked upon the politician as the person whose help was necessary to get "pull at the [police] station." Others apparently went to him seeking even more direct aid for their dance-hall business. But both by action and by precept it was agreed that a very important aspect of the dance-hall business was acquiring political influence.

> When you go into this business be sure you got plenty of pull. The laws are pretty hard on this business and a man's got to have real good friends if he makes the breaks. That's the reason I made a success of this place. The first thing I did when I came here was to get solid with the politicians. Then when I saw that I was fixed up all right I went out to rent a hall.[2]

[1] Interview of an investigator with a proprietor.

[2] Interview of an investigator with an early organizer of taxi-dance halls in New York and Chicago.

TAXI-DANCE HALL AND THE PUBLIC

The police, as a whole, do not appear always to have been regarded as "friends" in the same sense as the politicians or to have enjoyed the same confidence which the proprietors placed in their political friends. But it was recognized that the police were persons in authority with whom proprietors had to have dealings, and friendly overtures were often made to them.

We didn't pay any regular amount to the police. However, John, my partner, made a practice of giving $25 to the captain and $5.00 to each patrolman as a Christmas present. If he had to put in any special calls to the police he would pay each cop who came $5.00. Then on Christmas we often gave each policeman a box of cigars, and we always had a box of cigars hidden away to treat any cop or detective who came around. John kept a little book in which he had the birthdays of the cops and their children, and he made it a point to remember and give them birthday presents.[1]

The amounts of money reported to have been paid policemen at certain times justify the term "shakedown"—a word frequently used by proprietors to describe these financial contributions.

A social worker reported that one of the men employed in the _____ Dancing School told her that they paid $200 to $300 a month to the _____ Police Station, and were not afraid of the Juvenile Protective Association. The police officer with whom she talked also told Miss X that they had protection from the _____ Police Station, and that he was told to come in frequently to see that things were all right. The sergeant and captain also come in frequently.[2]

Whether because of a feeling of inability to gain "justice" by any other means, or because of a desire for special favors, the proprietors seem to have accepted periodic "shakedowns" as a necessary and inevitable way of doing business.

[1] Interview with a former dance-hall proprietor.
[2] Adapted from Juvenile Protective Association records.

The social reformers and private law-enforcement agencies have usually been much more of an uncertainty to proprietors than the politicians and many police officials. There was at first a disposition to treat private protective social agencies in the same manner as the police.

One evening I called at the ———— Dancing School and talked to Mr. O. D., junior partner. I had little fault to find with his supervision or upon the equipment, and spent most of my time complimenting him. I only remained for a few moments. As I was leaving he called me back and pressed a ten-dollar bill into my hand. I was so surprised I jerked my hand away and allowed the bill to fall to the floor. Then I tried to explain that I could not accept the money. He seemed completely mystified concerning my unwillingness to accept it, and followed me to the stairway, still holding out the money. I really believe he was sincere in not being able to understand why I could not accept it.[1]

But the proprietors did not continue this approach for long. Finding themselves unable apparently to comprehend the attitudes and ideals of the protective social agencies, especially the Juvenile Protective Association with which they were in chief contact, the proprietors for a time resisted all reform efforts. The Juvenile Protective Association, because of its success in establishing satisfactory ballroom supervision in the "dance palaces" of the city through fostering the National Ballroom Managers' Association,[2] sought to establish similar conditions in the taxi-dance halls. The proprietors' first reaction was one of resentment and hostility.

The next time I see Miss M. of the Juvenile Association was after I opened my new hall. She come up one day and said she had some complaints about my hall and that I should get some "nice women" to help me run it. I told her that I'm not making much money yet and

[1] Interview with Mrs. Elizabeth R. Crandall, formerly supervisor of dance halls, Juvenile Protective Association of Chicago.

[2] See later discussion of this program on pp. 274–76.

maybe later I can do it. I asks how much it would cost and she says "five dollars a night," and I said I cannot afford that. . . . .
But I tell her that I'll think about it, and maybe later when business is better I can do something. I didn't see nothing of her for two or three weeks. But I talks to some of the girls and some of the men that come to my hall and I ask them if they want a womans to come to run the school. The men say, "No!" They don't want a womans. Then the girls say "No!" They don't want a womans neither. So for why should I have a womans?

Then one night Miss M. comes up, and walks in like she owned the place, and tells me I got to get a womans right away. But I tell her I can't afford it. Then she walks over and sits down by two of the girls and asks them why they don't get a "good job" and "work days" —and things like that. She got them all scared and three girls quit the next day. . . . . But it was the way she [Miss M.] acted that made me mad. So, finally, I goes up to her and says, "Miss M., if I never see you again it will be too short a time." Then she talked like she'd have me closed up if I didn't hire a womans. But I knew she wouldn't, because I was solid with the captain [district police captain].[1]

Though these personal animosities served to precipitate active conflict, there was nevertheless under the surface the feeling that there existed a fundamental conflict of interest which could not be resolved.

During this period, however, there was one effort by a proprietor to modify his policy in such a way as to incorporate the program sponsored by the Juvenile Protective Association. A woman of mature years, selected by the Association but paid by the proprietors, was placed in a taxi-dance hall on Saturday and Sunday nights. This experiment is recorded in the Juvenile Protective Association files as follows:

[1] Extract from a conversation of a dance-hall proprietor with an investigator. The social worker discussed in this report was only temporarily employed by the Juvenile Protective Association and is no longer engaged in this type of work.

Visited Park Dancing Academy, arriving at eight o'clock. Worker went into the checkroom as the girls were taking off their wraps. . . . . Told them that we had been asked to make an investigation on account of the two girls who had been arrested . . . . , and that we were anxious to help. Asked them what they thought of having a fine woman there for their protection. All the girls said they thought this would be a very good thing to do, and that the two girls had asked Filipinos to take them out and that the boys were not as much to blame as the girls. Talked to the proprietor, and told him that unless he did everything possible to safeguard the girls and improve conditions that he was liable to be closed up. . . . . He said that he would be glad to have a hostess, not only to protect himself but the girls. He said that he is a married man with a family and is anxious to run a decent place.[1]

As a result of this understanding with the proprietor, a Mrs. C., a Juvenile Court Officer, was assigned to this hall for Saturday and Sunday nights, her salary to be paid by the management. Shortly after, for extraneous reasons, Mrs. C. was transferred elsewhere and a Miss D. was sent to succeed her. Miss D. was soon found to be unsatisfactory to the proprietor and a third woman was sent.

Mr. D. [proprietor] said that he would be glad if Mrs. C. would come back or if he could have someone else furnished him as hostess, as he does not like Miss D. In her zeal she has waxed indignant over the mixing of the races and has advised a number of girls to stop working there. We told him it could be arranged and later telephoned Mrs. E., who consented to go to work on the following Saturday night.[2]

But even Mrs. E. was not wholly satisfactory. She remained for several months, but had increasing difficulty in managing the girls, and finally resigned. The proprietors of this hall, now quite disgusted with their difficulties with women supervisors, swung back to their former plan. However, for the last five years a woman, professionally trained as a dancing teacher, has been successful in this establishment in meeting

[1] Adapted from Juvenile Protective Association records.   [2] *Ibid.*

TAXI-DANCE HALL AND THE PUBLIC

the exigencies of supervision satisfactorily to all the conflicting interests.

During this second stage in the history of the taxi-dance hall there was no attempt to justify the taxi-dance hall to the larger "public" outside the dance-hall world. Toward this unknown and uncertain "public" a characteristic attitude developed which subsequently became a part of the code of the taxi-dance hall.[1] The "public" was to be feared, and a direct conflict with it should be avoided at any cost. When in a situation of probable conflict, discretion was admitted by these practically minded proprietors to be the better part of valor. Discretion required that they should keep at least all external evidences of their activities well within the bounds of conventional propriety; and that in time of stress and strain they should seek aid and comfort, i.e., "protection," from their friendly enemies the police.

Yet the "public" was never objectively conceived. To some of the early proprietors, at least, the "public" remained a host of rather meddlesome oppressors, who were eternally "on the job."

No, it don't pay to try to get the girls by want-ads..... The big trouble is they don't bring the girls—they bring investigators instead, and God knows we got enough of them already. If it ain't some "feisty" woman it's a half-baked "nut" from some preacher college.

[1] The terms "code" and "policy" are here used to denote two distinct types of adjustments of an institution or organization which is to some extent in conflict with forces in its immediate environment. While the code serves to define the situation and to state the principles of conduct chiefly for those who are "on the inside" and whose fortunes are bound up in the institution, the policy is a public representation of the activities and purposes of the institution in a manner least antagonizing to outsiders and to the public. Thus, in this instance, the code of the taxi-dance hall may be said to be the body of unwritten principles and standards by which the institution is preserved; while the policy is the formulated statement or statements of its principles and standards as revised for public consumption.

I never had so much trouble myself because I never advertised for girls, but I heard tell of a fellow that put in a want-ad and got six investigators and one girl.[1]

Lacking a more objective point of view toward society, their difficulties with the "public" were explained by personalizing the conflict in terms of certain familiar newspaper "stereotypes."[2] These early dance-hall proprietors, most of them recent immigrants, came to think of the "public" in terms of "prohibitionists," "priests," "preachers," "puritans," "women reformers"—these being almost the only ones of the larger American public with whom they were brought into vital contact.

Since "religious fanaticism" and "hypocrisy" were thought to be securely in the saddle, the only possible adjustment for the proprietor was to protect himself in the best way possible from the present-day reformer. Especially it appeared to be necessary to protect his establishment against the unfavorable reports of casual visitors and investigators by insisting that all conspicuous conduct in his establishment be made to conform to the accepted canons of respectability. At the same time, he was torn constantly between the double dilemma of trying to satisfy the public which demanded conformity at any cost and the patrons who paid the bills and frequently expected something other than dull respectability.[3] As a result he led a "Dr. Jekyll and Mr. Hyde" existence, all the while fearful of what an inquiring stranger

[1] From the conversation of a former dance-hall proprietor with an investigator.

[2] See Walter Lippmann's discussion of this concept in his *Public Opinion*, Part III.

[3] It is interesting to note in this connection that Gregory Mason in an article entitled "Satan at the Dance Hall," *American Mercury*, II (June, 1924), 175–82, says that this same problem is found even in the dance palace. He quotes a Chicago proprietor of a dance palace who instructed his employees to "keep this place clean—but not too clean."

might discover, yet anxious that his patrons should have a good time.

The proprietor remained constantly apprehensive lest that larger public outside his dance-hall world become interested in his enterprise. An experience of the writer during the summer of 1925 reflects this attitude.

Mr. Philocrates was loath to tell more concerning his business. He again asked why I wanted the information, and I again tried to explain that I was making a study of this business in the same way as I might the confectionery business or the drug-store business, and that I was doing it as part of my study at the University. He wanted to know what I was to do with the information. I told him that it would be written up and placed in the University Library. "Then you're going to write a book?" he asked. Hoping to lessen his apprehension, I explained that I did not think it would be important enough for that, but that it probably would be more like a magazine article. "Oh, that's worse!" was his quick reply. "Nobody will read a book, but everybody reads a magazine."[1]

For the time being, at least, the proprietor sought to resolve his problem by attempts to restrain publicity and by efforts to maintain publicly the "dancing-school" fictions. Through this ruse it was possible for the cloak of conventionality to be spread over activities much more dubious and varied than had been tolerated in the past in bona fide dancing schools. Thus the intermingling of the proud young Oriental and the Polish girl from "back of the Yards," the middle-aged Slavic immigrant and the runaway girl from a Minnesota farm, the old man and the giddy flapper, are at least given a specious explanation in the public eye. In this way the institution could be protected against frequent invasions and questions from the public and could be enabled to develop its functions, structure, code, and policy with a minimum of interference from outside.

[1] From records of the writer.

CHAPTER X
COMPETITION, CONFLICT, AND SPECIALIZATION AMONG TAXI-DANCE HALLS

From a period when proprietors of taxi-dance halls seem to have been chiefly concerned with the reactions of patrons, politicians, police, other law-enforcing agencies, and the general public, the proprietors have now swung to a third stage in the institution's natural history in which intense competition, specialization, and other accommodations are the chief interest. This period of ruthless competition seems to have been brought about by the increasing movement of patrons and taxi-dancers from dance hall to dance hall and by the general recognition on the part of proprietors that all the taxi-dance halls could not survive. It was seen, apparently, that under the policies and practices then in vogue there would not be sufficient patronage for all and that in the end competition would make inevitable a bitter struggle for survival between establishments. Even the fact that all but two or three of these proprietors were of the same nationality—Greek-American—does not seem to have been sufficient to have restrained them. More recently, as an accommodation to the struggle there can be seen a strong tendency toward specialization in function and patronage among the taxi-dance halls. This whole development can best be seen by a review of the events themselves.

Before 1923 there were but two taxi-dance halls in Chicago sufficiently well established to be money-making concerns. These were the Athenian Dancing Academy,[1] the first suc-

[1] See chap. viii, pp. 186-87.

COMPETITION, CONFLICT, SPECIALIZATION 211

cessful taxi-dance hall in Chicago, subsequently located at 1321 North Clark Street, and the American Dancing School, situated near the corner of Robey Street and North Avenue. The Athenian was first established in a small room of the Haymarket Burlesque Theater Building, located on the hobo's "main stem"[1] along West Madison Street. The first proprietor, Mr. Nicholas Philocrates, remained there only a short time, and is reported to have sold his hall to Messrs. Philip and James Menestratos.[2] Philocrates continued his Athenian Dancing Academy at the new address on North Clark Street, the "Rialto of the Underworld,"[3] while the Menestratos interests, as soon as their lease expired, moved to new quarters in the great Polish settlement on the Northwest Side and established there the American Dancing School.

At about the same time a number of other taxi-dance halls opened—to survive only a few months. This was a time of high mortality for newly established halls. The reputable Colonial Dancing Academy,[4] in the Masonic Temple Building in the Loop, which had figured so prominently in 1921 as a transitional institution from the dancing school to the taxi-dance hall, was sold to a man who subsequently conducted it as a taxi-dance hall, combining the ten-cents-a-lesson ticket system and the frequent reselection by patrons of dance partners. But this dance hall survived only a short time. A number of other halls also had a sporadic growth and quick death. The first short-lived taxi-dance hall of which there is

[1] See Nels Anderson, *The Hobo*, chap. i, pp. 4-5; chap. iii, p. 27.

[2] For much of the factual data in this chapter the writer is dependent upon the records of the Juvenile Protective Association of Chicago.

[3] See Harvey W. Zorbaugh, *The Gold Coast and the Slum*, pp. 105-26.

[4] See pp. 184-85.

record was a "private dancing club" for Greeks only, called the Apolon Dancing Club,[1] located near Hull-House in the Near West Side Greek colony. It was in reality a taxi-dance hall, there to provide dancing for the homeless Greek immigrants of the vicinity. The Apolon antedated the Athenian Dancing Academy of Mr. Philocrates by several months, having been opened in the early spring of 1921. However, it maintained only a very uncertain existence[2] until its final demise in February, 1922. Only two months after the opening of the Apolon, the New England Dancing Studio[3] was opened on Halsted Street midway between Hull-House and the Athenian Dancing Academy just then getting a start in the Madison Street "hobohemia."[4] The New England Studio was also conducted by a Greek-American. It survived only a few months and was closed, to be reopened again the following year under new management—rechristened the La Gloria Dancing School. The La Gloria lasted through one winter only.

The spring of 1923 witnessed the first conscious competition among Chicago's dance-hall proprietors. Prior to this time the struggle for existence had been against other elements of the local environment. Each of these early taxi-

[1] See Juvenile Protective Association records.

[2] "I was acting as a case-worker and investigator for the Juvenile Protective Association at the time the Apolon Dancing Club was in existence. It occupied very crude, unattractive quarters on the second floor of an old building. There were seldom over three or four girls in attendance at any time. They were a coarse lot; some of them seemed physically dirty as well. They were drifters themselves, I learned. They were paid three cents a dance and had to dance with all-comers" (interview with Leslie Lewis, formerly director of the Committee of Fifteen of Chicago).

[3] See Juvenile Protective Association records, Case No. 44195.10.

[4] Anderson, *op cit.*, chaps. i and iv.

COMPETITION, CONFLICT, SPECIALIZATION 213

dance halls had secured its patronage exclusively from the neighborhood in which it happened to be located. But by the spring of 1923, the area from which patronage might be expected was sufficiently recognized to invite the establishment of several halls within a competing zone—and the resulting competition was soon felt by the proprietors.

The first tendency in this direction appears to have been the establishment of the Majestic Dancing School in the "bright-light" area of the Polish Northwest Side, only a few city blocks from the earlier American Dancing School. But the Majestic did not fare so well, and the "school," in true American fashion, closed its doors for a summer vacation. In the fall of 1923, however, the hall again opened, rechristened the New Majestic Dancing School. At this time, also, Mr. Nicholas Philocrates, who had founded the Athenian Dancing Academy, sold his interest in it and shortly after established the Royal Dancing School on the northwestern margin of the Lower North Community. But these were not the only changes. To the south of the Athenian a few blocks, and in the very heart of Chicago's North Side underworld, two other halls, the Palace d'Arts Dancing Academy and the Apollo Dancing School, came into existence. In the Loop the Up in the Clouds Club—actually a taxi-dance hall—found a place for itself on the twenty-first floor of the City Hall Square Building.

The two succeeding years showed persistent expansion in the business. Only one hall failed, and at least three new establishments appeared. In the Loop the La Marseilles Dancing Academy made its bow to the public on the third floor of an old building on Randolph Street. Two halls were established along Madison Street in the section just west of "hobohemia." At this time the unsuccessful attempt was made to reopen the old Victoria Hall, located on the corner of Madison Street and Western Avenue, first as a conventional dance hall, later as a taxi-dance hall.[1] Also, Philip Menestratos, who had been conducting the American Dancing School in the Polish Northwest Side, moved southward and acquired Victoria Hall. Here he opened his second taxi-dance hall, the New American Dancing School. His old hall, the American Dancing School, was continued, though very soon the New American Dancing School became a much more lucrative enterprise.

With the establishment of several competing taxi-dance halls along Madison Street in the Near West Side during the fall and winter of 1925-26, the period of bitter competition between establishments and proprietors may be said to have begun. Mr. James Pittakos, the proprietor of the Ashland Dancing School located at the corner of Ashland Avenue and Madison Street, joined with two compatriots, William Agoratos and George Androdamos, to found the Madison Dancing School, on the second floor of a new two-story building six blocks farther west on Madison Street. The Madison opened in the early fall of 1925 and soon had a promising patronage. The Menestratos interests, not to be outdone, made an effort to throttle the new venture by establishing a competing hall just east of it. In this way the New American Dancing School No. 2 came into existence near the intersection of Madison and Robey streets and directly opposite Lewis Institute. Competition went merrily on with the Madison Dancing School located midway between the Menestratos' two New American dancing schools.

It was a period of intense competition which in the summer of 1926 culminated in the establishment by Mr. Ago-

[1] See pp. 192-94.

COMPETITION, CONFLICT, SPECIALIZATION 215

ratos, one of the proprietors of the Madison, of another taxi-dance hall, the Sacramento Dancing Academy, at the corner of Sacramento Boulevard and Madison Street, just a few blocks farther west than the Menestratos' more westerly New American. Thus at one time there were five taxi-dance halls ranged along this section of Madison Street. The Ashland and the Sacramento failed shortly after because of lack of patronage, and the Madison was closed in August, 1926, by order of the chief of police because of incriminating evidence supplied the Juvenile Court by a former taxi-dancer.[1] The Pittakos-Agoratos-Androdamos combination was broken, and the Menestratos interests reigned supreme on Madison Street in the fall and winter of 1926-27.

While the intense competition along West Madison Street was the outstanding development of 1925 and 1926, it must not be supposed that there were not other changes going on in this most changeable business. In the Loop, the La Marseilles Dancing School found it increasingly difficult to meet its financial obligations. However, during the fall of 1925 it was closed by the police because of "immoral conditions." Shortly after, the Chicago Dancing Academy, under the proprietorship of the Isagoras Brothers, was opened on the sixth floor of the Childs Restaurant Building at the south margin of the Loop.

Under the strain of competition with these new halls, some bona fide "dancing schools" of longer duration felt compelled to instal the "ten-cent-lesson-ticket-system" and to offer the patrons a choice of dance partners. An American-born dancing master who had conducted dancing studios for years in Chicago introduced the plan into his Loop establish-

[1] See Juvenile Court and Juvenile Protective Association records. A partial account of this case is found in the document on pp. 237-38.

ment. At the Empire Dancing School on the sixth floor of an old building in the West Side "hobohemia," another dance-hall proprietor who for several years had been conducting "dance classes" used the ten-cents-a-lesson ticket system and the "line-up" routine formerly employed at the Colonial.[1] But with the competition of the "choose-your-partner" establishments he too swung over to the whole plan as used in the taxi-dance hall.

There were also during these years, 1926 and 1927, a host of "mushroom" dance halls that sprang up over night—only to disappear as suddenly shortly after. Though there is no reason to believe it complete, the list is definitely known to include at least fourteen such transient establishments. These failures were due to such factors as poor location or equipment; the lack of a personal following; insufficient capital to maintain the business until a patronage could be established; local opposition to the establishment; an inability to pass the requirements for a city-license permit; or the lack of sufficient means or influence to be enabled to operate without a license.

With the increase in the number of competing establishments, it was not possible to maintain the standards set during the earlier period and even the ties of nationality and religion do not seem to have been sufficient to ameliorate conditions. It was—literally—a case where Greek met Greek,[2] and where native shrewdness and strategy was its own reward. Competition was virtually unrestrained and some instances of "corrupt practices" resulted. Proprietors were frequently accused of deliberately cultivating gossip

[1] See pp. 184-85.

[2] Except for possibly one or two halls, all the establishments had been developed by Greek-Americans.

COMPETITION, CONFLICT, SPECIALIZATION 217

damaging to a competitor's hall. Some tried, by fair means or foul, to bring their competitors into difficulty with the law and thus to force them out of business.

Occasionally an individual proprietor was accused of using both fair and unfair methods to induce popular taxi-dancers to transfer from a competitor's hall and to bring their "following" among the patrons with them to the other establishment. Likewise, it was reported that certain proprietors offered special inducements to encourage their own taxi-dancers to attract their most popular girl friends from competing establishments. During this period special efforts were made by each proprietor to outdo his competitors in supplying his patrons with unusual variations and excitement. "Double dances" for the price of one, lottery devices, and special features on the different evenings of the week were all introduced. These innovations were immediately copied by competitors and in turn became standardized.

Certain other results of this intensive competition could be seen in the patronage and conduct in the halls. Most significant was the surprising mobility among establishments, of both patrons and taxi-dancers. Girls found in one establishment one week could frequently be discovered in two other halls the next week. Men changed about almost as frequently as the taxi-dancers. Among the patrons, the Filipinos proved the most mobile. At this time Filipinos and other Orientals were admitted to almost any of the taxi-dance halls and special efforts were made by proprietors to attract their patronage and to hold their good will.

The proprietors very willingly advertise in the local Filipino magazine, and often contribute the largest amounts to any "relief fund" being raised at the Filipino Clubhouse. If a dance is given at the

Clubhouse some of the proprietors are almost certain to be on hand to pay their respects, and to support any interest of the Filipino group.[1]

Before long the gangs of Italian and Polish boys became incensed over the presence of Filipinos and other Orientals and their interest in certain of the girls. Frequently gang fights resulted, both inside and outside of the halls, in which knives, iron knuckles, and even guns played a part. In several instances there were near fatalities.

Three men were stabbed and seriously wounded last night in a riot which started in a pay-as-you-go dance hall on North Clark Street, when a Filipino group from the West and South Side tried to monopolize the dancing girls. When the police arrived in force a pitched battle was still in progress in the hall and on the steps. The combatants were quelled and nine of the Filipinos, said to have been the aggressors, were arrested.[2]

These serious outbreaks were frequently the climax of a series of more trivial altercations, in which the Filipinos were seldom the aggressors. A Filipino's story of these petty disturbances which led to the dance-hall battle, recorded above, was as follows:

The Pinoys [Filipinos] have been molested for many months by these gangs of white fellows. They get after the Pinoys because they can get dates with some of the girls and the gangsters can't. So they began attacking Filipinos when there were only one or two together. They would jump on a couple of Pinoys and tear their clothes and take their money. Just last week two boys were caught and beaten up so that the doctor had to take stitches. . . . . The big fight on North Clark Street came as a reprisal. Just the night before a quiet little Filipino was asked by his roommate's girl to take her home because she didn't want to go with the Italian boys who were after her. He chartered a cab and was to meet her on a certain corner. Just as the cab stopped, this gang pulled him from the cab and beat him up and

[1] Records of the writer (1925–26).
[2] News item, *Chicago Tribune*, January 3, 1926.

he was left unconscious on the sidewalk. They took his money and watch, also. The big fight was to get even for that and to show them that we'd fight them if we had to. . . . . We were prepared for anything. The boys carried iron knuckles, knives—and guns were hidden away in the cars downstairs.[1]

Sometimes, however, the gangs of boys persecuting the Filipinos were actuated more by a motive of deviltry than because of animosity toward them.

Us guys was standing outside one of those dance halls on Madison Street waiting for the "niggers" [Filipinos] to come out. When our gang goes to one of those halls we just about run it. These "niggers" came out and they said real polite like, "We don't want to fight. We want to be your friends." They would have gotten away with it, but somebody yelled, "Don't let them get away so easy!" So we all chased after them. One "nigger" was wearing a big new topcoat, and a big fellow from our gang chased after him, and would have caught him. The Filipino took off his coat as he was running, and threw it right into the big fellow's face. Of course the "nigger" got away but the big fellow didn't care because he had a good topcoat.[2]

These tendencies toward criminal assault, intimidation, and stealing could only result in "bad business" for the proprietors of the dance hall. Gang fights drove away rather than aided business; yet as long as Slavic and Italian youths and hot-headed Filipinos were allowed to mingle together on the same dance floor, frequent disturbances were inevitable. In a similar way, the practice of sensual dancing, while it attracted some patrons, antagonized many others. For these reasons it was apparent that a segregation of the different types of patrons, morally and racially, into different halls where they would have a minimum of harassing con-

[1] Interview with a Filipino leader in the dance-hall fight to which previous reference has been made.

[2] Interview with a seventeen-year-old Polish boy, reported by Mr. W. R. Ireland, Northwestern University Settlement House.

tacts with one another, would serve best the desires of each group, and also would redound to the financial interests of the proprietors.

This trend toward a segregation of conflicting types of patrons into different establishments is clearly the present tendency. In the struggle for a maximum profit the different establishments are yielding to that group which promises immediately the most satisfactory patronage. Some halls are seeking to meet the needs of the Filipino and his friends, while other establishments serve those who are antagonized by the presence of the Oriental. Some managements permit only conventional dancing while others specialize almost exclusively in patrons who seek sensual dancing. Thus, several recent establishments in Chicago have become notorious for the conduct they have permitted. Likewise, there are now taxi-dance halls which will permit only conservative forms of dancing and where only Caucasians with at least a certain minimum of decorum and manners are admitted. In this way, through the exigencies arising in a competitive struggle for survival and profits, several types of taxi-dance halls have been evolved.

Along with this tendency toward specialization there has occurred also a movement toward combination and consolidation among establishments. On West Madison Street at one time the Pittakos-Agoratos-Androdamos combination controlled three halls while the Menestratos interests operated two resorts. Since 1929, however, these proprietors and their combinations have disappeared. New organizations and new proprietors have now come to the front. Yet even in the short time in which they have been in business the same tendency toward expansion and the operation of chains of taxi-dance halls can clearly be seen. In one

COMPETITION, CONFLICT, SPECIALIZATION

instance, at least, this expansion has extended to the operation of dance halls in other cities.[1]

It is also significant that there has been a change in the nationality of the proprietors. Instead of being Greek-Americans, these recent proprietors are of either Irish or Italian extraction. These new men are reported to have alliances or "understandings" with powerful underworld figures[2] or with corrupt political interests in Chicago. Instead of being headed by Greek immigrants, whose political influence was relatively slight, we find upon investigation that today the taxi-dance halls which pander openly to sensuality are in the hands of those known to have influential political affiliations. Because of the large profits which it is now seen can be gained through operating taxi-dance halls promoting sensual dancing, these more powerful interests have recently been attracted into the field. Their greater political influence also enables them to cope more successfully with police surveillance, court cases, and with dance-hall licensing.[3]

In other cities the natural history of the taxi-dance hall, as far as the data at hand reveal, appears to have been rather similar to that in Chicago. In every instance there has been the initial uncertainty, the discovery of techniques of control, the development of an informal code, and, when possible, the trend toward expansion and specialization among establishments. The developments in some cities

[1] A taxi-dance hall in St. Louis, for instance, has been operated by those interested in taxi-dance halls in Chicago.

[2] "The Club Floridan [described as 'one of the vilest hell holes in the city'] is reported to be owned and operated by the Capone syndicate" (*Chicago Tribune*, April 19, 1932).

[3] An account of the methods recently used in Chicago to circumvent public efforts at control is given on pp. 270-71.

may have progressed much farther along this cycle of evolution than in others, but they seem to be in conformity with this sequence.

On the other hand, even a superficial survey of taxi-dance halls in other cities reveals differences. In some cities the taxi-dance hall seems to have been imported from other places when at a relatively late stage of development, while in others it has evolved with little or no contact with other cities. In some places the taxi-dance hall has been less identified with the dance school in its development than was true in Chicago. In them it was associated more clearly with the deteriorating public ballroom or with the old "forty-nine" or "Barbary Coast" dance hall. Likewise, there have been taxi-dance halls which made little or no effort to camouflage the nature of their functions; and in certain cities specialization has progressed farther than in Chicago.

In New York City, for instance, there is much more specialization among the halls, some being exclusively for Orientals and others concentrating upon sensual dancing for white men only. Still others are ornate establishments with elaborate dining and lounging facilities where only conventional ballroom conduct is tolerated and where none but the more decorous white man is welcomed. New York's taxi-dance halls seem also to have advanced farther along the cycle toward expansion and consolidation than is true in most cities. In July, 1931, there were reported to be nearly one hundred taxi-dance halls operating nightly in Manhattan and Brooklyn alone and it is estimated that from 35,000 to 50,000 boys and men frequent these halls each week.[1] These were reported to be operated as one or more

[1] See *Annual Report for 1930 of the Committee of Fourteen of New York*, p. 20.

COMPETITION, CONFLICT, SPECIALIZATION 223

"chains" of taxi-dance halls and protected by influential political figures. In one instance it was intimated that a New York City magistrate who had been especially lenient in cases involving the taxi-dance hall had been found to be associated definitely with a taxi-dance hall syndicate.[1] These "chains" of taxi-dance halls are judged to have become so influential that the New York Committee of Fourteen considers them partially responsible for a recent increase of vice in that city.[2] Recent developments in New York City suggest clearly the probable future of the taxi-dance hall in other municipalities—if the institution is allowed to expand uncontrolled and unsupervised.

[1] See account of the Seabury investigation in *New York Times*, July 20, 1931, and *Annual Report for 1930 of Committee of Fourteen*, pp. 26–28.

[2] See *Annual Report for 1930 of the Committee of Fourteen of New York*, pp. 28–29, and pp. 40–41; also, Virginia Murray, "Relation of Prostitution to Economic Conditions," a paper read before the Regional Conference of the American Social Hygiene Association, New York City, January 22, 1932.

CHAPTER XI

THE LOCATION OF THE TAXI-DANCE HALL

The taxi-dance hall, like other institutions of the city, has its characteristic location. It finds its root in the central business district and the rooming-house area, near the residence of a majority of its regular patrons. Just as the "wonder ballrooms" or dance palaces in Chicago prosper only in the "brightlight centers" at considerable distance from the central business district, so the taxi-dance hall seems to flourish exclusively in the zone of furnished rooms and in the central business district. Map V, which shows the location of the unsuccessful and successful taxi-dance halls of Chicago, reveals that with but one possible exception all financially successful taxi-dance halls have been located in the Loop district itself, or well within the rooming-house area.

It is also suggested by this map that a location too near the periphery of the zone of furnished rooms is an uncertain venture. Thus the Royal Dancing Academy on West North Avenue, at the edge of the rooming-house district, in spite of excellent management, was unsuccessful and was finally abandoned. The three or four efforts to establish a successful taxi-dance hall in a West Side location at the intersection of Sacramento Avenue and Madison Street have all proved futile. It is, apparently, too near the edge of the rooming-house district and hence fails through lack of patronage. Likewise, the best efforts of the proprietors to establish the Moonlight Dancing School near the intersection of Chicago

MAP V

SMALL CAPS: Showing the Location of Chicago Taxi-Dance Halls in Relation to Rooming-House Areas, 1927–30

LOCATION OF THE TAXI-DANCE HALL

and Western avenues came to naught, apparently for the same reason. On the other hand, a location in the Jewish West Side, on Roosevelt Road near Hamilton Street, was apparently too far south to reach the rooming-house population. The taxi-dance hall that was started there soon failed. Even the Lane Dancing School, which for a time carried on an uncertain existence in the Lower North Community, on Division Street near Lane Technical High School, does not seem to have been sufficiently within the rooming-house area to be successful.

The only exception to the generalization that the rooming-house area and the Loop are the characteristic locations for successful taxi-dance halls is the New Majestic Dancing School, located in the East Humboldt Park Community at the intersection of Milwaukee Avenue, Ashland Avenue, and Division Street. This is the most important trading center for the large Polish community on the Northwest Side and is entirely different in general complexion from a rooming-house area. Although this is a family area, nevertheless many unmarried men live as boarders in the homes of others of their nationality. With this patronage nearby the New Majestic maintained itself for a period of five years.[1]

A second factor in the success of the taxi-dance hall is the adequacy of cheap late-night transportation facilities into all the sections of the city from which patrons come. Even though a majority of the patrons may come from nearby rooming-house areas, a significant number reside beyond

[1] A survey in the winter of 1925 of the attendants at the New Majestic revealed that on the evenings when investigators visited the hall, fully nine-tenths of the patrons were either recent immigrants who had not yet gained an ordinary command of English or boisterous youths from that section of the city. The New Majestic is no longer in operation.

these regions. The extent to which this is true is suggested by Map VI. This spot map shows the residence of a sample group of a hundred patrons. It will be noted that while a majority come from within the rooming-house sections of the city, there are still many whose homes are in family areas beyond the habitat of the homeless man. These patrons are usually either the immigrants, the "slummers," or the physically handicapped. Thus the taxi-dance hall, to avail itself of this patronage, must be easily accessible to those who come from other sections of the city.

In Chicago, inexpensive and frequent transportation during the late night hours is provided by the surface lines which radiate from many subcenters outside the Loop. Thus the location of a hall near several different street-car lines is an important factor in success. The Plaza Dancing Academy on North Clark Street, near Division Street, for instance, is located near the intersection where the Clark Street cars, the Division Street trolleys, and the State Street and Broadway cars meet. The New Majestic Dancing School, in the East Humboldt Park Community, was located at the intersection of important street-car lines running in six different directions. Likewise, the New American Dancing School No. 1, at the intersection of Madison Street and Western Avenue, and the New American Dancing School No. 2, near the intersection of Madison and Robey streets, both commanded[1] direct access to the residential areas served by important street-car routes.

The generalization may safely be made that the taxi-dance hall thrives best when its location affords ready access to cheap and frequent late-night transportation service to the residential sections from which patrons come.

[1] These were lucrative dance halls until closed in 1930.

MAP VI

SHOWING THE RESIDENCES OF TAXI-DANCE PATRONS EXCLUSIVE OF FILIPINOS IN RELATION TO ROOMING-HOUSE, NATIONALITY, AND RACIAL AREAS

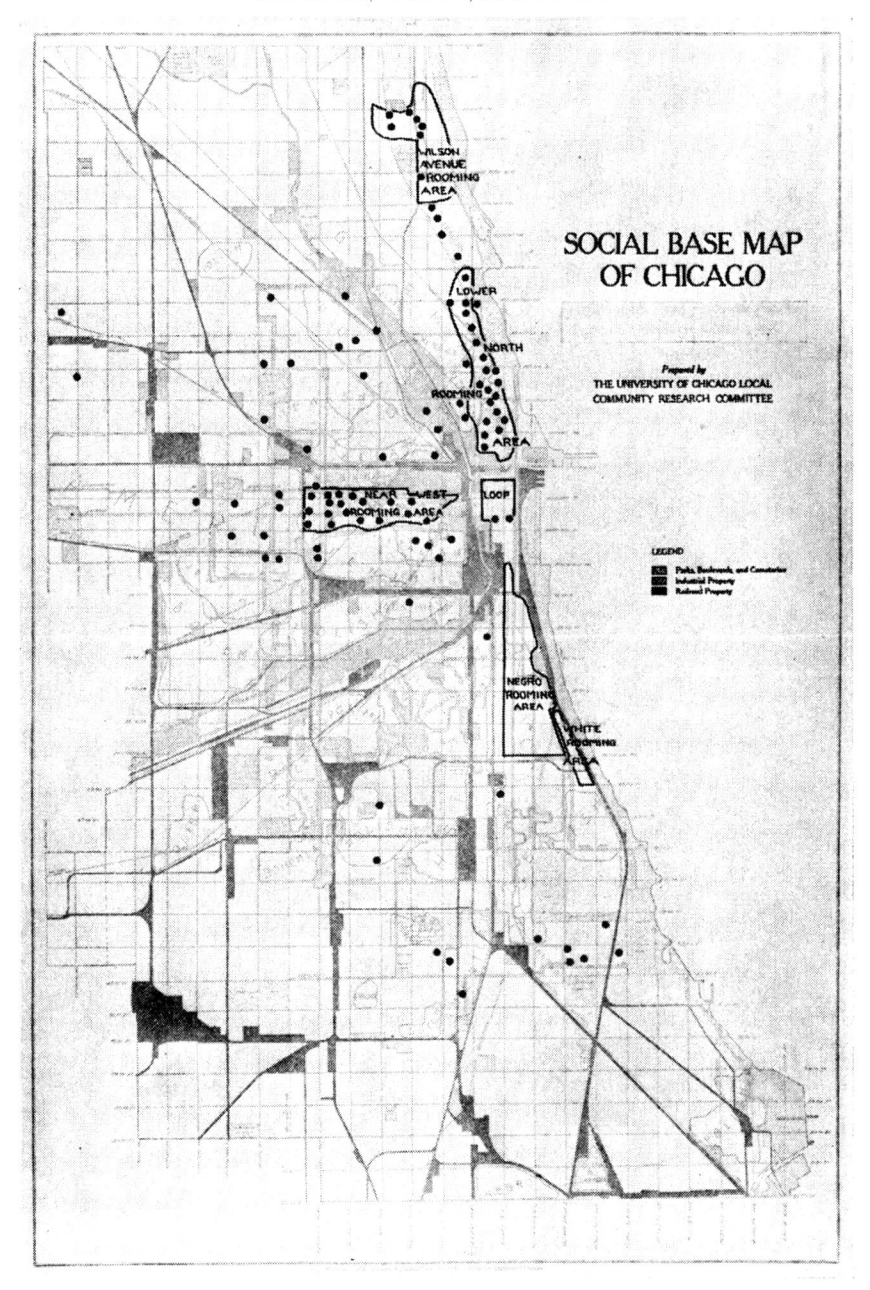

LOCATION OF THE TAXI-DANCE HALL

A third fundamental principle is that the taxi-dance hall must be located in an area of high mobility in which rental values are nevertheless relatively low. The taxi-dance hall cannot afford to pay extremely high rentals. Yet it must be easily accessible to as large a number of potential patrons as possible. As a result it seeks out a second-floor location in a second-rate business district near the Loop, or lodges on an upper floor of a skyscraper. In either case the dance hall, so located, is made accessible to a great number of possible patrons, yet at a fairly low rent. This rental varies within a narrow range, below or above which profits tend to diminish.

A study of the rents paid by the different establishments would be of value. But because of an inability in the past to secure the co-operation of proprietors rents cannot readily be determined. But from estimated land valuations[1] upon property in which taxi-dance halls are located, some suggestive information can be secured. By restricting this inquiry to the dance-halls outside the Loop where a second-floor location is almost universal, it is possible to gain some insight as to the maximum and minimum front-foot valuations at which it has been profitable for taxi-dance halls in the rooming-house areas to locate.

The data at hand, while insufficient for careful generalization, suggests that there is not as wide a range in the optimum land valuations as would naturally be supposed. In the years from 1921 to 1928 no halls had been successfully established in the rooming-house sections[2] of the city in

[1] The George C. Olcott annual *Land Values Maps of Chicago* have been used throughout as the basis for these estimated land valuations.

[2] There was one other hall which was begun on property worth more than $500 a front foot—the New Majestic Dancing School, at 1214 North Ashland Avenue, which has already been cited as an exception in another regard

property which at the time had an estimated valuation below $400 a front foot or above $500 a front foot. Indeed, in only one instance did a hall seem to have even temporary success when started on property having a higher valuation. This one establishment, located on North Clark Street, just north of the river, was begun on property having a front-foot valuation of $950 and continued intermittently under different managements until 1925, but was never truly a financial success. Even more surprising is the fact that in no instance did a taxi-dance hall located on property worth less than $400 a front foot give any impression that it might survive.

The uniformity in the estimated land values of buildings in which successful taxi-dance halls were established is shown in Tables II, III, and IV. The land values for the years in which a taxi-dance hall existed on the premises is underscored once, and the initial year for each establishment is underscored twice.

The list of unsuccessful taxi-dance halls is a record of ill-advised efforts. In some cases the establishments were located on sites with land values entirely too high for the new establishment. In other instances the halls were established in places where certain conditions—as reflected in low land values—were not conducive to the success of the institution.

An examination of the tables also suggests certain other possible interpretations. It is an interesting fact that where the dance hall was especially successful there was an accompanying rapid rise in land values. Conversely, those es-

---

(see p. 225). It will be noted, however, that while it was outside the Loop and in a typical second-floor location, it was an anomaly in being successful, in a small way, even though it was not within the rooming-house area.

LOCATION OF THE TAXI-DANCE HALL 229

tablishments which were failures or doubtful successes did not experience, in most instances, a similar pyramiding of land values. Thus, the Athenian entered its quarters on North Clark Street when land values were estimated at only $400 a front foot. In three years' time these valuations

TABLE II

SUCCESSFUL TAXI-DANCE HALLS BEGUN WITH ESTIMATED LAND VALUES OF $400–$500 A FRONT FOOT

	1921	1922	1923	1924	1925	1926	1927	1928
Athenian or Plaza N. Clark St.	$350	$400	$750	$800	$900	$ 900*	$1,100*	$1,200*
Ashland W. Madison St.	350	350	500	500	500	1,250	1,250	1,250
Royal W. North Ave.	300	300	400	400	500	500	500	650
New American No. 1 Madison St.	300	500	500	500	500	1,000	1,000	1,100
Madison Madison St.	300	300	350	450	450	550	550	550
New American No. 2 W. Madison St.	300	300	400	450	500	600	600	600

* Changed to more attractive quarters near by and continued under the new title Plaza Dancing Academy.

had more than doubled. After another three years, during which it moved across the street to a more important location and changed its name to the Plaza Dancing Academy, the estimated value of the property it occupied was reported to be $1,600 a front foot, four times its property value of seven years before. Likewise, the land values of the New American Dancing School No. 1, at the intersection of

Western Avenue and Madison Street, doubled during the three or four years during which that establishment occupied the building. On the other hand, the Royal Dancing School, on North Avenue near Sedgwick Street, which was at best only an indifferent success, experienced little increase in land values. In contradiction to this, however, it should also

TABLE III

UNSUCCESSFUL TAXI-DANCE HALLS OUTSIDE THE LOOP FOUNDED
WHERE ESTIMATED LAND VALUES WERE
ABOVE $500 A FRONT FOOT

	1921	1922	1923	1924	1925	1926	1927	1928
Grand N. Clark St......	$800	$900	$ 950*	$1,200*	$1,200*	$1,200	$1,300	$1,500
Belvedere N. Clark St......	600	600	1,000	1,000	1,100	1,200	1,200	1,200
Paulina-Madison W. Madison St...	350	350	500	500	800	1,250	1,250	1,250
Lakeview Belmont Ave....	200	300	400	400	600	800	1,000	600
New American No. 3 W. 63d St.......	300	325	1,750	1,500	1,500	1,750	1,250	1,000

* Operated only irregularly over a three-year period and by several proprietors.

be noted that other establishments failed even when there was a general increase in land values. Thus the Grand, the Belvedere, and the Lake View dancing school failed even though there seems to have been a general increase in property values in their neighborhoods. The explanation for these failures can perhaps be found among the other factors which make for success.

It is apparent that, with the small number of establishments, it is impossible to generalize with any scientific caution regarding the optimum land valuations for taxi-dance halls. Yet the fact no doubt remains that at any given time there is a rather definite limit to the range of possible rents and land valuations under which it is profitable for the taxi-dance hall to operate.

TABLE IV

UNSUCCESSFUL TAXI-DANCE HALLS* FOUNDED WHERE LAND VALUES WERE BELOW $400 A FRONT FOOT

	1921	1922	1923	1924	1925	1926	1927	1928
Moonlight Chicago Ave..........	$ 90	$125	$200	$225	$300	$250	$300	$250
The Lane W. Division St........	200	250	250	250	300	300	500	500
The Washington Blvd. W. Washington St....	80	80	115	115	150	150	225	225
Starry Roosevelt Road......	60	70	70	70	100	100	100	100
Oakland E. Pershing Road.....	300	150	150	200	200	200	150	300

* This list does not include ten or more transient institutions which were begun on property having less than a $400 front-foot valuation but unquestionably were outside any rooming-house area.

A final principle regarding the location of the taxi-dance hall may now be stated. This type of dance hall must seek out those sections of the city which will tolerate it. As a form of commercialized recreation held in grave suspicion by the general public the taxi-dance hall at present finds it desirable to locate in those "interstitial areas"[1] of the city

[1] For a discussion of social disorganization as it relates to the interstitial areas of our cities see F. M. Thrasher, *The Gang*, pp. 22–25, and Harvey Zorbaugh, *The Gold Coast and the Slum*, pp. 69–86 and 105–26.

where community consciousness is weak. Since the rooming-house district is an area of great mobility in which there is usually an almost complete absence of community interests, it provides the safest location for the taxi-dance hall. Thus, protection against opposition, as well as nearness to possible patrons, induces proprietors to locate in the zone of furnished rooms.

There are instances also, in which sections of the city outside the rooming-house areas have tolerated the institution. This has been true in the East Humboldt Park Community, in the West Humboldt Park Community, and in some residential parts of the Near West Side. But the taxi-dance hall has met concerted opposition from the East Garfield Park Community, just west of the Madison Street taxi-dance hall center. This community has been aroused on several occasions by threatened invasions of these dance halls.[1] The East Humboldt Park Community, on the other hand, while tolerating the institution does so only when there is a distinct understanding that Filipinos and other Orientals will not be admitted.

However, a large majority of the communities in the residential sections of the city at present would under no circumstances permit the taxi-dance hall to continue within their neighborhoods. Woodlawn, the South Side area immediately south of Washington Park and the Midway Plaisance, is a case in point. It now is fast becoming an area for small apartments, furnished rooms, and inexpensive residential hotels. Several years ago a successful dance-hall proprietor took steps to open a taxi-dance hall there. The

[1] See records of these efforts along with other material regarding this community in the files of the Local Community Research Committee of the University of Chicago.

LOCATION OF THE TAXI-DANCE HALL

older residents, who remembered Woodlawn as a community of homes with a vital civic life and a community consciousness, succeeded in preventing the opening of the establishment. They met, passed resolutions, and petitioned the mayor to refuse the taxi-dance hall a license. A concerted action of this kind may serve to withstand fundamental ecological changes for a short while.[1] Yet, inevitably, as the old residential population retreats to other sections of the city and the new hotel and rooming-house population streams in, it is probable that the day will soon come when the taxi-dance hall will no longer be excluded.

[1] It is interesting that two new taxi-dance halls were reported during the summer of 1931, only five years later, to have opened in Woodlawn.

PART V
THE TAXI-DANCE HALL PROBLEM

CHAPTER XII

PERSONAL DEMORALIZATION

For a large proportion of the taxi-dancers, and for not a few patrons, the experiences in the Chicago taxi-dance halls are demoralizing. The records of the Juvenile Protective Association, the Juvenile Court of Cook County, and the Morals Court of Chicago give ample testimony that all is not well with the taxi-dance hall. In the years 1926 and 1927, for instance, at least forty-six taxi-dancers are known to have come to the attention of these agencies. Their average age was nineteen, and their length of stay in the dance hall, at the time of the investigation, rarely exceeded three months. The following newspaper account is quite typical of these youthful delinquencies, except that the men involved are not always Orientals.

Assistant State's Attorney Marie C. Anderson today took in hand three young girls under 18 years of age, who were arrested just preceding the padlocking of the Madison Dancing School. The three were "teachers" at the "academy," although 17-year-old Stella Stepanski said "you didn't have to know how to dance any."

Vivian Robbins, who in two weeks' time will be 18 years old, was won over to an insistent promise that she would frequent no more closed dance halls and sent home with her mother. Vivian, a slender, unusually pretty girl, left home weeks ago. She obtained a job in the dancing school and was taken by the police who, at her mother's petition, were looking for her.

Mother and daughter found each other in the juvenile home and cried as they exchanged promises, the daughter to remain with her mother, and the mother to watch and guide the daughter.

Two little girls in crisp, blue uniforms, their countenances devoid of rouge and lipstick, were brought into the office. Clara Marowiski, 15 years old, lived on North Robey Street until she ran away from home two weeks ago.

"I could not get along with my big brother," said Clara in her childish way. "But, I could now if they'd only let me go back. Some girls told me about the Madison Dancing School, and you don't have to know how to dance any to be a teacher there. You just walk around and call it a dance."

"We met Esteban . . . . there and he invited us over to the Filipino Club. We just danced there. Then he invited us to go to his room. . . . . After we got there, he told me to go home, but I wouldn't go.

"I don't want to go back to grammar school," sighed Clara. "I wanta go to continuation school, if I gotta go to school at all. Grammar school is simply awful."

Clara insisted that the Filipino had not made love to her. Police arrested her in his room Wednesday night. She was on the list of missing girls. Clara told the proprietor of the dancing school not to worry about her working certificate . . . . because she was past eighteen. The proprietor was discharged when arraigned on a charge of contributing to Clara's delinquency, but he has lost his license to operate his "school."

Stella Stepanski, Clara's girl friend, is 17. "I had a quarrel with my married sister," said Stella. "You see, it's like this, she and her husband live with us. Whenever she and I quarrel, her husband butts right in. If I stay out late, my ma bawls me out. We're always quarreling at home.

"Neither Clara nor I worked during the day. We liked it all right at the dancing school. Everybody was nice to us, and nobody insulted us. Oh, I guess they did some of the girls, and some of them weren't decent, but we were. Clara said she was going to leave home, so I thought I might as well too."[1]

Other taxi-dancers, however, are not so fortunate as were these three girls. The social agencies, courts, and police

[1] Newspaper story, *Chicago Daily Journal*, August 22, 1926. The newspaper account is here altered only by the substitution of fictitious names and the elimination of street addresses.

reach only a few of the girls, and many taxi-dancers do not come into touch with corrective agencies until much later in their checkered career.

DeLoris Henderson, twenty, and Peter Marcos, forty-six, appeared before Judge Hayes at the Harrison Street Police Court, charged with living together although unmarried. DeLoris testified that she had met Mr. Marcos at a taxi-dance hall, where she was a taxi-dancer, and that he had asked her to share a furnished apartment.

She stated that she lived with him from August 28 until October 14, when visited by detectives and arrested. Mr. Marcos operates several shoe-shining parlors in the Loop. Mr. Marcos, through his attorney, pleaded guilty but petitioned for grace on the claim that he had never given her money, and in reality had only paid the rent.

DeLoris admitted to the judge, upon his request, that she saw nothing attractive in the short, stocky, middle-aged Greek, with whom she had been living. Her elder brother and sister, both holding responsible positions with business firms in the city, were at the hearing, and seemed anxious that the judge dismiss the case. The brother promised to be responsible for her conduct and she was dismissed, while Marcos was committed to the House of Correction for six months.[1]

The experiences of many patrons and taxi-dancers in the dance hall do not, of course, constitute their initial entrance into unconventional conduct. Many of the more sophisticated patrons and taxi-dancers are already accustomed to the type of life revolving around the institution. The taxi-dance hall may meet a want which has already been created by other associations and institutions. Thus to many sexually irregular taxi-dancers, entrance upon this form of livelihood means merely a transfer of their center of activity from a restaurant, a hotel, an amusement park, or a regular dance hall to the taxi-dance hall. The standards, practices,

[1] Adapted from Juvenile Protective Association records. Names are here altered.

and ideals of these taxi-dancers and patrons are already crystallized, and are the same whether they frequent a taxi-dance hall or any other resort.

Thus for the inexperienced girl and youth the taxi-dance hall may constitute the means of their breaking away from social conventions, while for another group it makes possible the continuance of habits already firmly established. For both groups the associations of the taxi-dance hall tend to be personally demoralizing.

The solution to this problem cannot be found merely by condemning the taxi-dance hall. It has arisen in response to definite trends in urban life, and it possesses the characteristics of most urban institutions. In its catering to detached and lonely people, in its deliberate fostering of stimulation and excitement, in its opportunities for pseudo-romantic attachments, it may be seen as an epitome of certain phases of urban life. On the periphery of the respectable, tolerated but not condoned by the community, it gathers to itself those who have failed to find a place in the more conventional groups and institutions of the city, and who yet need the satisfactions which inclusion in such groups affords. The taxi-dance hall, before being summarily dismissed from thought as a "den of iniquity," should be analyzed in terms of the human relationships which it fosters and in terms of the effect of these associations upon the personality and character of patrons and taxi-dancers.

Among the forces of demoralization in dance-hall associations may be mentioned, first, the anonymity of the situation. In the taxi-dance hall as in other public dance halls, young people are enabled to meet each other, socially, without any more knowledge of the background and previous activities of each other than can be gained by a moment's observation of their appearance and conduct in the ballroom. Associations of an intimate sort may quickly be formed between two people who later find themselves very incompatible or even at opposite poles in cultural or moral values. The unsophisticated adolescent and the hardened *roué* may meet on equal terms. Also, the anonymity of the dance hall serves to protect both patron and taxi-dancer from the censure of family and community. They may, if they wish, keep their dance-hall life a secret. While leading a conventional life in family and community, they can yet disregard moral standards in the dance-hall world. For them the dance hall becomes a means of escape from the restrictions upon conduct which, while necessary in a well-ordered society, nevertheless are felt by them to be oppressive. Thus the taxi-dance hall, like other types of public dance halls, presents two problems arising from these anonymous contacts: first, the uncontrolled associations between people with widely different backgrounds and standards; and, second, the possibility of leading dual lives. Each situation constitutes a strain upon the integration of personality and opens the way for a breakdown of stable habits and standards.

It should be noted, however, that the taxi-dance hall, unlike other types of public dance halls, places a special restriction upon the freedom of the woman. The taxi-dancer may maintain her separation from her family by the use of fictitious stories and name, but by her continued employment at one place she is forced into a certain consistency in the rôle she maintains in the dance hall. She comes to have occupational interests which may at times restrict her personal freedom. As an employee the taxi-dancer discovers very quickly that in the world of the taxi-dance hall she must maintain a certain consistency in her conduct, and that her success in this has a definite bearing upon her income. She learns that—like the actress—she has a "public" which she must consider.

The men patronizing the taxi-dance hall, on the other hand, have a greater opportunity to maintain an anonymous relationship. Especially when the patron is a "slummer," a "globe-trotter," or one in flight from justice, his sojourn in the taxi-dance hall may be entirely under the protection of anonymity. Even with such men, if attendance is continued for any length of time, anonymity inevitably breaks down and is replaced by something more personal. Because of the natural human tendency to classify and to individualize those whom we see repeatedly,[1] the patron may actually acquire a different personality in the dance hall. Lacking other information, the taxi-dancers and other patrons may learn to identify him wholly in terms of his activities and associates in the dance-hall world. Perhaps without foreseeing it, he eventually becomes so associated in the minds of others in the dance hall with his past activities and interests there that he may acquire a nickname or, perhaps, be identified as "Helen's boy friend" or even as "Fish No. 7." Though the regular patron may intend to remain anonymous and detached in all his relationship within the taxi-dance hall, his plan eventually breaks down and he acquires, in spite of himself, a certain dance-hall personality.

Herein is a demoralizing aspect of the taxi-dance hall. The patron is often attracted to the institution because it offers him certain pleasures to be enjoyed without disclosing his identity and without the need for becoming involved with those met in the resort. But as a regular patron of the

[1] See N. Shaler, *The Neighbor*, pp. 207–27.

halls, he finds himself drawn almost irresistibly into more permanent associations. He finds that, without knowing it, certain of the girls have begun to manifest toward him certain personal interests not in keeping with his anonymity. In turn he, too, either wittingly or unwittingly, gives special attention to certain of the taxi-dancers. Personal interests and affection spring up, and the cycle of activities which may mean demoralization for some patrons is begun.

The following case is typical of the process by which many patrons who, though originally intending to remain detached from the dance-hall life, nevertheless eventually become absorbed in it.

I first noticed Joe in the fall of 1925 at the taxi-dance hall on the West Side. His dark complexion, black eyes, tall slender frame, his elegant clothing, and polished manners made him a striking figure. He appeared to be about twenty-two years of age.

My efforts to make his acquaintance met with rebuff. He seemed diffident and fearful of anyone met in the dance hall and appeared to have no friends among the patrons. He came alone and left alone. He spent most of the time on the dance floor, but changed partners frequently.

Two months later I again found Joe in the establishment. But this time he seemed in a much more talkative and confidential mood. He said he was a native-born Mexican and indicated that he was from a Spanish family of social position and of some wealth. He lived with his family in an uptown community.

"The girls here aren't bad to dance with," he confided. "I come here once every little while to dance. My old man thinks I'm taking a course in the evening school [in the Loop] to make up a course I missed last year. He'd beat me if he knew I came here. . . . . He asks me why the evening school costs so much and I tell him that the professor changed his mind about the books, so I have to buy different ones. My old man doesn't know American schools and he believes me," he explained laughingly.

"I don't try dates with the girls. They are good to dance with, but I don't want to go out with them. They're not the kind I could take home to my father. . . . . They don't know how to act in good society. My father has planned for me to marry a rich Mexican girl. She's a nice girl. She is in a convent school now. But I cannot be free with her like I can with these girls. . . . . Anyway I like the blue eyes. My girl is Spanish; she has dark eyes."

Some time later I again found Joe in the dance hall, but this time his manner was quite different. He had little time to talk to anyone except a certain rather attractive young woman, a Celtic type, with whom he danced entirely. "Catherine is my girl," he later confided to me proudly. "She lets me take her home every night now. She's a nice girl, a pretty blue-eyed kid, and knows how to act. I'm going to introduce her to my father when I get the nerve. The old man is already mad over the money I'm spending, but he doesn't know about the girl yet."

A month later I visited the hall at a time when Joe had not yet arrived and talked with Catherine. "Joe is a nice boy," she confided, "but he's so young and so inexperienced. He's in trouble with his father now, because of me. You know, his people are real high-class people on the North Side. He's promised to take me up there but he keeps putting it off. I think he's afraid."

Later, I learned from Catherine that Joe had had a serious dispute with his father and had left home. Shortly afterward he quit school and went to work, taking employment at a place located in the vicinity where Catherine lived.

Subsequently, Catherine left the dance hall, and I learned through mutual acquaintances that she and Joe were living in a West Side apartment. Joe was reported to have joined a "beer racket." A year after they drifted apart.[1]

The maintenance of contradictory "personalities" and interests is emotionally disturbing for even the hardiest persons. Most patrons soon find it necessary for their peace of mind, if for no other reason, to resolve the tension by some form of readjustment. The patron may decide that the clandestine activities are not worth what they cost, renounce these alliances, and return to conventional life.

[1] From the records of an investigator.

PERSONAL DEMORALIZATION

> I don't think I shall look up any taxi-dancers on this visit to the city. I got into more than I was bargaining for. Long before I got through with the girl I had before, I decided that if I was once free I'd stay free. Of course it was an interesting experience, but it cost quite a lot of money and—worse yet—there was a lot of worry. Ann wasn't in the least interested in my work. In fact, she seemed to be deliberately pulling me away from it. Then I was always worried lest somebody would find it out. I ended my stay in the city about a thousand dollars poorer and without accomplishing anything worth while.[1]

Occasionally the patron, after becoming seriously interested in a taxi-dancer, may resolve the tension by deliberately bringing his conduct into conformity with established conventions and mores. Marriage and the introduction of his wife into his own circle of associates are the results. "Marrying out of the life" is, for the girl, a frequent means of exit from the taxi-dance hall.

A third possible way of resolving the tension is an acceptance of the dance-hall interests as the major consideration. The patron merely forsakes whatever contacts and activities are necessarily incompatible with his dance-hall interests and gives himself wholly to them. According to the parlance of the Filipino, he becomes a "drifter" or a "vagabond." In this way the student may forsake his ambitions and permit the taxi-dance hall to become his controlling interest.

A second significant force in demoralization is the wide divergence of the world of the taxi-dance hall from anything to which many patrons or taxi-dancers have previously been accustomed. For the patron it means that he comes into intimate association with standards, practices, and points of view toward life too completely differentiated from his own to make possible any effective integration. Starting, perhaps, with some rather insignificant dissatisfaction in his

[1] Case No. 58.

old life, the man who regularly attends the taxi-dance halls may eventually find himself unhappily adjusted both to the more normal world in which he had lived and to the dance-hall life as well. He discovers that he has become so habituated to the life of the taxi-dance hall that it provides him certain basic satisfactions and pleasures. At the same time these are often not as completely satisfying for the man as for many of the taxi-dancers,[1] and he finds that other sides of his nature crave outlets not available in the dance-hall world. Yet the contradictory standards and practices and the philosophy of life of the dance-hall world only serve to undermine the patron's effectiveness in attaining his vocational and social ambitions. Engaged in solving the riddle of these contradictory ways of life, he loses step in his occupational advancement.

I was engaged to a fine girl, but we began having quarrels and finally she broke the engagement. The worst of it was that I couldn't see that anything I had done was wrong. In a dim sort of a way I saw that the trouble had something to do with the "psychology of sex." I knew physiology, of course, but the more important side, the "psychology," was a closed book. I resolved that I would never again permit myself to become seriously interested in a girl until I had prepared myself. It was only fair to any other girl I might later become interested in, and to myself, to get educated. But I soon discovered that there was nothing written which helped very much.

About this time I heard of the taxi-dance halls and began going. I had an abnormal curiosity at the time, and soon became interested in the taxi-dancers. There was something satisfying about the open and frank, yet not indecent, way in which they discussed sex. There was none of that barrier and reserve which had made it impossible for my fiancée and me to talk out our difficulties. I was merely "playing around" with the taxi-dancers; they knew it and I knew it, but never-

[1] The taxi-dancer's active interests are usually rather completely served. See discussion, pp. 32–33.

theless they were just what I needed. They educated me—though fortunately I never allowed myself to become involved with any. I now feel that I am psychologically prepared to make a happy marriage. But I have paid a price for this knowledge. I haven't associated with the kind of girls I should marry for so long now that I feel ill at ease in their presence. Most of them are so unsophisticated that I can't get up any real interest in them, except intellectually. Certain personality traits of theirs aren't as interesting as the taxi-dancers'. On the other hand, the dance-hall girls are so impossible in other ways I have sense enough not to become seriously interested.

Then there is something nerve racking about dance-hall life. The girls aren't really permanently interested. At least they're not interested in a man's future and his ambitions. He's just a temporary attachment and they don't have the interest in his future which a wife or fiancée does. They're always bleeding him for as much of his time and money as they can get at once. A man tends to lose his perspective. He thinks only of tonight and tomorrow night, not of ten years from now. Instead of helping him this kind of a life holds him back. The affections are a strong influence which helps a man forward if they are hooked up with his career, through marriage, for instance; but they're a millstone around the neck of a man who gets interested in the kind of girls whom, for other reasons, he can't afford to marry.[1]

For the taxi-dancer the wide divergence of the standards, practices, and philosophy of life of the world of the taxi-dance hall from anything to which many taxi-dancers have previously been accustomed is, similarly, a cause of demoralization. The old standards and attitudes which had proved satisfactory in other social groups are not practicable in the dance hall. When followed in this radically different social world they result in pain, misunderstandings, and disillusionment. In the words of one young woman, the taxi-dancer soon discovers that in the taxi-dance hall "it doesn't pay to trust anybody—not even your own sister—much less a man!"

[1] Case No. 45.

In her discouragement the new girl quite willingly gives ear to the suggestions of the more mature and successful taxi-dancers. She quickly acquires the ways of acting, the language, the attitudes, and the standards of conduct of the successful young woman and gives little thought to where this type of life may eventually lead. These other taxi-dancers provide for her not only acceptable modes of behavior and conduct but also a scheme of life and a philosophy of life, suitable to the world of the taxi-dance hall, which again make possible a satisfying adjustment of the taxi-dancer to the life around her. Strange as it may at first seem, the philosophy of life and the standards and practices which she acquires are for the time quite satisfying, and instead of being disorganizing are in reality reorganizing, because they again bring the taxi-dancer into effective relationship with her immediate social world, that of the taxi-dance hall.

The modes of behavior, attitudes, and philosophy of life of the taxi-dancer do not, however, appear to be desirable as permanent aspects of personality and character. Foremost among these undesirable traits are the attitude of extreme individualism and the philosophy of exploitation. It has been indicated elsewhere[1] that a rationale of exploitation is apparently basic to the enterprise of the taxi-dance hall. Associated with it everywhere is the practice of the "sex game,"[2] which serves to prepare the way psychologically for more serious sexual misconduct. Prostitution and allied forms of immorality very naturally follow. But other consequences of the rationale of exploitation and the practice of the sex game are not so readily seen. This scheme of life may pave the way, not only for a commercialization of

[1] Pp. 39–42.   [2] See pp. 46–48.

PERSONAL DEMORALIZATION 249

sex, but for a criminal career of other varieties as well. In the following case a period of several years of exploitation in the taxi-dance hall was but a schooling for later organized criminal activities.

Gertrude Mueller was the oldest daughter of a widow of German extraction living in a suburb of Chicago. There were several younger children and family finances at times were in a precarious condition. The wages which Gertrude could earn by leaving school and going to work at fifteen years of age were needed.

When hardly seventeen years of age Gertrude entered the taxi-dance hall and somewhat later began her most unique adventure in exploitation—that of marrying or living with young men in order to "fish" them. According to the information supplied by one taxi-dancer who knew her well she would find some young man who was enamored with her, "had a bank account," was "easy," and would then establish an alliance. In a short time she would appropriate the man's savings and desert.

She is reported to have exploited several young men in this way. For a time she is said to have "married" a young man by the name of Johnny Smith whom she soon deserted. Then, under the name of Bobby Dixon she was married to an Italian youth, whom she later deserted. Since then she is reported to have established other alliances and marriages under other names.

Later, she became associated with a gang of youths engaged in criminal activities. She is reported to have been the leader of the gang. . . . . After committing a number of robberies and holdups the gangsters were arrested and several of them convicted. Gertrude, now styling herself Billye Dixon, was convicted along with three of her men confederates.[1]

Another undesirable aspect of the taxi-dance hall is the rôle of sophistication and cynicism which seems almost a universal pattern among taxi-dancers. The cynicism is frequently evidenced in the attitudes of girls toward one an-

[1] From information gained from Juvenile Protective Association records and newspaper accounts. Names and addresses altered.

other and frequently reflects their own attitudes on matters of feminine virtue. The following excerpt suggests this attitude of cynicism and reflects the round of interests by which the taxi-dancer's life is ordered.

> The talk of the girls makes me sick. It's always the same. About the cabaret parties they've been to, and how much they drank, and how much the men spent on them. If it isn't that it's about how they "fished" a man for a ring with a big "rock" in it, or how they worked another for a watch. And so on. All the time they're talking as though they got these things just because the guys were "fish." We sit around and act like we thought what the girls were saying was the truth when we know all the time that they had to do a lot of hustling to get the "rocks."[1]

An even more frequent note in the philosophy of life of the taxi-dancer is a justification of promiscuity, together with a denial of the sanctions of ecclesiastical marriage.

> One thing the church people back home and all the other hypocrites say that I never could understand was why it was so all-fired holy to love a man after a preacher has said a few words over your head, but downright wicked five minutes before. Love seems to me a lot more precious than a few words that somebody says over your head. What's more, I don't see why I shouldn't do what I want to. It's nobody's business anyway.[2]

In a social world in which the use of contraceptives is common knowledge, a philosophy of promiscuity and freedom in love may gain some headway. This seems to be particularly true of the world of the taxi-dance hall.

A third demoralizing aspect of dance-hall life, especially for the younger girls, is the constant exposure to the contradictory ideals, beliefs, and standards of conduct present within the dance-hall world itself. A dance-hall group is a

[1] Case No. 13.   [2] Case No. 10.

heterogeneous assemblage, and has among its personnel representatives of many contradictory ways of life. Few of these are wholly consistent within themselves, yet they all embody points of view, rationalizations, and schemes of life which are readily available for the young girl to use in justifying her conduct.

But these contradictory points of view serve further to confuse the young girl. For these bear upon problems which, to the taxi-dancer, are not minor considerations at all. Should she dance with, "date," or perhaps marry a Filipino or other Oriental? Should she engage in sensual dancing and in other immoral conduct in order to add to her income? To what extent can she be expected to be "loyal" to a former lover or husband when making her way in the taxi-dance hall? These and other critical questions present themselves. In the maze of contradictory paths suggested it is not easy for anyone to select deliberately a wholly consistent and permanently satisfying plan of life—and even more difficult for an impulsive and untutored young girl.

On such an important question as the basic conception of marriage itself there is no agreement. Many young women even in the taxi-dance hall retain apparently the conventional conception of marriage. Frequently, however, the taxi-dancer seems to favor the companionate. In this social world, marriage with the definite understanding that there will be no children is a natural adaptation to conditions of life. There is yet another conception of marriage which is, in reality, a much more radical departure from the traditional idea of the family than the companionate. As yet, it appears to be a point of view which is not at all common, even in the dance halls. Nevertheless it is significant in that it suggests the wide range of possible standards within the taxi-dance hall. In direct contrast with the companionate, which regards marriage as an institution for the legitimatization of sex life and intimate companionship, and not for the rearing of children, this new point of view conceives of the family as an institution *exclusively* for the rearing of children.

There is no reason to get married unless people want children. That's what marriage is intended for anyway. . . . . The trouble with the country now is that people are getting married too quickly. If they waited until they'd had time to try each other out thoroughly then they would know better whether they ought to get married . . . . . I don't see anything in the companionate marriage idea because that just means making people get married before they're sure of each other, and before they're really ready to have children.[1]

In a social world in which modified promiscuity is common, even such a revolutionary point of view is a natural development. It reflects one extreme in the contradictory conceptions of marriage and the family to which the girl is exposed in the taxi-dance hall.

The effect of the young girls' contact with these contradictory ways of life can be seen in part in their hasty and illogical behavior. With only a limited experience and ineffective parental instruction to guide them, these young people frequently follow the whim of the moment and make interpretations and decisions of the most foolish character.

Anna was a young girl of Polish parentage, not over eighteen years of age, who entered the taxi-dance halls and there made the acquaintance of Filipinos. In the early spring of 1926 three couples of girls and Filipinos were spending a Saturday night at a "black and tan" cabaret.

In the conversation they began talking of marriage. One of the

[1] Case No. 11.

other girls "dared" Anna to marry her escort of the evening, a young man whom she had not met until a few hours before. Anna accepted the challenge, and in turn, by similar tactics, induced the other girls to consent to marry their Filipino friends. As a result, they chartered a taxi-cab, drove to Crown Point, Indiana, and were married early Sunday morning. These couples never attempted to establish residences. Within a few days the girls were each anxious for a divorce.[1]

In the following instance, a Dutch immigrant girl, in this country less than two years, apparently accepted "girls' gangs" and "fist fights" among taxi-dancers as legitimate means for maintaining her claim that she was a "lady."

I suppose you know we had a fight here last Wednesday. It all got started back in the restroom. You notice most of the girls won't speak to me. That is because I have nice things and they are jealous. There was a girl back in the restroom. They call her "Red." She called me a dirty name and it made me mad and I kicked her. Then all of her friends jumped on me, and pretty soon we were biting and scratching and pulling hair. Then somebody said the orchestra had started up again and for us to settle our fight outside afterward.

"Red" got her gang together, and I got mine. But "Red" had more girls than I had. We got to fighting as soon as we got down the steps. I got knocked off the sidewalk into the ditch and got my dress all dirty. Somebody struck me hard on the face and somebody else struck me in the stomach. I also lost my pocket-book with fifteen dollars in it. I got it back the next day but my money was gone. But I don't care about the money or the dress. I showed them I wasn't a coward, and anyway they won't ever say I'm not a lady any more. . . . . You know, I really am a lady; I live with my mother.[2]

These are literally "wild young people," with no universally accepted code or body of practices to guide them.

Another evidence of the disorderly life resulting from the conflicting codes and groups within the taxi-dance hall is the discovery in it, occasionally, of the exclusively girls'

[1] Records of an investigator.

[2] Case No. 60, assembled from the reports of special investigators.

gang. This is, indeed, a unique phenomenon. Thrasher, in his study of 1,313 gangs in Chicago, found only five or six exclusively girls' gangs. His interpretation is that the gang behavior of girls is opposed by a much greater weight of tradition and custom and that, in even disorganized areas of the city, girls are much more carefully supervised than are boys.[1] But for the taxi-dancer, who probably lives away from home much of the time, and is economically independent of her family, the restraining influences of neighborhood and family are of slight consequence.

Other factors in the dance-hall situation also favor the development of the girls' gang. For girls as well as boys the gang seems to thrive only in a situation of conflict and as an "interstitial group."[2] Exposed to the contradictory standards and practices of the taxi-dance hall, and necessarily in conflict with some, the girl finds in the gang a basic group affiliation of vitality and of some permanence. The gang gives protection to its members, and supplies the girl with a satisfying conception of herself and the outside world. More than that, it provides the taxi-dancer with a standard of conduct, i.e., a code accepted by all the members and enforced by the gang, and makes possible a certain amount of order in the disordered world of the taxi-dance hall. Likewise, the taxi-dancers' gang is an interstitial group. It functions in an environment which is an "interstitial area" par excellence—the disordered taxi-dance world and the deteriorating sections of the city.[3]

In contrast with the boys' gang, the girls' gang of the type found in the taxi-dance hall is unstable and transient, principally because of the development of romantic attachments conflicting with gang allegiance. Thrasher has point-

[1] Thrasher, *The Gang*, p. 228.   [2] *Ibid.*, pp. 22–25.   [3] See pp. 231–33.

ed out that in the case of the boys' gang it is the romantic interest and marriage which constitute the disintegrating force.[1] Similarly, for the taxi-dancers, a romantic interest is fatal to gang allegiance. Hence, the exclusively girls' gang in the world of the taxi-dance hall is found only among those taxi-dancers whose interest in the patron is utilitarian and exploitative.

There are several organized groups among the taxi-dancers sufficiently well recognized by the girls, both inside and outside, to be termed "gangs." In their own way the girls apparently recognize that these "gangs" have leaders. For they are known by the name or nickname of the leader. Thus there are at present certain embryo gangs of taxi-dancers which are referred to as "Red's Gang," "Rose's Gang," and "Minnie's Gang."

The gangs are formed in the dance hall and among a group of congenial girls who frequent the same dance hall. These girls in their association with patrons seem to be motivated wholly by utilitarian or exploitative interests. In some instances the girls of a gang are reported to be living together in apartments. They are reputed to be some of the most active in "fishing" gullible patrons.[2]

The taxi-dancer's gang, in its organization and method of discipline and control, is patterned after the boys' gang and the criminal gang. The following incident suggests a deliberation and organization not ordinarily found among a group of young women.

"Red" and two of her cronies had secured the permission of the proprietor to leave early. At eleven o'clock in the evening they were wearing their wraps and were standing near the door. "Red" signaled for me to come over. After a moment's conversation she said: "There's going to be a fight here in a minute. Watch that black-eyed kid with the white dress. Our gang is down on her and we've decided that Stella is to go over there and give her a good punch. Stick around and you'll see some fun."

[1] Thrasher, *op. cit.*, p. 242.   [2] Records of an investigator.

I waited and watched. A moment later the dance was completed and the "black-eyed kid" stood on the side lines talking to a patron. Then I saw Stella stroll over in her direction and without any formalities deliver one vigorous well-aimed blow at the "black-eyed kid." She crumbled to the floor, and Stella strolled triumphantly away to join "Red" and her cronies, who disappeared down the stairs a moment later. The "black-eyed kid" was carried to the restroom, and after a time was able to go home.[1]

Irrespective of its picturesque character, the gang behavior of the girls is significant evidence of the conflicting standards and groups found in this social world. Despite its temporary effect in bringing a certain amount of order into a disordered world the girls' gang in the end serves as an influence toward further demoralization in the taxi-dance hall.

A fourth factor contributing to the demoralization of the taxi-dancer is her economic position in the institution. To make her sojourn in the dance hall profitable the girl must in some way meet the commercial demands of the patrons. Whatever may be her personal inclinations or ideals, the taxi-dancer is expected to accept conditions as she finds them and to do everything possible to make certain that the patrons "have a good time." She must dance with all who so desire, and under no circumstances may she "insult" a patron.

The first night I was here a fellow insulted me. I slapped him across the face just like I would any other fellow who started anything. He got sore and took a "pass" at me but I dodged him. Then the floorman stopped him. When he learned that I had slapped him he told me to go in the office and see the boss. Well I went in there and he bawled me out. He said I'd either act all right, no matter what the fellows said, or I could get out. I've got to put up with a lot to stay in this place.[2]

[1] Records of an investigator.

[2] Comment of taxi-dancer to investigator.

These administrative requirements in themselves should not be taken too seriously, for the girl has devices for meeting most of these unpleasant situations. But behind these is the entire economic situation which—irrespective of other values—places the premium upon whatever dance-hall activities will realize the most in profit to proprietor and taxi-dancer. The struggle of the veteran taxi-dancer to "get the dances,"[1] the necessity of lowering occasionally her rôle in the dance-hall world,[2] and the whole "retrogressive life-cycle"[3] reflect the immutability of economic forces in the dance hall.

So far, dance-hall developments seem to show that in most instances the greatest immediate profit, at least, is gained through permitting some questionable conduct. Certainly, in many cases, proprietors acting of their own free will have not been backward in encouraging taxi-dancers to make the most of the economic opportunities which the taxi-dance hall affords.

We asked Jim [for positions as taxi-dancers] and were informed that we would probably be taken on as dancing instructors when the place opened for the winter at a price of a nickel a dance, and a "chance to make anyway five dollars a night," and more too if we "had a mind to."

When I asked him what we had to "put our mind to" in order to increase our nightly stipend he was noncommittal, telling us that we were smart and ought to know.[4]

Out of the economic requirements of employment in the taxi-dance hall arises a fifth factor in demoralization—the necessity for casual intimacies with the many patrons who present themselves. It is necessary for the taxi-dancer to manifest toward each of her clients a certain measure of

[1] See p. 98.   [2] See pp. 101–5.   [3] See pp. 86–94.
[4] Report of Investigator B (*Chicago Journal*, August 16, 1926).

personal interest irrespective of her real feelings regarding them.

> Most of my patrons "fall" for my "line." A girl's got to "kid" the fellows along a lot. That's what most of them want. If a girl can just remember the first name of a lot of the boys who come up occasionally it helps a lot. I like it when I happen to take a fancy to a boy. But when I don't like him, it goes against me to have to "kid" him along so much. But they "fall for it" just the same. But then that's the only way to make a living out of this hall. "Business is business" you know![1]

These promiscuous intimacies, though sometimes innocent enough, often result in unfortunate and embarrassing experiences. The following is but an illustration of the difficulties which may develop:

Evelyn Henderson is in wrong with the Austin police. Police say her story of having jumped from the frying pan into the fire by accepting a ride from two men she didn't know after refusing to ride farther with one she did, in the wee small hours of yesterday morning, puts a bit of a strain on their credulity.

Evelyn is 20, by her own story, and is a taxi-dancer, earning her nickel a dance as an "instructress" at a hall on West Madison Street. By her costume of blonde satin with voluminous chiffon sleeves and high-collared neck, she might be a Paris mannequin and her ultra blasé manner would do credit to a gold coast hostess.

Her explanation of her presence in an automobile loaded with loot from drug stores, including fountain pens, five gallons of alcohol, cigars, cigarets, and $26 in small change, when it was halted after a mile chase by a squad car from the detective bureau, was given with an air of slightly annoyed condescension.

She had a date with a man she had danced with frequently, she said, and after she left the dance hall they drove out beyond the end of the Crawford Avenue car line, where her escort attempted familiarities. After an argument, she jumped from the car and began to walk back toward the car line, where she was overtaken by the two men in the automobile, who invited her to ride with them, she said.

[1] Case No. 10.

PERSONAL DEMORALIZATION 259

They seemed all right, she said, so she accepted the ride, and they had gone nearly to Madison Street when they sighted the squad car, and the driver stepped on the gas.[1]

Casual intimacies often make for breakdowns all along the line. Even though she may engage in casual associations with patrons only because of her economic interest and with firm resolve not to let them disturb the other provinces of her life, there seems to be an almost inevitable tendency for them ultimately to make inroads upon her private life. Elements in the social situation of the taxi-dancer seem almost to make necessary an inconstancy in her affections.

I never did love my husband, I guess, but we were getting along pretty well. . . . . My husband was always close about money matters when it came to me. He'd raise all kinds of trouble if I paid two dollars for a pair of stockings, even if he did understand that I had to look attractive at the dance hall if I was to get enough money to buy the groceries. . . . . Then we'd quarrel about my escorts. If he wouldn't come down and get me at closing time I'd have to have someone else bring me home. I couldn't walk down Clark Street alone at one o'clock in the morning, and so I'd have to get some boy friend to bring me home. . . . . Then my husband would get "sore" if he found I hadn't told the boy I was married. But I couldn't always get a man to bring me home if I told him I was married and living with my husband.[2]

The effect of these necessary personal associations is seen in the distraction and disorganization of individual taxi-dancers.[3] The effect can also be observed in the philosophy

[1] News story, *Chicago Tribune*, March 22, 1929. Name changed and addresses deleted.

[2] Case No. 10.

[3] It is quite possible that these forces of disorganization may sometimes lead to complete mental breakdown. Suggestive in this connection is the fact that in a single public institution for the insane in New York City four former taxi-dancers have been admitted as patients within the past year and a half. Dr. Nobe E. Stein, Senior Psychiatrist of the Manhattan State Hospital, Ward's Island, New York City, in an interview concerning these

of life of exploitation and in the techniques of exploitation which characterize the life of the taxi-dance hall. It has been suggested[1] that these rationalizations and practices may at first seem to the taxi-dancer to be satisfying because they again bring her into an effective adjustment with the social world in which she is living. Fundamentally, it may also be said that the philosophy of life and practices of exploitation are felt by the girl to be satisfying because they serve to protect her against a dissipation of her affections through the casual intimacies required of taxi-dancers. Yet, in spite of this temporary boon, the standards and practices of exploitation—along with the casual intimacies which give rise to them—influence in the end toward further demoralization.[2]

In review it may be stated that there appear to be at least five forces in the taxi-dance hall making for demoralization. Even though it is conceded that in certain instances they do not actually bring about a disorganization of the individual, it is nevertheless true that these forces do exist and do tend to demoralize those whose standards and practices are not already of a sort suitable to life in the taxi-dance hall. In the order discussed, these forces are as follows:

First, the condition of anonymity provides for the patrons a release from the usual social restraints, an opportunity for

---

cases stated: ".... They ranged in age from eighteen to twenty-five years. Two were manic-depressive, manic type and two were schizophrenic; all quite typical of their respective groups, i.e., extrovert and introvert. Life in the taxi-dance hall, involving overwork, irregular night hours and drinking could be considered one of the precipitating factors in some of the psychoses, for which, however, these patients were fundamentally predisposed." A careful study of the incidence of insanity among former taxi-dancers would be an interesting program for further research.

[1] See pp. 247–48.   [2] See pp. 42–48 and 52–53.

living "double lives" and for making contacts of a sort which in the end cannot but be at least partially disorganizing. A *second* force abetting demoralization for both patrons and taxi-dancers is the wide divergence of the standards and practices of this social world from that to which many have been accustomed in other groups. A *third* element in the situation is the existence within the dance-hall world of contradictory standards and beliefs. The girls' gang arises in the taxi-dance hall as a reaction to these contradictory ways of life. It makes possible a certain amount of order in the disordered world of the taxi-dancer, yet in the end it may serve as a further agent in demoralization. A *fourth* possible influence making for disorganization is the economic position of the taxi-dancer. In the dance hall the premium in the form of maximum immediate profits for taxi-dancer and proprietor is often placed upon questionable conduct; and the opportunity to turn to this source of revenue is always closely at hand. *Finally*, the casual familiarities with many patrons required of the taxi-dancer exposes her to intimate approaches from questionable characters and serves to place her in a social situation which seems almost to make necessary a certain inconstancy in her affections. All these factors make for conflict, both for the taxi-dancer and for the regular patron, between the attitudes and patterns of behavior in dance hall life and in family and community circles. This social conflict, no matter how sedulously these two social worlds may be kept apart, inevitably results in moral conflict, to a degree which often spells personal demoralization.

CHAPTER XIII

THE TAXI-DANCE HALL AND SOCIAL REFORM

Any recreational institution so contradictory to traditional American standards as the taxi-dance hall could not arise in the cities of the United States without calling forth opposition to it. From the very first the taxi-dance hall was suspected by officials and social workers of harboring immorality and prostitution. The fact that taxi-dancers were required to dance with all-comers, that the establishment was closed to women patrons, and that proprietors did not favor women supervisors furnished grounds for these suspicions. Nevertheless, it should be recognized that the taxi-dance hall structure did not develop in Chicago as a deliberate attempt to circumvent conventions but rather grew out of certain competitive exigencies and the concentration in certain areas of an unassimilated male population. The taxi-dance hall may thus be viewed as a natural outgrowth of certain urban conditions rather than as a moral violation. Its control can then be sought with a recognition of underlying conditions.

I. CHARGES MADE AGAINST THE TAXI-DANCE HALL

Many charges during the last years have been leveled at the taxi-dance hall. These can be reviewed briefly and without elaboration, since material bearing upon most of the points has already been presented.

One of the charges made most frequently against the taxi-dance hall is that it is "closed to women patrons." It should be noted, however, that the taxi-dance hall was not the result of a deliberate attempt to exclude women patrons but was rather a means by which dance partners might be secured for men who could not otherwise obtain them. The absence of other women in the taxi-dance hall is due, historically, to the fact that women refused to dance voluntarily with certain types of men, rather than because of an unwillingness of patron or proprietor to have them there.

A second charge is that taxi-dancers are compelled by the management to dance with any patron who may so desire, irrespective of their personal wishes. From a commercial point of view, however, some such requirement as this is necessary if the taxi-dance hall is to serve its patronage, since the men who attend this type of hall are those who cannot secure dance partners easily in the large public ballrooms. In practice, however, the clever taxi-dancer does not dance long with anyone who is positively distasteful to her.

There is, in the third place, a disposition on the part of many people to regard the absence of women supervisors and chaperons as *ipso facto* evidence that the taxi-dance hall is at least questionable. Since many prosperous ballrooms have recently employed women supervisors or hostesses, it is only natural to expect that taxi-dance halls should do likewise. Certain factors, however, differentiate the supervision problem of the taxi-dance hall from that of the public-dance palace. There is no known clientèle which is attracted to the taxi-dance hall because of the presence of chaperons, as is true of the dance palace. In other words, the box office gives little or no encouragement for the employment of hostesses. A second factor is the difference in the relative cost of employing a woman supervisor in the small taxi-dance hall as contrasted with the large dance palace. While the taxi-dance hall may have only a few hundred patrons, the large dance palace may count its patrons by the thousands. For it the salary of the supervisor is a much smaller item in the total expense than in the case of the smaller taxi-dance hall.

A fourth and more serious charge, frequently leveled at the taxi-dance hall, is that because of its very structure and its method of paying taxi-dancers, it must—of necessity—be an institution in which there is a great deal of prostitution. This assumption appears to have arisen from a recognition of the similarity of the social situations of the prostitute and of the taxi-dancer. In each instance the types of social contacts which are possible, the interests, and the social forces molding their lives seem to be very much the same. Further, the taxi-dance hall situation embodies the three essentials of prostitution as given by Flexner[1]—barter, promiscuity, and emotional indifference. The association of patron and taxi-dancer is based upon economic ties, and the bargaining and higgling typical of the market place inevitably results. Also, the taxi-dancer is required to be familiar and affectionate with many men and to simulate at least a personal interest in each; yet if she is truly successful in her trade, she must be one who does not discriminate among her patrons and is in fact rather emotionally indifferent to them.

This marked similarity between the social situation of the taxi-dancer and the prostitute is at least a partial explanation for the universal belief that much regular prostitution is to be found in the taxi-dance hall. Actually, however, the professional prostitute is seldom discovered in a taxi-

[1] Abraham Flexner, *Prostitution in Europe*, p. 11.

TAXI-DANCE HALL AND SOCIAL REFORM 265

dance hall. While promiscuous sex behavior and extramarital alliances of varying types are all too frequent,[1] prostitution of the older forms[2] is not common.[3]

The explanation for this fact can be found in part in the differences in income afforded by the two livelihoods. A young woman willing to become a prostitute can in this way secure an income much greater than that of the taxi-dancer. Moreover, because the two occupations are pursued during the same hours of the day, they cannot be engaged in concurrently. Nor can the prostitute, when her day of popularity is over, return to the taxi-dance hall. When she has reached such a low estate in her own profession that the

[1] For discussion of these forms see pp. 48–49.

[2] The chief type of activity in the life of the taxi-dance hall which can be classed unquestionably as prostitution is the late-night or overnight auto or rooming-house engagement, characterized by barter (bargaining) and emotional indifference. The following may have been merely an instance of "fishing," or may have been the beginning of conduct resulting in overt immorality. "The two girls who had been seen talking to the two young fellows who had said that they were 'picking up' came out of the restroom and headed for the two chaps. The larger one spoke up, 'We decided we'd go out with you, but you guys have got to give us our five dollars before we start' " (news story, *Chicago Journal*, August 18, 1926).

[3] There is reason to believe that in some cities much more prostitution has been associated with the taxi-dance hall than has been true of Chicago. The explanation for this difference is not as yet entirely clear, but very probably could be understood in terms of the differentiating factors in the local situations.

In New York, where it has been maintained that the prostitute is less accessible, the Committee of Fourteen, in its *Annual Report for 1930* reports: "Many of the halls 'sell' the hostesses to prospective customers who do not wish to remain for dancing, but desire to take the hostess out for a few hours for immoral purposes. The usual charge is a flat rate of $15, although some charge on an hourly basis. Of this the dance manager receives from 50 to 60 per cent. . . . . Curiously enough, it is exceptional in the halls where the worst public conduct prevails."

earnings of the taxi-dancer are attractive, the prostitute will no longer possess the personal characteristics which make for success in the taxi-dance hall.

On the other hand, it must be recognized that considerable clandestine prostitution and the practice of "overnight dates" are to be found associated with the taxi-dance halls. The "occasional prostitute," the one who ventures occasionally into prostitution as a means of meeting special financial needs and then returns to her former life and activities, is sometimes found. But if the young woman continues indefinitely in prostitution she usually gives up taxi-dancing for the more lucrative means of support.[1]

A fifth charge against the institution, closely associated with the previous accusation, is that even though a great deal of prostitution, strictly conceived, is not to be found in the taxi-dance hall, it is for many young girls nevertheless a "school" preparing them for prostitution and for allied forms of sexual misconduct. Immediately it must be conceded that there is much truth in this accusation. It is, in fact, one of the more important charges—if, indeed, not the most important—which can be made against these resorts. The data substantiating this accusation have been accumulating until now there is an impressive array of evidence. First of all, the social world of the taxi-dance hall embodies many factors which influence toward prostitution and sexual misconduct. One such factor is the attitude of cynicism and sophistication current almost universally among the girls. Associated with this is the scheme of life of exploita-

[1] It should not be inferred that there are not other forms of sexual misconduct often associated with the taxi-dance hall. Taxi-dancers engaging in these may frequently continue indefinitely in the taxi-dance hall (see pp. 48–49).

tion and the "sex game." These, too, provide standards of conduct and rationalizations which may very easily lead toward misconduct. Finally, the social forces of the dance-hall world are such that it is only a question of time until the taxi-dancers are forced to gravitate toward less desirable activities or groups, or to leave the dance halls entirely. For those who pursue taxi-dance hall life to the end of its retrogressive cycles,[1] prostitution or other forms of sexual license appear almost inevitable.

Two other social judgments which can be made regarding the taxi-dance hall, as at present conducted, still remain. These, by some chance, have not come to the attention of many who have inveighed against the institution. Yet they seem to be judgments which are entirely in accord with the facts revealed.

In the first place, it may be said with certainty that the taxi-dance halls serve to bring into intimate association people from widely divergent social groups who in the normal course of events would never meet. Under the cloak of anonymity, and with the form of social acceptability bought at the box office, any kind of man may have the opportunity to make his overtures to young women serving as taxi-dancers. Thus, taxi-dancers are exposed to approach from thieves, pickpockets, holdup men, bootleggers, and even procurers.

The young girl is also exposed to those who would seek to exploit her sexually in other ways. Recently there has developed about the taxi-dance halls of New York and Chicago a scheme by which a gang of fellows are able sometimes to secure a taxi-dancer even against her will. Known in the vernacular as the "line-up," it is perhaps the experi-

[1] See pp. 86–94.

ence most dreaded by many young women.[1] This is but another hazard to which the girl is exposed in the taxi-dance hall.

In a like manner the young girl may become intimately associated with men of alien culture and race. Thus the daughter of Polish peasants, living in the Stock Yards district, may become romantically attached to a member of another race. Or, again, the son of a proud family in the Philippines may abruptly terminate his college career because of his infatuation for a girl of little culture or education whom he has discovered in a taxi-dance hall. These are but examples of the incongruous matches which are regularly seen in these establishments. In the light of the racial prejudices, the standards of propriety, and the mores which—whether we think them right or not—will certainly function in well-ordered social life for some time to come, we may well ask whether it is wise to tolerate an institution which most certainly fosters unwise marriages and increases appreciably the marital disorganization of present-day life.

A final charge which can justly be made against the taxi-dance hall is that it provides a focal point for the congregation of those who, at least at the time, are impelled by interests and desires inimical to social welfare. Here they find others who either have the same dominant interest or are willing to accommodate themselves to it for money. Under the protection which the anonymity of the institution provides they are enabled to make clandestine contacts of a

[1] The information being collected as a part of the Boys' Club Study, New York University, under the direction of Professor Frederic M. Thrasher, reveals that this practice is much more common in New York than had been supposed. In Chicago this practice was brought to light in the instance of a taxi-dancer who leaped from a third-floor window to escape attack (see *Chicago Evening Journal*, September 12, 1928).

sort which in the end cannot but be disorganizing to many. In other words, the taxi-dance hall by its universal practices of using young women as the lure for trade, by maintaining an established location in the city, and by its policy of remaining open during the leisure hours serves in reality to facilitate contacts of the sort which progressive communities are seeking to suppress. To these places are gathered some of those who seek illicit stimulation. Matured individuals here find conveniently located for them an outlet for vagrant impulses; and young people may discover in this circumscribed social world a sanction for conduct which may ultimately result in thwarted ambitions and personal demoralization.

2. THE PROBLEM OF SUPERVISION

Taxi-dance halls have not fared well at the hands of private protective social agencies. While it has often been possible to establish satisfactory relationships with politicians and police, the protective social agencies have been less co-operative.[1] Sometimes these agencies have made thorough investigations before steps have been taken to close the dance halls. More often agencies have proceeded with very little knowledge of the life revolving about the establishments.

Protective social agencies, for the most part, have inherited the attitudes of social workers of fifteen and twenty years ago, who looked with dubious eye upon all com-

[1] It should be noted that recently the Chicago Police Department, under the leadership of those personally opposed to the taxi-dance hall, has been found by unscrupulous proprietors to be anything but co-operative. The Police Department has pursued questionable taxi-dance halls unremittingly and has co-operated at all times with the Juvenile Protective Association, according to a statement issued in 1931 by Jessie F. Binford, executive director of that agency.

mercialized recreation, especially theaters and dance halls. It is not surprising, therefore, that the dominant attitude of protective social agencies at the first was one of opposition. In other cities, as in Chicago, much effort was expended to bring about the closing of certain establishments.

In addition to the effort to eliminate the taxi-dance hall whenever possible, the Juvenile Protective Association has sought to use various means to restrain the development of the taxi-dance hall and to control and supervise it whenever possible.[1] An attempt was made to force taxi-dance halls to secure city amusement licenses such as held by other commercialized dance halls. In most instances the taxi-dance halls had successfully represented themselves as educational institutions, i.e., "schools of dancing," and were not required to secure an amusement license. As a result, the corporation counsel of Chicago was requested to render a decision upon this controversial point. Subsequently all taxi-dance halls, even though styling themselves "schools of dancing," have been considered amusement establishments, and have been expected to come under the regular licensing provisions of the city.[2]

Then began a whole series of strategical efforts on the part of Chicago taxi-dance hall interests to circumvent the licensing requirements and to defeat the various attempts at control. Because the halls often were very profitable, taxi-dance hall interests apparently considered it worth while to spend considerable money to secure licenses or to prevent their revocation.[3] The influence of these expendi-

[1] For an account of one such effort see pp. 205–7.
[2] Corporation Counsel Decision, No. 842.
[3] For much information regarding the strategy employed by proprietors to circumvent licensing and supervision the writer is indebted to Jessie F. Binford, director of the Juvenile Protective Association of Chicago.

tures was hard to combat, especially when this money made it possible to bring political pressure to bear upon city courts and licensing officials. A second type of strategy used by proprietors was the mandamus suit to compel the city to issue a license, or to show just cause for not issuing it. If the proprietor appears to be questionable, but is a man about whom little concrete information is known, it is most difficult to oppose the suit. Only as unfavorable data can be gathered quickly has it been possible to defeat the suits of mandamus.

When failing in these efforts taxi-dance hall interests have turned to a third tack: placing forward as the titular head of the establishment a man about whom nothing unfavorable is known. The tie between this "straw man" and the more notorious individuals who may really control the resort is, of course, not revealed. Unless this hidden relationship can be established in time or the applicant shown to be incompetent or unfit, it has been impossible to prevent the granting of a license. Recently another form of legal strategy has developed: securing an injunction against police interference and surveillance. Under the claim that police visits to public dance halls "hurt business," injunctions have been granted by friendly courts, and police officials have been prevented from entering.[1]

These latter efforts of taxi-dance hall proprietors have been hampered considerably through police reports and through the independent investigations which private protective agencies, especially the Juvenile Protective Association, have been making for some years. There is now on file

[1] To circumvent these injunctions Chicago police officers in 1931 began picketing the entrance ways to these resorts, dissuading people from entering. In April, 1932, however, four taxi-dance halls were reported to be still operating under injunctions (*Chicago Tribune*, April 20).

a rather complete record of many different dance halls and of the men who have been identified with each. This in itself is found to be of value when new applicants for dance-hall licenses are considered.[1] Also, private protective agencies, through the fact that their investigators are unknown and unidentified, have been able to send investigators even into the resorts which have been protected by injunctions against police visits.

Out of these experiences in dealing with public dance halls, and especially the taxi-dance hall, a new point of view is developing. While still pushing prosecutions when the conditions seem to warrant, there is now discernible among social-reform groups a disposition to study more thoroughly the entire situation of the taxi-dance hall with a view toward a better understanding of the problem. Associated with this trend has come a willingness to offer the opportunities for dance-hall supervision to taxi-dance hall proprietors as well as to the proprietors of the larger public ballrooms. The Juvenile Protective Association, while not approving the structure and organization of the taxi-dance hall, has taken the position that until these establishments are prohibited by local ordinance it will do everything possible to assist proprietors who desire to introduce standards of supervision similar to those found in the approved ballrooms of the city.

This new policy seems in general to have been affected indirectly by the new trend in the attitude of the protective social agencies toward all commercialized public dance halls. The blanket opposition to these establishments seems to

[1] The fact that Chicago police officers are now instructed to consult Juvenile Protective Association records before recommending the issuance of dance-hall licenses may be regarded as a recognition of the practical value of thorough investigations and record-keeping.

have given way before the increasing recognition that many types of commercialized public dance halls are permanent units in the recreational structure of the city. Instead of wasting effort in fruitlessly fighting them, these organizations have sought to establish in them satisfactory methods and standards of supervision. In this way it has been thought that the young people attending might be protected against the worst dangers in commercialized recreation. As a result protective social agencies have been able to develop methods of ballroom supervision in which these social agencies, or their appointees, can function unofficially. The movement has resulted in at least two outstanding plans: the "San Francisco plan" and the "Chicago plan."

San Francisco plan.—Under this arrangement the dance-hall supervisors are given police power and work in direct co-ordination with the Police Commission, but are privately supported, or are paid by the proprietors. This plan as developed in San Francisco was applied first to taxi-dance halls, and only later extended to other public dance establishments.

The San Francisco Center of the California Civic League [in 1918] appointed a Public Dance Hall Committee; .... its chief interest lay in being of service to this group of girls [taxi-dancers]. It recognized at the outset that the halls were furnishing amusement of a sort to a considerable proportion of the population, and therefore did not ask for the abolition. It requested from the Police Department an order to install a woman "supervisor," with police power, in each place to protect the interests of the girls; to prevent exploitation of the clientèle by avaricious and unscrupulous interests, such as dope sellers, panderers; to enforce the law prohibiting the attendance of minors.

A triangular plan of administration has been worked out including the Police Commission (granted power to regulate the halls by the City Charter); the Chief Supervisor of Dance Halls, employed by and responsible to the Public Dance Hall Committee of the San Francisco

Center; and the supervisors of the individual halls. Supervisors are paid a moderate monthly salary by the halls, and are on duty every night the halls are open. . . . .[1]

Maria Ward Lambin in her study of San Francisco dance halls evaluates the plan as follows:

The unique feature of the San Francisco plan is the social case work of the supervisors. All of the social problems of modern life are met within the dance hall: sickness, marital difficulties, unmarried motherhood, unemployment, vocational maladjustment, desertion, feeblemindedness, poverty, ignorance of social hygiene, of American manners and customs, lack of sex education. The dance hall supervisors, who are experienced in case work methods, are able to deal with these problems both scientifically and sympathetically.[2]

Chicago plan.—The "Chicago plan," on the other hand, was applied first to the "dance palaces" and only later attempted with the taxi-dance halls. The plan does not include the city police in its organization and is in fact simply a co-operative understanding between the social agency and the proprietors of the public ballrooms by which they jointly establish standards and practices which they all agree to uphold. On the basis of these standards the officers of the social agency may then feel free to make criticisms and suggestions to individual proprietors. The plan developed out of conditions in 1922 and 1923 when many proprietors of the large Chicago ballrooms recognized that they could prosper most by establishing good reputations for their establishments. From the point of view of the social agencies it was, in the words of one leader, a time when "we proceeded upon the novel assumption that the proprietors were just as interested in establishing good conditions as we were."[3] As a result of this new co-operative attitude it was possible to

[1] *Report of the Public Dance Hall Commission of the San Francisco Center.*
[2] Adapted from *ibid.*   [3] Jessie F. Binford, *Survey*, LIV, 98–99.

TAXI-DANCE HALL AND SOCIAL REFORM 275

create a ballroom managers' association which looked to a protective social agency for advice and assistance. An account of this development, given by Jessie F. Binford, director of the Juvenile Protective Association, is as follows:

> Having formed the Ballroom Managers' Association, the proprietors turned for help to the organization which had perhaps taken the greatest interest in dance halls, although the men had never before regarded it as a friendly interest. From the very beginning a representative of the Juvenile Protective Association attended all the meetings. Reports were no longer made secretly, from a detective point of view, and they were no longer filed away to be used as clubs. They were laid on the table as we all met together to decide whether these great ballrooms could eventually become assets in our community life.
>
> We began by barring bad dancing, questionable conduct, and, perhaps the most important move of all, placing in the ballrooms women supervisors who had had social service training and experience. Under the new method of reform from within, our dance halls have prospered as never before; small undesirable halls have gone out of business.[1]

Following the success of the "Chicago plan," as applied to the large ballrooms of the city, an effort was made to deal with the taxi-dance halls in very much the same manner. There was, however, this outstanding difference: the taxi-dance hall proprietors were not invited into membership in the National Ballroom Managers' Association. However, one taxi-dance hall voluntarily asked for membership and for the opportunity of having a woman supervisor. The proprietors of the Park Dancing School on North Clark Street in 1923 came to the Juvenile Protective Association and asked that someone be recommended to serve as a supervisor. Since then several women have been employed in this capacity,[2] and have served as well as could be expected. For it should be noted that an essential element in the

---

[1] Adapted from *ibid.*   [2] See pp. 205–7.

"Chicago plan" is missing when the proprietor is not a member of the group of ballroom managers who support one another in maintaining standards. Instead of having the coöperation of his taxi-dance hall competitors, the single taxi-dance hall proprietor may feel that he is sacrificing profits by insisting upon supervision. In attempting to adapt the "Chicago plan" or any similar plan[1] to the taxi-dance hall situation, several problems present themselves. First, the woman supervisor alone in a taxi-dance hall, dependent upon the proprietor for her livelihood, and with no organization of managers to support her, may sometimes find it impossible to uphold high standards and yet retain her position.[2] Another is the difficulty of appearing overinsistent upon details of conduct which in themselves may seem of little consequence, yet must be insisted upon if supervision is to be effective. Also, in the taxi-dance hall where the mingling of the Oriental and the American girl is countenanced, the supervisor experiences difficulty in dealing fairly, yet not too drastically, with this anomalous situation.

Another major problem arising with any such plan of

[1] In New York City, in reaction to a public attack by the police commissioner, fifteen taxi-dance hall proprietors in September, 1931, were associated together into the Five Boro Ballroom and Dancing Academy Owners' Association. It is their reported plan to establish standards of supervision to which they will all agree to adhere. Another suggestion has been that the Association employ women investigators unknown to the individual proprietors, to secure positions as taxi-dancers in the different halls and to make confidential reports to the central committee of this Association. The New York City Police Department in the summer of 1931 assumed the responsibility for licensing and inspecting dance halls.

[2] It is significant in this connection that Ella Gardner in her survey of public dance halls for the United States Children's Bureau (Pub. 189) suggests that the difficulty of insuring effective supervision when the woman's salary is paid by the management of the ballroom is the critical problem in this type of dance-hall control.

supervision is the adjustment of the reciprocal relations of social agency and proprietor in such a way that the highest possible standards of supervision can be attained, yet without the chance that the methods and purposes of the social agency will be misconstrued. This problem is seen most clearly in the occasional public indorsement of individual dance halls by the social agency. If the management of a certain ballroom is known to be doing everything possible to maintain wholesome conditions, it seems only just that the establishment should be defended against the consequences for the occasional misfortunes of its patrons for which otherwise it might be held accountable. From one point of view this appears as only simple justice. But for those of a more cynical turn of mind it may appear as something else. Some may even see in it a slightly camouflaged scheme for granting illicit "protection" through a public indorsement made doubly valuable because of the prestige of the social agency.

An interpretation of this kind is, in most instances no doubt, a rank perversion of the truth. Yet the fact remains that a policy of even occasional and judicious public indorsement serves to provide individual dance halls with a form of "protection" against the hazards of the business which, in some cases, is more effective than any which might be "bought" from grafting politicians or police. It should be noted that by this procedure the indorsing social agency serves the interests of both the sincere dance-hall proprietor and the public by making unnecessary this form of petty grafting, which cannot but be demoralizing to all concerned —police, politicians, and dance-hall proprietors.

It should be noted that the petty contributions to corrupt political interests for "protection," made by honest and sincere dance-hall proprietors, can be exacted from them chiefly because of the traditional stigma associated in the public mind with public dance halls. This aspect of the problem, as well as the practical way in which dance-hall men look at the matter, is revealed in the following document. Unfortunately, in this instance, the dance-hall proprietor adopts a misleading attitude of cynicism toward his competitors. This should not, however, be permitted to obscure in any way the point that, after all, the judicious granting of public indorsements by an upright private social agency does serve a justified purpose in making unnecessary the paying of "graft" to protect legitimate interests.

I'll tell you how the dance-hall men happened to get hooked up with the Juvenile Protective Association. . . . . You know the dance-hall business is a funny game. We've got a bad name and so everything that happens that has anything to do with a dance hall is blamed on to it. . . . . A boy and girl meet in a dance hall and later get into trouble and the dance hall is blamed for it. . . . .

Now that means that the dance-hall men to protect themselves have to keep on friendly terms with the police and the politicians. Of course, ordinarily it doesn't cost so much, but it's twenty-five dollars here and twenty-five dollars there and it soon counts up.

That's where the Ballroom Managers' Association and the Juvenile Protective Association come in. These fellows who first supported the plan weren't any more righteous than the rest of us. They just saw the point first and then the rest of us got wise and jumped in, too. We just figured that the Juvenile Protective Association would give us better and cheaper protection than the police and politicians do.[1]

With the practically minded proprietor, "protection" was recognized to be a vital factor in his business. Like insurance, "protection" was a way by which the dance-hall proprietor could reduce the factor of risk in his business to a minimum. Thus in addition to idealistic considerations,

[1] From an interview with a dance-hall proprietor.

there was a very practical utilitarian interest to induce proprietors to follow policies which might occasionally receive the commendation and indorsement of protective social agencies.

Another administrative difficulty arises from the fact that public indorsement of individual dance establishments by reputable social agencies virtually eliminates the necessity for the form of "protection" which corrupt police and politicians can provide. Social agencies may in this way come to be viewed as competitors with corrupt officials in distributing "protection." This is especially true when in the practical carrying-out of a "Chicago plan" the social agency finds it desirable to engage in activities and to establish ties and obligations which—even though the entire procedure has been above reproach—may later prove to be embarrassing. Political foes of the movement are thus provided with an excellent prima facie case against the social agency.

Such an interpretation can be given to the public altercation three years ago between a city prosecutor—a William Hale Thompson appointee—and the Juvenile Protective Association. In a public letter to the director of the Association, protesting against charges alleged to have been made in its annual report, the prosecutor cited by way of rebuttal certain anomalous relationships which he claimed existed even under the Juvenile Protective Association policy of occasional indorsements. These counter charges involve, in part, the supposed policy of the Juvenile Protective Association in "protecting" against legal action the Park Dancing Academy, the one taxi-dance hall which had been interested in securing and maintaining a woman supervisor.

One taxi-dance hall owner has protested, saying that they have a working arrangement with the Juvenile Protective Association whereby their moral status was firmly established, and that they did not therefore consider any other regulation necessary. . . . .

This department is desirous of protecting from unjust criticism legitimate dance halls, the owners of which maintain high standards. By the same token this department is determined to stamp out all vicious, lawless, immoral and dangerous dance halls and dancing without regard to who may be involved and without regard to the sponsorship or recommendation of women acting as supervisors in them. . . . .

It may be interesting to note that the Morals Court recently sent two girls to my office in the custody of the police, after they had stated in the Morals Court that they were instructors in this particular dance hall. The officer stated that upon complaints from the neighbors he and other officers had raided a flat which resulted in the arrest of a Hawaiian and a Filipino, one of which men was fined $5.00 and costs and the two girls ordered to leave the city.

In the face of this and other information, I cannot understand why you persist in a further dispute of the character of this particular place, but in your last communication, you still charge that "we are honest enough to recognize a sincere effort on the part of one of the proprietors to give supervision and protection to the girls who act as instructors and to have good conditions generally. The proprietor of this hall has done that."

This department, as all departments under the present administration, seeks to co-operate with and give recognition to all proper efforts of every reputable agency of Chicago. On the other hand, this department does not propose to assist or recognize any agency which, under the guise of social service, receives support for itself or for its employees [dance-hall supervisors] from the very institutions which in its program of alleged social service it is supposed to regulate, investigate, or prosecute. . . . .[1]

The limit to which a private agency may go in giving public indorsements of certain dance halls is most difficult to determine. Such an agency is constantly confronted by a double dilemma. Without yielding in the least to dishonest

[1] Adapted from an open letter of a former prosecuting attorney to the director of Juvenile Protective Association under date of March 24, 1928.

or unworthy motives, it is possible for the organization, on the one hand, to err by refusing to grant enough public indorsements, and, on the other hand, it is equally possible to err on the side of too frequent indorsements. By not giving enough indorsements the agency tends to lose its very power for influence over the dance halls themselves; and by too frequent or too indiscriminate indorsements the agency lays itself open to the accusation of being a racketeering organization trading on public indorsements and "protection." In this situation there is a grave danger that the organization through a popular misunderstanding of the activities may even lose the public support by which it is able to exert influence with the proprietors themselves.

This policy of judicious indorsements is obviously difficult to administer in as dubious a situation as that presented by the taxi-dance halls. It is apparent that the "Chicago plan," if it is to succeed, must be administered not as a matter of routine, but with a viewpoint of practical expediency. As long as the taxi-dance hall problem presents itself, each instance of possible indorsement must be viewed in the light of the total situation and with a consideration of the different community changes from time to time. It follows, therefore, that the "Chicago plan" to be successful must have the support of social leaders who are constantly at work studying the ever changing nature of their problem and who remain equally active in informing the more intelligent public of the complexity of the social forces which social workers must face in the modern city.

3. THE PROBLEM OF A SUBSTITUTE

It is certain, from the information which has been amassed, that the unsupervised taxi-dance hall is frequently morally degrading and disorganizing. If the taxi-dance hall were eliminated, it is clear that many would be spared demoralization in this way at least. Yet it should be noted that there are also patrons and taxi-dancers for whom the taxi-dance hall is not disorganizing. Many are already adjusted to the type of life revolving about these places. Others among the patrons are so situated that taxi-dance hall life, even at its worst, is superior to what they might otherwise experience. For some patrons the taxi-dance hall is the only opportunity for feminine society outside the brothel. And among those men who will not resort to prostitution can be found some for whom the taxi-dancer affords the only opportunity for affectional ties of a heterosexual character. For certain of these the taxi-dance hall, instead of promoting demoralization, no doubt actually prevents the establishment of emotional adjustments even less wholesome. Yet the fact remains that the taxi-dance hall in a majority of cases contributes appreciably toward further demoralization.

Social judgments such as have just been given are of value in helping to define the problem; yet it should be noted that they were not the chief aim of the study. Rather it was hoped that a more thorough descriptive analysis of the taxi-dance hall, its origins, evolution, policies, standards, practices, and methods of control, might in the end be of greater value. In a very real sense, the research was based upon a conviction that even such an anomaly as the taxi-dance hall is but the natural result of certain social forces, of certain basic human desires and interests, and of human nature itself when confronted with a particular physical setting and with certain social situations. The belief prevailed that it was only as the taxi-dance hall could be seen in its entire setting, as a natural development and as a normal manifestation of human nature in certain situations, that we could hope to get any real control over the problem.

It is well to note that in spite of its serious faults the taxi-dance hall can serve the legitimate needs of certain groups: older unattached men who wish to dance, men who are socially handicapped by an unattractive personality, small stature, language difficulties, or by physical disabilities; detached immigrants who no longer find social life among their own nationality entirely satisfying; and, finally, the young men of oriental races, who because of their isolation in America feel most keenly our social exclusiveness and our racial prejudices. The taxi-dance hall is the only dance institution which makes a place for all these groups, the only social opportunity afforded them in which they do not feel tinge of pity, repulsion, or social condescension. Any comprehensive social program for eliminating the taxi-dance hall must make satisfactory provision for the needs of these groups.

Non-commercial agencies in Chicago have made few efforts to meet the recreational interests of patrons of the taxi-dance hall. Occasionally, perhaps, social settlements and religious agencies have shown a sporadic interest in some of them. But probably the most significant of these efforts is the Lonesome Club, Inc. Since its inception in 1915 it has conducted weekly dances to which men and women of any age are invited. Its object, from the beginning, has been to facilitate the social contacts of those who are alone and without friends in the city.

The Lonesome Club was organized largely as a result of a series of articles written by Elizabeth Guyon Dormer in the *Chicago Evening Post*, telling of the loneliness of strangers in Chicago. At a banquet held in the Crystal Room of Hotel Sherman on the evening of October 9, 1915, the organization officially came into existence, but was not incorporated until June, 1917. During the war the activities of the Lonesome Club were broadened to include the service to soldiers and sailors on leave.

But throughout the years the chief interest of the Lonesome Club has been to provide "one happy evening a week for all." According to its motto it seeks to provide "A Bright Spot in a Blue World." Supervision of the highest order has been consistently maintained. A number of "hosts" and "hostesses" mingle with the throng, making the acquaintance of the new or backward and introducing them to others.

The duty of chaperonage is taken seriously by the directors of the Club, who think of themselves as social workers. Mrs. Alice M. Buck, the president of the Club, has been active in the organization for many years, and can tell interesting stories of the personal problems solved, romances begun, men and women helped through contacts made in the Lonesome Club.[1]

The success of the Lonesome Club has encouraged the growth of rivals. Chicago at different times has had a Get-Acquainted-Club, a West Side Social Dancing Club, and a Middle-aged Dancing Club, all patterned after the original Lonesome Club.

In New York there has been even less effort to meet the social and recreational needs of these isolated groups. The Y.W.C.A. organizations of New York City, as well as those of Chicago, have sought to provide facilities for bringing together socially unaffiliated young men and women of the city—but the most significant development which has come to the attention of the writer is the "99 Steps Club" of the Times Square district.

Organized as a part of a program to provide social contacts for the young people of New York who turn to the Times Square "bright lights" for their social life and recreation this club in the three years

[1] Adaptation of information secured from interviews with officers of the Club, from newspaper accounts, and from social case records.

of its existence has served over 1500 individuals. Under the leadership of the Reverend C. Everett Wagner, the club is sponsored by the Union Church (Methodist Episcopal), "99 Steps West of Broadway" on Forty-eighth Street as a part of a unique church program. Young people are sought through want-ads in newspapers, and applicants are interviewed and investigated by trained social workers. Members, ranging in age from 18 to 40, are grouped in chapters according to age, interest, and apparent congeniality. The activities are not confined to social dancing, but also include amateur dramatics under professional direction, discussion groups, swimming, bowling, bridge, ping pong and pool.

However, it should be noted that these clubs do not meet all the needs served by the taxi-dance hall. In fact, they serve only the stranger in the city, the unattached person, and the one somewhat older than the typical dance-hall patron who nevertheless desires to dance. Younger men and those not at ease in a social gathering or not possessing the social graces required for acceptance in the Lonesome Club group do not find their wishes satisfied. Neither does the one handicapped by physical disabilities or abnormalities, the immigrant with an imperfect command of English, nor the Oriental find a satisfying place in such clubs.

Aside from the recreational programs of social settlement houses, the activities of nationality fraternal orders, and the social life incidental to Americanization programs, little is done to serve the recreational needs of the immigrant. For the young Oriental in America, even less is attempted. The only social life provided him is that which is associated with Cosmopolitan clubs, the International Houses of New York and Chicago, and the international discussion groups sponsored by the Y.M.C.A.[1] and the Y.W.C.A. All further

[1] There was, however, one effort on the part of the Chicago Church Federation and the Foreign Student Department of the National Y.M.C.A. Council to promote a separate religious organization for Filipinos in Chicago. It was hoped that these religious services might provide the basis for building

efforts to provide Filipinos some opportunities for wholesome association with young women have met formidable opposition in our racial mores. No organizations or leaders have been willing to undertake the responsibility of providing suitable American girls for these young men.

In a most significant sense it may be said that the taxi-dance hall affords eloquent testimony to the inadequacies of present-day life for its patrons and to the maladjustments and unhappiness which many have experienced. Whether it be the Filipino for whom socially we do not make a place, or the European immigrant who seeks so desperately to achieve what he considers "Americanization," or the man distraught by marital shipwreck or goaded by some bitter sense of incapacity or failure, the patrons of the taxi-dance hall present a panorama of the maladjustments typical of urban life. Even those who come seeking sensuality cannot justly be regarded as depraved. More often than not they are merely men who feel themselves beaten down by the adversities of life and who have had the normal avenues for affectional life closed to them. In the monotony and humdrum of the mechanized city they play no significant rôle and their experience in the taxi-dance hall may sometimes make it possible for them to feel that life after all is worth while. Similarly the young men of sixteen and eighteen who attend reflect maladjusted homes, unresolved conflicts of Old World parents and American-born children, and the failure of the community, the church, and the school to awaken in youth a

---

up a better morale among Filipinos. Filipino student ministers are appointed and carry on religious services under the name of the "Filipino Christian Fellowship." While of great value, some of these efforts have not reached the great mass of Filipinos in Chicago. A large majority are Roman Catholics, and a form of worship borrowed from Protestant churches no doubt has not had a great appeal for them.

zeal for right living and for the compelling interests and activities that in the end make life significant.

In the last analysis the problem of the taxi-dance hall can be regarded as the problem of the modern city. Just as in the problem of crime, of vice, and of family disorganization, we find in the taxi-dance hall the same social forces which operate in all city life. There is, first of all, mobility, impersonality, and anonymity. As never before people are able to conduct activities in many places at the same time. They may move in and out of the mosaic of contradictory moral worlds which constitute the city and yet be relatively free from detection. Others find in the city's anonymity an opportunity for the submergence of their ego. In this microcosm—the taxi-dance hall—is to be found additional testimony to the isolation, the loneliness and the distraction of the city; of its failure to satisfy normally the basic cravings of human nature. In the abnormal behavior found in life in the taxi-dance hall is seen again the failure of the city to meet in a wholesome way the fundamental wishes of its people. Toward misconduct such as is associated with the taxi-dance hall it would be easy to advocate some form of repression. But a policy involving repression alone would never be wholly successful. It does not get at the heart of the problem, for the problem is as big as city life itself.

The problem of the city and of city life remains the unsolved riddle about which these lesser questions revolve. This strange structure of iron and steel, brick and mortar, of skyscrapers and traffic lights, has potentialities for weal or woe. Now that man has built the city, can he thrive in it? For countless ages man has prospered in a rural or a village situation. In this setting he has worked out through the centuries the accepted standards and practices, the mores of society. Now, suddenly transplanted to the unfamiliar urban setting, will modern man be able to adjust his "rural heritages" to urban life; or, like so many city civilizations of history, will the present also disintegrate? Today with the radio, the telephone, and the automobile urbanizing the entire country, the question becomes even more crucial. Will modern man be able to readjust his standards and practices in such a way that he and his descendants will prosper? This is the problem implicit not only in the development of the taxi-dance hall, but in almost all maladjustments in city life.

The taxi-dance hall also reflects in the extreme the commercialism and the utilitarian considerations which characterize the city. In it even romance is sold on the bargain counter. The adaptability of commercialism is also seen. Just as the flophouse for hobòs and the sale of protection and favoritism by politicians are ingenious adaptations of commercialism in the big city, so the organization of the taxi-dance hall is an adroit adjustment to a previously unrecognized demand. Commercialism, in its freedom to follow unrestrainedly wherever the profit motive seems to lead, appears to have the advantage over other city forces and institutions. Long before most social agencies, for instance, had even considered meeting the needs of this unassimilated male population, commercial interests had responded to it and by slight adaptations of other enterprises had begun to serve the newly discovered demand. This commercial responsiveness and adaptability is another aspect of the impersonal city and is one making doubly difficult the whole problem of community control.

It is also apparent that the very nature of city life makes necessary and inevitable some system of formal dance-hall

TAXI-DANCE HALL AND SOCIAL REFORM 289

supervision. For city people the dance hall is but an incidental experience in a life packed full of stimulating human contacts. Hence, their associations with people met in the dance hall are usually casual and anonymous. Often people meeting in this way have little abiding interest in one another and are not greatly concerned regarding the judgments which others met in the dance hall may make of them. The dance-hall activities are but a segmental aspect of their experiences and may often seem to have little bearing upon the main current of their life-careers. For this reason the village concern, of time immemorial, "What others might think," becomes of little significance in the transient world of the ballroom. Instead, the impulse becomes strong to "let go," to give vent to forms of self-expression one ordinarily would not permit one's self. Moreover, in the transient contacts of the ballroom one feels no personal responsibility for the conduct of strangers seen there. As a result, any effective control which is exercised must be formally imposed from without, either by the manager himself or by others whose interest is that of civic welfare. Thus, the informal social control arising naturally and without special concern in the village situation must be supplanted in the urban dance hall by formal regulations, by institutionalized methods of supervision, and by systems of control imposed forcefully and externally upon the dance-hall patrons.

The taxi-dance hall reveals, again, the passing of traditional forms of prostitution and the development of new substitutes. With the virtual disappearance of the professional prostitute and the segregated vice district a host of variants has arisen. The sensual dancer in the unsupervised taxi-dance hall, the "charity girl,"[1] the "gold-digger," and

[1] See Harvey W. Zorbaugh, *The Gold Coast and the Slum*, pp. 75–81.

the "occasional" and the "clandestine" prostitute are some of these. For many of these women the taxi-dance hall, the night club, the roadhouse, the beer flat, and many public ballrooms provide hunting grounds where they can seek out their clients while unidentified and unembarrassed by popular stigma. The taxi-dance hall becomes also a place where girls and young men may be approached easily and solicited. It is thus a recruiting ground for many illicit activities. Moreover, the habitualized sensualism tolerated in many dance halls suggests another adjustment to the new order. With the prostitute more inaccessible than ever, new accommodations have been worked out. The taxi-dance hall, unsupervised, is one among several institutions which are apparently a product of the new order and which function in harmony with it.

The practical problem presented by the existing taxi-dance hall yet remains. If the institution did not serve the legitimate interests and needs of a significant number of patrons, if it were not true that the taxi-dance hall undoubtedly prevents emotional adjustments even less wholesome than those possible through this institution, it would be a simple matter to advocate elimination. If it were not probable that a widespread program of repression would only force these interests and activities into institutional forms more difficult to control,[1] one could much more easily recommend the abolition of the taxi-dance hall. Had the experience of social agencies not demonstrated that it was quite possible to purge the public dance hall of many of its

[1] The private "night club" which admits only members and their friends is a form into which taxi-dance hall patrons might easily be absorbed. Because, in theory at least, it is not open to the general public, the private night club has often been able to evade much routine public supervision (see pp. 23–24).

worst evils through vigorous supervision, a recommendation favoring the extermination of this enterprise might be considered.

However, the success of the Chicago plan and the San Francisco plan in dealing with dance palaces and the profitable operation of well-conducted taxi-dance halls in both New York and Chicago give reason to believe that many taxi-dance halls can be operated in an acceptable manner. A vigorous social program involving thorough investigation and supervision of individual establishments would quickly eliminate the undesirable institutions and also most of the unwholesome practices in others, but at the same time would hold open the taxi-dance halls which serve the legitimate interests of men whose needs are not met elsewhere. It should be noted, however, that such a policy is successful only to the extent that it is supported by vigorous and continued supervision. In the social control of commercialized dance halls, as elsewhere, eternal vigilance will always be the price of our liberties.

There is some reason to believe that supervision in the taxi-dance hall, if honestly and thoroughly administered, might prove even more successful than in the dance palace. The economic necessity in the taxi-dance hall that the girl be casually affectionate toward many patrons, with all that results from this in an inconstancy and dissipation of her affections[1] and in the philosophy of life and practices of exploitation,[2] would continue, no doubt, to be a serious force in disorganization. But other demoralizing influences in the present-day taxi-dance hall could be eliminated or greatly reduced by vigorous and sincere supervision. Questionable conduct in the hall, the presence of the conspicuously im-

[1] See pp. 256–61.   [2] See pp. 42–48.

moral girls and others indorsing demoralizing patterns of life, and the attendance of patrons whose influence is obviously bad could easily be eliminated. Positive social case work with each taxi-dancer through investigation of the past conduct and family backgrounds of each applicant, continued surveillance of the taxi-dancer's association with patrons outside the hall, aggressive job-finding for girls who can no longer succeed in a wholesome way in the taxi-dance hall, and a unified insistence by proprietors that the girl not be allowed to follow indefinitely the retrogressive life of the dance-hall world would do much to obviate the institution's deleterious influence.

In the possibility for social work is the hopeful side of the picture of the taxi-dance hall. For, in this institution, the fact that all the women are employees gives an opportunity for supervision of the feminine part of the dance-hall population not found in other types of establishments. Contrasted with the large dance palace, for instance, where the anonymity of both men and women patrons makes effective control over conduct difficult and uncertain, the opportunity in the taxi-dance hall to prevent much illicit conduct through a rigorous supervision of every taxi-dancer affords a basis for optimism. Unfortunately this possibility has not been tested by experience. Public opinion has not been mobilized as yet to demand effective supervision, and the present proprietors have not seen fit to provide it voluntarily.

It is significant that Professor Arthur L. Swift, of Union Theological Seminary, who has been interested for some years in the problem of the intelligent control of commercialized dance halls, believes that there are valid reasons for the existence at present of the taxi-dance hall and that there is a possibility for regeneration through social regulation.

While it is true that the possibilities of social harm are greatest in these halls [taxi-dance halls], the writer sees no adequate reason why this type of hall should be singled out for abolition rather than, with the others, be subjected to regulation. His investigations show that certain of these halls are worse and certain of them are better than the average of all halls investigated. .... The proprietor who insists that his girls be of good character morally and who insists upon the observation of decent standards can successfully operate a closed hall [taxi-dance hall]. This is proven in the case of one such hall investigated. ....

.... The closed hall serves certain valid social ends. It provides a way by which the socially ill-adapted youth may adapt himself to the social customs of the group to which he rightfully belongs. And it provides for certain men, in the absence of women of their own race, opportunity for social intercourse with the opposite sex without necessarily involving them in immoral relations.[1]

Ultimately the solution to the taxi-dance hall problem must come through meeting more wholesomely the special recreational and social needs of each group of patrons. Even with the very best supervision, the taxi-dance hall can never be entirely satisfactory as a substitute for normal social life. For both taxi-dancers and patrons the institution, even with the best of supervision, can never be entirely free from moral danger and from the hazards involved in promiscuous acquaintanceships. The situation presents a challenge to the best social planning of which we are capable. Sociologists no doubt should have some valuable suggestions to make. But in the end the problems presented by the taxi-dance hall, if they are to be solved, must be met through the collective thought of our best "social engineers." Whether these individuals be classified technically as social workers, educators, clergymen, business men, editors, police officials,

[1] Arthur L. Swift, *The Dance Hall; a Problem of Social Control* (Columbia University M.A. thesis, 1925), pp. 41-42.

jurists, psychiatrists, or city planners, the solutions must arise through the co-operative planning of our civic leaders. This will require the unlimited confidence and the generous financial support of the community. It will also necessitate systematic planning by these leaders and—in addition—scientific efforts from time to time to measure the results of the programs and the institutions created to meet the patrons' needs. In the last analysis it is only by satisfying more wholesomely the legitimate desires of the men themselves that the taxi-dance hall problem will be met.

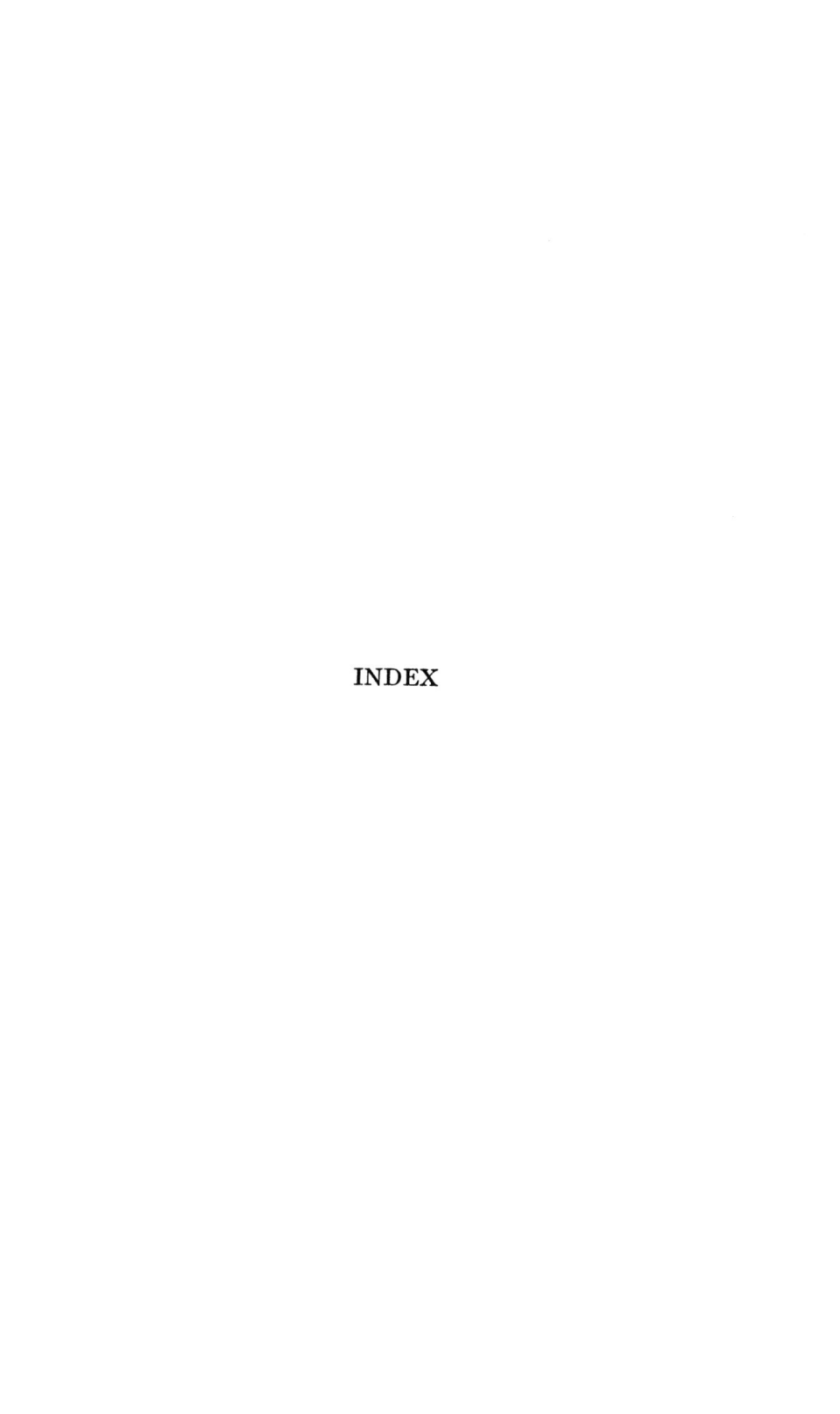

INDEX

INDEX

Anderson, Nels, 25 n., 211 n., 212 n.
Anonymity, 240 ff., 261, 287

Barbary Coast dance hall, 178, 179 ff., 195
Barrows, M. Alice, 180 n., 181 n., 182 n.
Basa, Aproniano A., 171
Binford, Jessie F., 269 n., 270 n., 275
"Black and tan" cabaret, 44, 90
Bogardus, E. S., 146 n.

Cabaret, 21. *See* Night club
Chicago plan, 274 ff.
Code, of taxi-dance hall, 207, 221
Committee of Fourteen of New York, 222 n., 223
Competition: beginning of, 212 ff.; institutional adaptation under, 188 f.
Concert hall saloon, 25
Conflict situations, in family, 59-72, 74-80, 237 f.
Crandall, Elizabeth R., 204 n.

Dance halls: closed, 17, 181; closed to women patrons, 262 f.; types of public, 20-23
Dance palace, 22
Dance pavilion, 22
Dancing, sensual, 45 f., 104 f., 220
Dancing academy, 20. *See* Dancing school
Dancing instruction, 131 f.
Dancing school, 4, 26, 182 ff., 215, 270
Degeneration, of dance hall, 178, 189-94
Delinquency, in taxi-dance hall, 237-39

Demoralization, in taxi-dance halls, 240-61
Dine-and-dance restaurant, 21

Exploitation: attitude of, encouraged by proprietors, 50; philosophy, rationale for misconduct, 39-49; scheme of life of, 39-42; of taxi-dancer, 267 f.

Filipino, chap. vii, 109, 197, 217 ff.; attitude of, toward American girl, 150 f.; Chicago settlements of, 152; intermarriage of, 167 ff.; legal and social status of, 146; "lost Filipino" in United States, 161-63; marriage of, to a taxi-dancer, 153 f.; as opportunist, 163-66; racial and marital status, of, 147 ff.; romantic impulse toward, 51, 85, 90; in taxi-dance halls, 152 f.; techniques of courtship of, 155-58; types of, 161-67; as vagabonds, 161 ff.; as victim of exploitation, 156 f.
Flexner, Abraham, 264
Forty-nine camp, 24-26
Forty-nine dance hall, 24, 182, 195
"Four Wishes," 33, 143
Fraternal dance, 20
Furnished-room areas, 56 f., 224-26

Gangs: fights among, 218 f.; gangsters, conspicuous by absence, 144; girls', 253-56
Gardner, Ella, 276 n.
Globe-trotters, 121 ff.
Guyon, J. Louis, 193

Harris, Mrs. E. W., 25 n., 183 n.
"Hostesses," in the dance palace, 24 f.
Hotel dance, 21

Interstitial areas, 231 f.
Irwin, Will, 179

Johnson, Godfrey, 184 n.
Juvenile Protective Association, 204, 237, 269 n., 270, 272, 275, 278 f.

Lambin, Maria Ward, 18 n., 27, 183 n., 274
Land values: of successful taxi-dance halls, 227 ff.; of unsuccessful taxi-dance halls, 230 f.
Lasker, Bruno, 145 n., 146 n., 147, 155 n.
Lewis, Leslie, 212 n.
Licensed dance halls, in Chicago (1910 and 1927), 189 f.
Licenses, evasion of, 270 f.
Life-cycle, of taxi-dancer, retrogressive, 86-94
Line-up plan, in dancing school, 186 f.
Lippmann, Walter, 208 n.
Location, of taxi-dance halls, chap. xi
Lonesome Club, 283 f.

Marriage: attitude of taxi-dancer toward, 251 f.; "marrying out of the life," 245; marrying a taxi dancer, Filipino's attitude toward, 153; marrying a taxi-dancer, immigrant's attitude toward, 113 f.; of taxi-dancer and Filipino, 167-74
Mason, Gregory, 208 n.
Mears, Eliot G., 146 n.
Municipal ballroom, 20
Murray, Virginia, 223 n.

National Ballroom Managers' Association, 204, 275 f., 278
Nationality: of patrons, 109 ff.; of proprietors, 188, 221; of taxi-dancers, 57 f.
Natural history, of taxi-dance hall, 177 ff.

New York City, 222 f.; Five Boro Ballroom and Dancing Academy Owners' Association, 276 n.
Night club, 19 n., 21 f., 44 f.
Ninety-nine Steps Club, 284 f.

Occupations, of patrons, 141 f.
Orientals, 109 f. See Filipinos

Patrons: the aesthete among, 133 f.; anonymity of, 242 f.; desire of, for physical exercise, 133; disorganization of, 242-45; Filipinos as, chap. vii; as fugitives from justice, 128 f.; globe-trotters among, 121 ff.; interests of, 129-41; married men among, 118 ff.; occupations represented among, 141 f.; older men among, 114; Orientals among, 42 ff.; personal freedom of, 136 f.; physically handicapped among, 126 f.; residences of, 225 f.; segregation of, 220; sensual stimulation of, 137 ff.; slummers among, 123 f.; stranger in the city among, 120 f.; transients among, 122 f.; types of, 109-29
"Picking up," 138 f.
Pleasure-boat dances, 22 f.
Police, 202 f.
Policy, of taxi-dance hall, 207 n.
Politicians, 202 f.
Private dancing club, 19 n., 23; first taxi-dance hall as, 212
Professional names, of taxi-dancers, 97
Prohibition, contemporary with, 178
Promiscuity, 250, 258 f.
Proprietors: attitude of, toward police, 202 f.; attitude of, toward politicians, 202; attitude of, toward public, 207 ff.; efforts of, to evade supervision, 270 f.; nativity of, 188, 221; "straw men", as, 271
Prostitution: in taxi-dance hall, 264-66; taxi-dancing, a preparation for, 266 f.

INDEX

Protection, 199, 203, 207, 277
Pseudo-club dance, 21, 23
Psychopathic family situations, 60 ff.
Public: attitude of proprietors toward, 207; taxi-dance hall and the, chap. ix
Public ballroom, transformation of, 189–94. *See* Dance palace

Rent party, 22
Rental values, 227–31
Residences, in Chicago: of patrons, 225 f.; of taxi-dancers, 56 ff.
Retrogressive cycles, 86–94, 267
Roadhouse, 19, 22
Rôles, among taxi-dancers, 101 f., 241 f.; "never-miss girl," 102 f.; "nice girl," 101 f.; sensual dancer, 104 f.; "smart girl," 102
Romance, in taxi-dance hall, 50 ff., 96 f., 129 f., 159 f.
Rooming-house areas. *See* Furnished-room areas
Runaway girls, as taxi-dancers, 55
Rural standards, conflicts with, 65 f.
Russell, Daniel, 201

San Francisco, 178–82, 183 f.; plan of, 273 f.
Seattle, 182 f.
Sex-game, 46 ff., 100 f., 139 f.
Sexual alliances, forms of, 48 ff.
Shaler, N., 242 n.
Slummer, 123 f.
Social agencies, 204, 238 f.
Social reform, chap. xiii
Social reformers, 204 ff.
Social service dance, 20
Social world, taxi-dance hall as, chap. iii
Sombart, Werner, 186 n.
Specialization among dance halls, 220–23
Standards and practices, contradictory, 245–56

Stein, Nobe E., 259 n.
Stranger: in the city, 120 f.; sociological and economic, 186
Substitute, problem of, 281–94
Supervision: 191, 199 f., 205 f., 263; problem of, 269–81
Swift, Arthur L., 292, 293 n.

Taxi-dance hall: admission to, 5; charges against, 262–69; code and policy of, 207 f.; conventions of, chap. iii; defined, 27; description of, 4–16; Filipino in, 152 f.; first in Chicago, private dance club, 212; land value of, 227–31; location of, chap. xi; natural history of, 177 f.; opposition to, 232 f., 272 f.; in the Philippines, 153; problems presented by, 14 ff.; proprietor's efforts to evade supervision, 270 f.; racial attitude in, 99; rental value of, 227–31; romance in, 39 f., 50 ff., 96, 113–17, 129 ff., 159 f.; as a type, chap. ii; unique meanings of conventional activity of, 36 f.; variants of, 23–26

Taxi-dancer: adjustment of, to family, 74–81; age of, 81, 198; breakdown of standards of, 85; as Chicago product, 54; code and techniques of, 38 f., 98–101; conflict situations in home of, 59–72; disillusionment of, 247 f.; disorganizing experiences of, before entering taxi-dance hall, 94 f.; dominant in taxi-dance hall, 37 ff.; double life of, four outcomes, 75 f.; economic position of, 256 ff.; economic relationship of, to family group, 59; employment as, only a few years, 84; upon entering taxi-dance hall, 94 f.; exploitation of, 39 ff.; exploitation of, encouraged by proprietors, 50; exploitation of Filipino by, 41–44, 98 f., 156 f.; family and social backgrounds of, chap. iv; family ties of, 58 f.; first experiences of, in taxi-dance hall, 95 f.; "getting the dances," veteran's problem, 98; how secured, 72 ff.; immigrant as, 56; interests and standards of conduct of, 32 f.; life-cycle of, chap. v; mental breakdown of, 259 n.; moving from city to city as, 105 f.; nationality of, 57 ff.; personal standards of, 85 f.; philosophy of life of, 39-42, 47, 248, 260; profits through questionable conduct of, 257 f.; racial attitudes of, 99; residence of, 54-58; retrogressive life-cycle hypothesized, 86-94; romantic impulse of, 50 ff.; romantic period of, 96 f.; runaway girl from other city as, 54 f.; significance of name of, 3; status of, 88 f.; techniques of, 38 f., 98 ff.; types of, 101-4

Techniques: of patron, 40, 140 f.; of taxi-dancer, 38-42, 98-101

Thomas, W. I., 33, 143 n.

Thompson, Edgar, 25 n.

Thrasher, Frederic M., 231 n., 254, 268 n.

Transients: as patrons, 121 ff.; as taxi-dancers, 105 f.

Transportation facilities, a factor in dance-hall success, 225 f.

Types: of patrons, 109-29; of public dance establishments, 19-24

Underworld alliances, 221

Utilitarian interest: of patron, 131-41; of taxi-dancer, 39 f., 42-44, 98-101, 104 f.

Vagabonds, among Filipinos, 161, 245

Vocabulary, of taxi-dance hall, 33-36

Wagner, C. Everett, 285

Wishes, Four: and the patron, 143 f.; and the taxi-dancer, 32 f.

Zorbaugh, Harvey, 231 n., 289 n.